Entangled Mobilities in the Transnational Salsa Circuit

With attention to the transnational dance world of salsa, this book explores the circulation of people, imaginaries, dance movements, conventions and affects from a transnational perspective. Through interviews and ethnographic, multi-sited research in several European cities and Havana, the author draws on the notion of "entangled mobilities" to show how the intimate gendered and ethnicised moves on the dance floor relate to the cross-border mobility of salsa dance professionals and their students. A combination of research on migration and mobility with studies of music and dance, *Entangled Mobilities in the Transnational Salsa Circuit* contributes to the fields of transnationalism, mobility and dance studies, thus providing a deeper theoretical and empirical understanding of gendered and racialised transnational phenomena. As such it will appeal to scholars across the social sciences with interests in migration, cultural studies and gender studies.

Joanna Menet is a post-doctoral researcher at the Laboratory for the Study of Social Processes at the University of Neuchâtel, Switzerland.

The Feminist Imagination – Europe and Beyond

Series Editors:
Kathy Davis
Senior Research Fellow, Vrije University, Amsterdam, The Netherlands
Mary Evans
Visiting Professor, Gender Institute at the London School of Economics and Political Science, UK

With a specific focus on the notion of "cultural translation" and "travelling theory", this series operates on the assumption that ideas are shaped by the contexts in which they emerge, as well as by the ways that they "travel" across borders and are received and re-articulated in new contexts. In demonstrating the complexity of the differences (and similarities) in feminist thought throughout Europe and between Europe and other parts of the world, the books in this series highlight the ways in which intellectual and political traditions, often read as homogeneous, are more often heterogeneous. It therefore provides a forum for the latest work that engages with the European experience, illuminating the various exchanges (from the USA as well as Europe) that have informed European feminism. The series thus allows for an international discussion about the history and imaginary of Europe from perspectives within and outside Europe, examining not only Europe's colonial legacy, but also the various forms of "cultural imperialism" that have shaped societies outside Europe. Considering aspects of Europe "abroad" as well as Europe "at home", this series is committed to publishing work that reveals the central and continued importance of the genealogy of feminist ideas to feminism and all those interested in questions of gender.

Published titles in this series:

Gendered Wars, Gendered Memories
Feminist Conversations on War, Genocide and Political Violence
Edited by Ayşe Gül Altınay and Andrea Pető

Translation and Travelling Theory
Feminist Theory and Praxis in China
Dongchao Min

Entangled Mobilities in the Transnational Salsa Circuit
The Esperanto of the Body, Gender and Ethnicity
Joanna Menet

For more information about this series, please visit: www.routledge.com/The-Feminist-Imagination—Europe-and-Beyond/book-series/ASHSER-1346

Entangled Mobilities in the Transnational Salsa Circuit

The Esperanto of the Body, Gender and Ethnicity

Joanna Menet

Routledge
Taylor & Francis Group

LONDON AND NEW YORK

First published 2020
by Routledge
2 Park Square, Milton Park, Abingdon, Oxon OX14 4RN

and by Routledge
52 Vanderbilt Avenue, New York, NY 10017

Routledge is an imprint of the Taylor & Francis Group, an informa business

The open access version of this publication was funded by the Swiss National Science Foundation.

British Library Cataloguing-in-Publication Data
A catalogue record for this book is available from the British Library

Library of Congress Cataloging-in-Publication Data
A catalog record has been requested for this book

ISBN: 978-0-367-43366-6 (hbk)
ISBN: 978-1-003-00269-7 (ebk)

Typeset in Bembo
by Integra Software Services Pvt. Ltd.

Contents

Figures and tables

Figures

Table

Acknowledgements

Engaging in the long journey of a dissertation and a book on and off the salsa dance floor would not have been possible without the support of many people.

I would first like to express my sincere gratitude to all the research participants who contributed to this study. Muchas gracias for the time spent discussing, for the trust and openness to share personal stories in interviews and of course for the many dances. Salsa photographer Valentin Behringer generously allowed me to use his photographs to add some images to the descriptions and analysis in this book.

My sincere thanks go to my thesis supervisor Janine Dahinden who trusted me in my choices and supported me throughout the thesis process. This work owes much to her close reading of numerous drafts and her guiding me to push further. I would also like to thank the three members of my thesis committee Kathy Davis, Ellen Hertz and Jonathan Skinner, who carefully read earlier versions of this work. Their detailed comments and questions were extremely helpful in reviewing the thesis for this book.

Upon arriving at the Laboratory for the Study of Social Processes, I had the chance to be surrounded by amazing colleagues. This book is not least the result of the fruitful exchange of ideas with them. In particular I would like to thank Matthieu Bolay, Aylin Eriksen, Carolin Fischer, Shpresa Jashari, Faten Khazaei, Anne Kristol, Joëlle Moret, Alain Mueller, Aurélien Petzold, Alice Sala, Martine Schaer, Marion Schulze and Marc Tadorian. A big shout out to the participants of our weekly writing spaces, whose friendship and encouragement at the right moment was central in making it through the thicket of academic writing.

I was lucky to present drafts and ideas from this book at several conferences, where I got valuable feedback from other salsa-dancing colleagues, notably Ruxandra Ana, Alice Aterianus-Owanga and Brigid McClure. In spring 2016 I had the chance to spend two months as a visiting research student at King's College in London. I would like to thank Ananya Kabir and her Modern Moves team for their welcome in an extremely stimulating research environment.

I would also like to acknowledge the funding bodies that partly supported this research: the Office of Equal Opportunity and the Donation Funds of the Swiss National Science Foundation at the University of Neuchâtel, as well as the Graduate School for Gender Studies at the University of Bern. The open access publication of this book was made possible through the Swiss National Science Foundation. I take the opportunity to thank Fiona Shearer, whose attentive copy editing was very precious. I would also like to thank the editorial team at Taylor & Francis for their attention to detail.

Finally, I am profoundly grateful to my family and friends for their continuous support in times of doubt just as much as joy related to this book project. I want to express my heartfelt thanks to Alessandro, whose encouragement and presence throughout these years was invaluable. Grazie mille.

"*Bailamos*, shall we dance?"

An ethnographic entry to salsa

It's a cold Saturday evening in February 2016 I am surrounded by small groups of people all heading towards the convention centre near the lake in the heart of Zurich. As I open the doors, I can immediately hear the rhythmic music drifting down the stairs. I pass beneath an arch of multicoloured balloons; this year the Salsafestival Switzerland celebrates its 15th anniversary. In the entrance hall, people are queuing for their tickets, but I already wear the wristband I put on the day before, allowing me access during the whole festival: three party nights and the workshops during Saturday and Sunday.

I take off my coat and warm boots and change into a pair of dance shoes, made of soft black leather, with heels low enough to make it through the night but high enough for me to be considered a salsa dancer. Around me women and men are doing the same, changing their street shoes for dance shoes and getting ready for "the biggest Salsa party in Europe with 4+3 dancefloors", as tonight's party is announced in the festival programme. People remove their coats and jackets to reveal short dresses, black trousers combined with fancy shirts and suits appear. The dancers have followed the motto of tonight's party, "dress to impress", and the sportswear dominating the look at the daytime workshops has completely disappeared. I look around, as people arrive in small groups or couples. I spot a familiar face and greet him with a kiss on each cheek. Next to us I hear others doing the same, speaking English and talking about the last salsa festival where they met – was it in Rovinj (Croatia) last summer, in Berlin last autumn or in Krasnoyarsk (Siberia) this winter?

I leave my coat at the cloakroom and walk up the stairs, taking a look at the large roll-up posters announcing future events in Bordeaux, Milan, Antwerp, London, Šibenik (Croatia), Düsseldorf, Sopot (Poland) and Paris. On a table by the wall, printed flyers further advertise festivals in: Limassol (Cyprus), Monaco, Vilnius, Frankfurt, Minsk, Warsaw, Graz, Prague, Kiev, Antalya, Stuttgart, Marrakesh, Hamburg, Dubai and Lebanon.

As I continue, the music gets louder and people rush up the stairs; it's almost 11pm; show time. I enter the big hall upstairs and pass the (now closed) booths where dancers can purchase all the dance shoes, CD and clothes they want during the day's workshops. I find myself immersed in a dressed-up crowd, feeling the excitement of a long dancing night ahead. Some people hold a drink, but most of them stand around the large wooden dance floor or have already formed a couple and started to dance: woman and man, often touching only with their hands, sometimes with a hand on a shoulder or their partner's back, they move quickly to the music, stepping forwards and backwards, changing place and turning around, flicking hair, smiling. They dance together for one or two songs, then separate when the music comes to an end and reform new couples. After a well-known salsa song ends, the DJ changes the music and the attention turns to the huge stage installed on one side of the room where the host welcomes the first performers to the stage.

During the next hour, different dance couples and groups successively perform their choreographed shows, dressed in colourful costumes. At the end the public applauds enthusiastically, whistles and screams and all the performers come back, but not on stage: instead, they walk directly onto the dance floor where they invite individuals from the public to dance with them. The DJ plays several songs and soon the whole room is transformed into a sea of moving bodies.

I decide to look at the other rooms, all named for different music–dance styles: the big room next to the main stage is decorated with palm trees and a huge poster of old cars and colonial-style buildings – the *Salsa Cubana* room. A bit further away I walk into a smaller room, named *salsa romantica*, next to the bachata room. I learn from the programme that there are more rooms downstairs: one for kizomba, and others for the *after party* that starts at 4am. Indeed, as I leave the party at 2.30am, there are still people arriving, taking off their coats and putting on their dance shoes.

(Edited Field note, 27 February 2016, Salsafestival Switzerland)

Looking at the social world through the prism of salsa dancing

This entry into the salsa circuit through a snapshot of a salsa congress is an invitation to an intellectual exploration of what I have come to term the salsa circuit and its "affective economy". In the early 2000s, salsa festivals or congresses like the one described in this field note started to appear in urban centres all over Europe, North America, Australia and some countries in Asia, fuelled by event organisers and salsa entrepreneurs. In the following years, the gendered partner dance has attracted ever more students circulating between the festivals, as well as taking dance holidays to what have come to be recognised as the birthplaces of salsa dancing: Cuba and New York, where dance studios proliferate. A new category of *salsa artists* started to circulate between festivals and dance studios, earning their living through teaching and performing. Salsa dance's commercialisation builds on a strong narrative of salsa as an inclusive *community* where people are united through their passion for salsa; as one dancer remarked, it is the *Esperanto of the body*.

When starting to work on salsa dance in 2013, I found that while the music and some local salsa scenes were a topic of scientific literature, the transnational circulation of dancers, dance moves and gendered representations in salsa had attracted astonishingly little interest from scholars. While there exists ample literature on transnational activities of migrants, musicians, religious groups or the so-called highly skilled, the mobile practices of salsa dancers, as well as their gendered performances, had prompted little scientific exploration.

Having started my research, I became more and more fascinated by the apparent tensions of the salsa circuit: its insistence on global connections between people across the world despite their highly unequal access to travel; the gendered performances in salsa dancing, seemingly at odds with any feminist sensibility; the celebrity cult around recognised *salsa stars*, reversing assumed power relations in post-colonial Europe. At the same time, I wondered: was salsa just another case of neo-colonial or "cultural appropriation" of others' practices by the West, through the exoticisation of "the other" (as Savigliano (1995) has put it for tango)? Did the commercialisation and sexualisation of the gendered dance moves lead to the reinforcement of harmful gender stereotypes? And: who were the dancers, who lived their lives travelling from event to event, particularly the highly mobile professionals who seemingly fit none of the categories that migration or mobility scholarship has theorised? These broad questions stood at the beginning of this book. During the research process, I honed the questions to the most salient, following the reading of studies on similar phenomena, the inclusion of theoretical perspectives and the twists and turns of empirical research.

The research rests on a qualitative, multi-sited study with the hitherto neglected group of highly mobile salsa dancers, including multiple research phases over a period of three years between 2013 and 2016. Semi-structured, problem-centred interviews and participant observation-observant participation were the primary research methods. I conducted interviews with 36 male and female salsa dancers of a variety of national origins holding different positions in the salsa circuit, including salsa dance professionals, students and event organisers. The short-term embodied ethnography took place at salsa congresses, in salsa studios and during salsa holidays in cities in Croatia, Cuba, Germany, Italy, Poland, Switzerland and the UK, as well as on Facebook. In order to explore the multiple dimensions of salsa, I draw on theoretical frameworks developed in diverse research fields such as research on migration and (im)mobility, ethnicity, gender, dance, music and art, as well as affect and tourism. This interdisciplinary approach allows for a broad perspective on the phenomenon of salsa dancing and the ways it connects different people and places.

Outline of the book

This book is divided into four parts, an introductory, two empirical parts, as well as a conclusion. Part I provides a theoretical, methodological and empirical introduction to the book. It develops a framework to study the salsa circuit and its underlying logics, to better understand how the salsa circuit is integrated into a larger web of globe-spanning power relations. Chapter 1 introduces the theoretical perspectives, followed by a discussion of the methodology and the chosen methods to conduct research. Chapter 2 consists of an empirical and contextual introduction to the salsa circuit, in terms of the "hubs" and circulating salsa students and imaginaries. Part II addresses the ways gender and ethnicity/race are negotiated in embodied ways, focusing on "conventions" of the salsa circuit, introduced in the introduction to Part II. To do this, it zooms in on the interactions of salsa dancers on the dance floor and in the workshop situation. Chapter 3 explores how salsa dancers negotiate "authenticity" and ethnicity, while Chapter 4 analyses how dancers are (un/re)doing gender on the dance floor. Part III addresses the transnational careers of salsa dance professionals, considering them in three phases. The introduction to Part III conceptualises the notion of transnational careers and provides an example of three portraits of salsa dancers' careers. In Chapter 5, the first status passage of "becoming a salsa dance professional" is addressed, while Chapter 6 explores the ways in which Latin American salsa dancers access the European salsa circuit, and Chapter 7 focuses on how reputation is constructed inside the salsa circuit. These three chapters of Part III thus focus exclusively on what I have termed "salsa dance professionals", while the other chapters deal with salsa dancers of different statuses, from beginning dancers to more experienced ones. Part IV, the Conclusion reviews the main findings of the study and highlights the books' contributions to contemporary academic debates.

Figure 0.1 Dancers at a salsa festival.
Source: © Valentin Behringer.

A note on videos and photographs

Although not the primary focus of interest of this book, visual content distributed through the internet plays an important role in the salsa circuit. In order to allow for visual impressions of the analysed interactions and to enhance the written analysis with sound and (moving) images, I include photographs as well as links to short videos of salsa dance professionals, publicly available on YouTube. In order to guarantee the anonymity of my research participants, I selected videos and photographs of different dancers. I also chose pictures that represent aspects I analyse in this book, taken by acknowledged salsa photographer Valentin Behringer at different salsa events in Europe and use them with his kind permission (Figure 0.1).

Part I

An introduction to the salsa circuit

1 Studying salsa

Through the entry point of salsa dancing, this book explores the circulation of people, imaginaries, dance movements, conventions and affects from a transnational perspective. It relies on an analysis that ranges from the intimate gendered and ethnicised moves on the dance floor to the cross-border mobility of salsa dance professionals (cf Cresswell 2006), and it thereby contributes to a deeper theoretical and empirical understanding of transnational social processes. In particular, it explores the negotiations of gendered, ethnicised and racialised representations in the salsa circuit and analyses the transnational careers of salsa dance professionals. Salsa thus serves as a case study to explore broader sociological questions related to current global transformations, mobility and immobility, social inequalities and their intersections.

Studies on salsa rarely theorise the dance in terms of the transnational connections, using the notions transnational, global and network as mere metaphors. Additionally, few studies on "global" worlds focus on the mobility of their participants, and this is therefore just taken for granted. This book argues that a transnational perspective combined with an (im)mobilities approach enhances our understanding of the shaping of these practice-based social fields, including an awareness of globe-spanning hierarchies and power relations.

In order to explore the multiple dimensions of salsa, I navigated between different theoretical approaches and fields of study, from mobility and migration to art and "cultural production" to specific literature on dance and particularly salsa. This interdisciplinary approach allows for a broad perspective on the phenomenon of salsa dancing and the ways it connects different people and places. In this chapter I discuss the key frameworks and theoretical concepts that inform my analysis, as well as methodology and methods I chose to conduct research. The first section introduces salsa, building on existing literature from a social anthropological perspective. The second section briefly clarifies the chosen theoretical perspectives concerning mobility, ethnicity and gender. In the third section I explain how I conducted short-term ethnographic research and qualitative interviews over a period of three years.

Salsa in the literature

In her analysis of tango, Savigliano (1995) discusses the difficulties of writing about the origins of tango in the following way: "In reconstructing roots, issues of inclusion and exclusion are at stake: It is easy to forget one group's participation and to exaggerate the protagonism of some others, and not always for innocent reasons" (32). Literature on salsa music and dance stresses the multiple influences that have led to the music and dance complex today called salsa. Among contemporary salsa dancers, salsa's origins are still hotly debated, including several circulating "origin myths".[1] These shared origin myths stress one element over another, often depending on the personal preferences of one salsa style or the associations individuals are able to construct with their own family histories, indeed in a not completely "innocent" way. Such often highly essentialised arguments can be understood as a playful way of performing salsa ownership as a "marketing strategy" (see Pietrobruno 2006) or even as a mode of resisting the commodification of dance through Western organisations (see Boulila 2018). In this way, the origin myths circulating in the salsa world tell us more about the positioning strategies and the striving for credibility of contemporary salsa dancers than about the historical trajectories of salsa music and dance. I therefore join Savigliano in her caution when writing about salsa's "roots".

Literature on salsa as well as broader studies on dance and nationalism have aptly demonstrated the ways dance has been instrumentalised in political projects of nation-building, as dance "is a powerful tool in shaping nationalist ideology and the creation of national subjects" (Reed 1998: 503). As dance historian and ethnographer Buckland (2006) states, "The use of dance as a symbolic political strategy in shaping a future society was particularly evident in the often integrated aims of research and reconstruction in the institutes and state dance ensembles of Cold War Eastern Europe" (14). Studies have analysed how folk dances in European countries are related to "everyday nationalism" (e.g. Kalegoropoulou 2013 on Greece) and "nation-building" (e.g. Wulff 2003 on Ireland). Through bodily movement, social identities are communicated, formed and negotiated (Desmond 1993), which explains dancers' sometimes strong insistence on salsa as the heritage of one particular country. Román-Velazquez (2002) noted that despite salsa's stylistic variation,

> academic writers and commentators have sought to categorise salsa as primarily Puerto Rican, Cuban, Latin-Caribbean or more broadly "Latin". Trying to label salsa in such a way can be viewed as an attempt to claim it for a singular identity, to fix its rather fluid character and to limit its capability to be transformed as it travels.
>
> (Román-Velazquez 2002: 212)

Due to all these reasons, in my research on salsa, approaching history proved to be particularly challenging, a point also raised by Mueller (2016) in his study on hardcore punk. Similar to the genealogies salsa scholars construct, he notes that "most research proposes a formal history of the subculture under study by articulating fragments of 'native' information into a logical, chronological account, conveniently forgetting that these sources are products of processes of negotiation" (Mueller 2016: 119). There exist numerous versions of salsa dance's origins and excavating them would be a research project in itself, partly done by others (cf Hutchinson 2004; McMains 2015; Pietrobruno 2006).

However, there exists a growing body of literature on salsa music and dancing, which includes the historical and socio-political context of its development and transnationalisation. I opted for a short discussion of this literature, distinguishing between three thematic strands of writing about salsa: the first includes literature particularly about music and dance as artistic forms and the question of how they emerged. The second body of (mainly ethnographic) literature tends to concentrate on localised salsa dance scenes[2] and negotiations of power relations in them, focusing on the question of how salsa interacts with specific local contexts. A last strand of literature analyses so-called *Latin* dances and the ways they are represented from a critical, post-colonial perspective.

Salsa music and dance

As argued in the literature, the history of salsa is inextricably linked to colonial history: its Cuban precursors (danzón, son) were a result of the fusion of European couple dances and African percussive traditions (Pietrobruno 2006) "brought to the Caribbean through slavery" (Kabir 2013: 267). Salsa has a complex history of circulation between the Caribbean and the US, and its evolution is thoroughly entangled with that of other musical styles, such as jazz, R&B and rock (Morales 2003: 33) as well as with the development of the recording industry (Waxer 2002a: 8). Migration movements and political conflicts, particularly the Cuban Revolution in 1959 and the following political and economic sanctions by the US, also shaped salsa's development. As the term salsa is used as a signifier of both music and dance, in historical accounts the two are often mixed up. For analytical reasons I separate the two in this discussion and will first focus on music and then on dance.

Covering the most-cited influences of salsa's formation, dance scholar McMains (2015) characterises salsa music as "an updated take on Afro-Cuban dance music, developed by Puerto Ricans living in New York" (1). For some of today's dancers, New York therefore holds as the "place of origin" of their dance practice, although most dancers acknowledge other "roots" entailed in salsa's complex history. Historically, the term salsa has been used as a commercial label since the 1970s, largely propelled by Fania Records, a New York-based recording company formed in 1964, which promoted almost every successful salsa musician of the time (McMains 2015: 1). Yet the term did not remain unchallenged: many musicians are said to have rejected the label initially, and musicologist Manuel (1995: 74) observes that the term salsa was often believed to be an artificial and commercial construct, designed to disguise the Cuban origins of the music. This "marketing trick" was thought to be necessary after the US government had declared an embargo on the import of all Cuban products, including music (McMains 2015: 52).

Earlier studies about salsa focus particularly on salsa music and its historical emergence, highlighting its role in ethnic and national identity constructions.[3] For the early years of its development in the US, according to research, salsa music was related to a political project of the affirmation and political consciousness of a working-class Latino identity in rejection of Anglo-centric assimilationism (Waxer 2002a: 4). "Many early salsa fans were second-generation immigrants who, coming of age during or after the Civil Rights Movement, began to question their assimilation into American culture and turned to salsa as a means of reconnecting to their cultural heritage" (McMains 2015: 80). Washburne (2008) also argues that in the 1970s salsa was defined by its association with marginalised working-class Cuban and Puerto Rican immigrants in New York City and soon came to encompass the experiences of working-class people throughout Latin America. This was also reflected in salsa lyrics, as Waxer (2002a) suggests: "Significantly, salsa's lyrics reflected the experiences of the Latino and Latin American black and mixed-race working class, and – in distinction to its Cuban antecedents – songs mirrored the violence and discontent of the inner city" (4).[4] On today's dance floors at salsa congresses in Europe, this so-called *salsa dura* (hard salsa) of the 1970s is the favourite music of many dancers (cf McClure 2015: 15). With the emergence of *salsa romantica* in the 1980s, a more lyrical and commercially successful style of salsa music, salsa became less politicised and more popular among a larger audience (Washburne 2008).[5] Meanwhile, in Cuba, music developed in other directions, where first *timba* and then *Salsa Cubana* bands became popular, both musical styles including aspects of Afro-Cuban religion (Klette Bøhler 2013).[6] On today's salsa festival dance floors, these three types of music (*salsa dura*, *salsa romantica* and *timba/Salsa Cubana*) are the most common styles. On such occasions, the live bands of the 1960s and 1970s have been replaced by DJs playing recorded music, and live concerts at salsa dance venues are rare.

The studies discussed so far are mainly concerned with salsa as a musical form and the ways it emerged in a specific socio-political context. As should be clear from this discussion, salsa music is often described as being caught up (from its very beginnings) between a commercialised goal of finding new audiences and the often politically inspired "identity projects" of creating a common denominator for groups.

When considering salsa dance's early genealogy, scholars of dance identify elements of both European and African legacy: the couple formation between a male and a female dancer touching one another is associated with European court dances (Daniel 2002: 43),[7] while the isolation of various body parts such as hips and shoulders that move separately are associated with African movement vocabularies (Pietrobruno 2006: 32). Dance scholar McMains

(2015), whose declared goal is to demonstrate the participation of all social groups in salsa's development (at least the actors in the US), cites mambo as an important influence of contemporary salsa dancing, which for her is a result of the intermingling of elements of the following dances: "Cuban *son*", "American lindy hop", "Cuban rumba", "Puerto Rican *bomba*" and "African-American jazz" (32). Later on, throughout the 1990s, dancers and salsa dance professionals performing staged shows also borrowed from ballet, jazz, tap and hip-hop (McMains 2015: 327). Two of the above-mentioned dances are worth a brief discussion, as they will be mentioned in the analysis throughout this study: mambo and rumba.

One of salsa's most-popular origin stories, especially of the New York or "On2" style, builds on the mambo craze of the 1950s and particularly the Palladium ballroom, New York's most popular dance venue for Latin dance music at that time (McMains 2015: 30). The Palladium still today figures as kind of a "multiracial utopia" (Hutchinson 2014b: 30), as it paved the way "for interracial social interaction that would not be realized in other social sectors or geographic locations for decades" (McMains 2015: 42). The Palladium ballroom, open from 1947 to 1966, is thus often described as a space of integration, where racial and class boundaries were blurred during social dancing on the dance floor, with participants of Puerto Rican, Cuban, Italian, African-American, Irish and Jewish descent (McMains 2015: 39). Despite mambo's success and such idealising depictions, García demonstrates that in US media representations of the time mambo and its dancers were racialised: mambo was described as a "primitive African" dance, which needed to be "disciplined" into a socially acceptable product (García 2009: 177). Such racist stereotypes from the discourse of African primitivism were in line with contemporary ideologies. Nevertheless, as Hutchinson (2014b) contends, the Palladium "remains in dancers' memories as the mythic point of origin" (32).

Another often-cited "mythic point of origin" is Cuba, where several of the dances that merged into salsa are said to have developed, such as the casino (sometimes done in a circle, called Rueda de Casino), a dance now often taught at salsa congresses under the label *Salsa Cubana*, and the danzón, son and rumba. The rumba in particular has been received with increasing popularity and accessibility among salsa dancers at congresses worldwide; as I observed, the festivals all scheduled workshops in so-called Afro-Cuban rumba. Rumba is a genre said to have developed in rural areas of Cuba, influenced by Spanish and Central/West African traditions (Daniel 1995). It has a complex history of colonial repression and stigmatisation, until its institutionalisation by the socialist government after the revolution of 1959.[8] The inscription of rumba on the UNESCO List of Intangible Cultural Heritage in 2016 further accentuated its public recognition. Foreigners' fascination with and interest in learning the rumba has led to it being more accepted in Cuba, yet its practitioners are still often racialised and associated with low social status (see Ana 2017). As I will demonstrate in Part III for some contemporary Cuban dancers, knowledge and skills in rumba dancing are crucial in the process of accessing the (European) salsa circuit, where these embodied skills are highly valued.[9]

In salsa dancers' origin myths, New York and Cuba both hold a special weight as places in which the dance practice supposedly originated. Yet other actors challenge such a linear construction of history (e.g. Hutchinson 2014a). As Mueller (2016) argues, historical accounts usually "come from people of higher status in the world under study, reproducing classical social biases such as white-, elite- or androcentric readings of the world" (120). For this reason I choose not to single out one history and present it as the most legitimate version, as this would attach more credibility to certain historical accounts. Hutchinson (2014a) also criticises a too-linear reading of salsa's history, dismantling the common narrative positioning salsa as a new style emerging in New York and later spreading throughout Latin America as only one version: "In fact, salsa was frequently experienced not as a break with but as a continuation of earlier dance practices" in countries like the Dominican Republic and Colombia (Hutchinson 2014a: 5). Salsa's formation can be understood in terms of a simultaneous development of salsa histories in different places; as in fact: "many people in disparate locations experience [salsa] as their own" (Hutchinson 2014a: 8).[10] It is in this understanding that I approach salsa and its history.

In this book, salsa is used as an umbrella term for different salsa dance styles as practised in the transnational circuit and learned and taught in a studio or workshop context. As this study examines salsa dance professionals and the construction of their transnational careers in the commercialised field of the salsa circuit, I do not include what Borland calls "street, freestyle, or untrained salsa, which encompasses a geographically diverse set of dancing practices" (Borland 2009: 467).

At today's salsa congresses and in salsa dance studios, several salsa dance styles are taught and danced. They have some common features, which distinguish them from other dance forms. Salsa dancing is characterised not only by the already mentioned couple hold, the gendered convention of leader and follower and the independent movement of body parts such as hips and torso. Salsa dancer and scholar Renta (2014) also points to the importance of improvisation, creativity and musicality as part of *sabor* (often translated as flavour), taking into account the "Latin-Caribbean cosmology on which salsa dancing is founded" (120). Indeed, salsa dancers often acknowledge improvisation, musicality and connection as criteria for competence in social dancing.[11] Most salsa dancers recognise a basic set of steps and figures as being salsa, while valuing creative adjustments and improvisation through individual dancers. Some of the mentioned elements are also important concepts in other dance worlds (such as connection in tango), but they are imbued with specific meaning in salsa dancing, as discussed in more detail in the analysis of Chapters 3 and 4.

For their adepts, salsa dance styles differ considerably and are used to distinguish themselves from other dancers. Technically speaking, salsa dance styles are either differentiated by the ways the two dance partners move on the dance floor or by the ways dancers interpret the rhythmical timing of the music (McClure 2015: 17). In *cross-body* or *line* salsa dance styles (including LA-style, New York-style and what is in Europe termed Puerto Rican-style), dancers change place in a linear movement, while in *Salsa Cubana* dancers move in a circular way.[12] The basic step (short-short-long) is the same in all styles, but the moment dancers move forwards or backwards may happen on the first and fifth or second and sixth beat of the bar. Before starting to dance on a dance floor at a congress, a new couple will therefore often ask each other "on one (On1) or on two (On2)?", to make sure they step back (follower) and forward (leader) at the same time and avoid bumping into each other because both step forward at the same time. Due to salsa dance's development and marketing, the different ways of dancing to salsa music are also named after geographical locations: New York-style (and Puerto Rican-style) salsa is linear, often in On2 timing; LA-style salsa is linear in On1 timing; Cuban-style salsa is circular and usually On1.[13] At congresses and particularly at competitions, the very fast Cali-style or Colombian-style salsa is also present, but less than the aforementioned styles. During my research I also observed a lot of mixing of these salsa styles with other dances, such as salsa–flamenco, salsa with hip-hop or just "salsa fusion".[14]

Ethnographies of salsa dancing

The second strand of literature on salsa developing over recent years is mainly comprised of ethnographies of localised salsa dance *scenes* in various places. It is mainly concerned with questions of salsa dance's local adaptation in cities across the US, the Caribbean and Europe. Studies focus on how dancers in different places relate to salsa, in terms of ethnicity, race, class and local identity politics. The edited volume *Salsa World: A Global Dance in Local Contexts* (Hutchinson 2014a), for example, collects case studies of various aspects of salsa's "global" spread in the US, Cuba, Puerto Rica, Colombia, the Dominican Republic, France, Spain and Japan.

Building on theorists of "cultural globalisation" (see e.g. Appadurai 1990; Hannerz 1996; Robertson 1992), several authors of localised salsa ethnographies are led by the question of how globalisation creates distinct practices and identities for people dancing salsa in these particular places. Skinner (2007), for example, examines salsa dancing in three cities (Belfast, Hamburg and Sacramento), to show how salsa is transformed and adapts to local contexts and how dancers use salsa to express identities and emotions. He discusses salsa in Belfast as "segregated" between Protestants and Catholics, and as "multicultural" and "cosmopolitan" in the two other cities. Skinner (2007) observes the globalisation of salsa teaching and merchandise, which for him shows

> that salsa has become a cultural product, one navigated by cosmopolitan artists and musicians, one relying on an international market economy and the existential needs of the public with time on their hands (Febres

1997: 177), a disposable income in their pockets, and seeking activities in which to come together, express their emotions, fulfil their fantasies and proto-narratives (Appadurai 1996), and to affirm self-identity in our late-modern world (Giddens 1991).

(Skinner 2007: 488)

Building on Hannerz (1996), he describes salsa dancing as a "decontextualised" knowledge, a "mobile skill" that can be carried and "recontextualised" in a new setting (Skinner 2007: 498). As Skinner (2007) argues, in this process emotions have become a commodity "explored and exploited by salsa promoters and instructors" (500).

My findings in the European salsa circuit echo Skinner's discussion of salsa dancing as a modern leisure pursuit that allows what he calls "cosmopolitan artists" to make a living while their "addicted" students in North American and European cities "follow their passions" and "pursue the identities of their imagination" (Skinner 2007: 503). At the same time, this study adds to the understanding of how salsa instructors construct their careers, and shows the ways in which these are considerably shaped by "regimes of mobility" (Glick Schiller and Salazar 2013) and social capital as well as the class-based, gendered and ethnicised/racialised logics of the salsa circuit.

Most studies on salsa dancing focus their analysis on the experiences of or interactions between salsa students (e.g. Bock and Borland 2011; Borland 2009; Bosse 2013; García 2013; Papadopoulos 2003). Bosse (2008: 46), for example, explores salsa and ballroom dancing in central Illinois, focusing on "cross-cultural borrowing and the ways in which new dance styles are generated", thereby also examining the "refashioning of identity" for its practitioners. As she describes, white North American salsa newcomers in particular explained their wish to learn salsa dancing with references to a metaphorical, alternatively racialised self (Bosse 2008: 58). Drawing on Gans' (1979) concept of "symbolic ethnicity", Bosse describes salsa dancers' wish to "get ethnic" (Bosse 2008: 60), to obtain the positively valued aspects of "Latin American ethnicity" through the performance of salsa. "Latin American culture" was hereby understood as a monolithic entity; it was associated with strong familial and community ties, a "living" culture of salsa music and dance and being physically and sexually relaxed (Bosse 2008: 59). Such depictions could be read as the wish for "consumption" of the thus created "other" and white North Americans' desire for a so-called Latin American ethnicity. However, in her discussion, Bosse nuances the picture, presenting dancers' wish to engage in salsa as an "affirmation of the existence of an exotic self":

They desired to construct for themselves an alternative sense of self that they perceived to be more 'vibrant' or 'alive', more physically integrated, and more sexually attractive. But there existed no language and few conceptual categories for such a construction of their own, largely unmarked identity.

(Bosse 2008: 60)

Bosse's analysis is supported by other authors, who argue that salsa dancers in Europe embrace dancing "for its exotic appeal" (e.g. Escalona 2014) and their desire to perform what Schneider (2013: 558) calls "traditional gender identities". While a few of my interviewees started salsa dancing due to similar motivations, the majority of participants had other motives, as the discussion in Chapter 2 will demonstrate.

Several studies dealing with salsa dancing also focus on gendered aspects of dancing, while some authors analyse particularly gendered dimensions, such as Wieschiolek (2003), Skinner (2008), Borland (2009), Schneider (2013) and McClure (2015). Some of the cited authors mainly focus on women's experiences of dancing and thus take an (often implicit) perspective of women's studies. While this perspective is framed by earlier feminist interests in "the politics of pleasure" (Gotfrit 1988), due to their focus, these studies leave male experiences underexplored. Furthermore, some of the studies tend to assume egalitarian gender relations in the countries where the studies focus and contrast them with the gendered structure of "imported" salsa, thus ascribing unequal gender relations to the supposed origin "culture" of salsa. While this study builds on the related literature, it seeks to develop an understanding of gendered processes encompassing male and female experiences and going beyond explanations of salsa's gendered roles through a recurrence to "foreign culture". In Chapter 4, I will discuss more of the relevant literature.

The already cited books by McMains (2015) and Pietrobruno (2006), along with the cited articles, are among a growing body of literature to focus on the local spread of salsa in specific urban centres.[15] Local salsa ethnographies are also written from a more critical perspective, which attests to salsa's erasure of certain dance practices (see Balbuena Gutiérrez 2014 on the commercialisation of Cuban casino) and bodies through its highly heteronormative discourses (see Boulila 2015 on lesbian salsa spaces).

Most of the cited ethnographies of local or national salsa *scenes* deal with salsa as a dance practice and/or dance students, their emotions, identifications and motivations to embrace salsa dancing. Primarily concerned with salsa in a specific local context, these ethnographies are less interested in the perceived "non-local" salsa congresses (cf Kabir 2013). Though some of them acknowledge the existence of a transnational salsa circuit (such as Skinner 2007), most of the above-mentioned authors further investigate neither the transnational relations between dancers based in these various places nor the professional careers developing in the circuit (an exception is McMains 2015). In a review of Hutchinson's edited volume (2014a), Fraser Delgado (2014) points to this omission, stating that

> nowhere is there a sense of what it feels like to live along the global circuit for those instructors and performers who boast on their Web sites that they have visited 60 countries or more. A separate study of the global network itself is called for.
>
> (108)

While it is not the goal of this study to give a historical account of the developments of the "global network", it addresses some elements of the transnational careers of the mentioned salsa dance professionals. Thus, though building on the cited existing literature on salsa dance *scenes*, this study adds several hitherto underdeveloped aspects, namely a focus on salsa congresses, an analysis of the transnational careers of salsa dance professionals (including the question of who has the possibility to access transnational mobility to participate in the salsa circuit) and their social capital in terms of (transnational) social networks, as well as negotiations around the gendered and ethnicised/racialised logics underpinning the affective economy of the salsa circuit.

The exoticisation of *Latin* dances

In line with the argument developed above, historical and critical scholarship on dance has demonstrated the significance of "dance as a site of considerable political and moral anxiety" (Reed 1998: 506) since the colonial era. For instance, colonial administrations were keen to reform or ban dances (Comaroff 1985), as they perceived indigenous dance practices as a political and moral threat (Reed 1998). In this line of thinking, Western dance practices were often seen as superior and contrasted with "primitive" dance practices (which prompted the US anthropologist Kealiinohomoku in 1983 to look at ballet as an "ethnic dance"). Interested in "the politics of dance" (Reed 1998), scholars have indicated the power relations imbued in the categorisation of certain dance practices or dance moves. Cresswell (2006) for example analyses how in early 20th century London forms of dance considered to be "American" were labelled as degenerate and the ways corporeal mobility was regulated in attempts to create an "English" style of ballroom dancing. Drawing on these historical analyses, scholars also indicate the continuing importance of colonial images in the evaluation of and fascination with certain dance forms: numerous studies on dance deal with the topic of "exoticisation". As they demonstrate, historically in Europe, non-European dances were often sexualised and represented as different from European dances: "Exoticization takes many forms, and the representation of the exotic Other, especially women, has been an important feature of both dance performances and visual representations of dance since at least the 18th century" (Reed 1998: 509). Exoticisation is often discussed related to so-called *Latin* dances, which are represented as particularly "hot" or "passionate" in their commercialised versions abroad (see for instance Savigliano 1995). Listing Argentinean tango and Brazilian samba, Hutchinson (2009) also argues that "few parts of the world are defined by dance in the same way and to the same extent as Latin America" (378). Dance has thus played an important role in the construction of Latin American national imaginaries, on site as well as abroad, a process highly interrelated with the history of colonialism and exotification (Hutchinson 2009).

Salsa is by far not the first "global dance craze" associated with Latin American countries, as the already cited examples of the rumba and the mambo as well as the ample literature on tango (Davis 2015a; Savigliano 1995; Törnqvist 2013) suggest:

> Twentieth-century American social dance history is rife with Latin dance "crazes", short-lived periods of frenzied obsession with hip-centric dances from Argentina, Cuba, or Brazil. For at least a century, starting with the tango craze of the 1910s and extending through the rumba, samba, and conga crazes of the 1930s into the mambo and cha cha crazes of the 1950s, past the lambada craze of the late 1980s, and onto the salsa craze at the turn of the millennium, Anglo-Americans have practiced dances borrowed from their Latin American neighbors.
>
> (McMains 2016: 480)

In this process, some of these dances were codified and adapted to the standards of the "ballroom industry" and then distributed in classes, books and performances, as McMains (2016) writes, a process clearly driven by economic motives.[16] In the process of commodification, elements associated with "Latinness" were particularly accentuated: the "Latin" section of ballroom dances is characterised by a "fetishized focus on movement of the hips" (McMains 2016: 481). Furthermore, competitors of "dancesport Latin" at ballroom competitions use self-tanning products – a practice with obvious "racially charged" effects (McMains 2001: 55). She therefore argues that the popularity of these dances is often based on harmful representations and stereotypes of Latin Americans as, among other attributes, passionate and sensual, but also dangerous and criminal – in short, emotionally uncontrolled. McMains (2016) analyses these stereotypes as serving "to justify not only North American superiority over Latin America, but also to reinforce ethnic hierarchies within the United States" (482).

The commodification and exoticisation of so-called Latin dances is also critiqued in Savigliano's (1995) analysis of *Tango and the Political Economy of Passion*. As the author demonstrates, in order to render tango dancing acceptable for a European audience, it had to be reshaped. Herein, dance masters in early 20th century Paris played a key role; they standardised the dance and simplified its improvisational characteristics into a morally acceptable set of steps, "a choreographic transformation suited to French manners and good taste" (Savigliano 1995: 122). Savigliano details the complex lives the tango has led in Argentina and in the cultural capitals of London, Paris and Tokyo, arguing that tango has been commodified for "imperial consumption". In her analysis, Savigliano (2010: 138) distinguishes between two groups of contemporary tango dancers: the European and North American "exoticizers" and the Argentinean "exotic others".

Taking a critical stance regarding the postcolonial critique of exoticism in tango, Davis (2015a) proposes to adopt a more empirically grounded approach and actually demonstrates how "exotic/erotic fantasies and desires of both Argentineans and their visitors are mobilized in complicated ways"

(Davis 2015a: 169). In this way, Davis (2015a) shows that exoticisation is a mutual process and an integral feature in the "transnational encounters" on the tango dance floor (175).

An important ingredient of exoticisation is "passion", as feminist and postcolonial scholars such as Savigliano have argued. As Davis (2015b) writes, feminist scholarship has been challenging "scientific authority that gave precedence to reason, objectivity, and value neutrality over emotions, subjectivity, and political engagement, thereby opening up space to explore embodied experience as a source of knowledge and a resource for a passionate and partisan feminist politics" (6). The "affective turn" in the social sciences in particular argues not to ignore sensory experiences in social analysis. However, as Davis (2015b: 6) continues, feminist scholars have been less concerned with "how passion feels or what it means in people's everyday lives", and they rather "tended to be interested in the ways passion is linked to power and how restrictive social norms and dominant hierarchies and exclusions get played out at an affective level" (cf Pedwell and Whitehead 2012 for a similar argument).

Departing from her own frustration with the one-sided feminist and postcolonial informed analysis of tango, Davis (2015b) draws precisely on the contradictions between *politics* and *experience*. She therefore uses a more empirically grounded approach to study dancers' passion for tango, exploring what it means for the people doing it (Davis 2015a: 15). She suggests developing a reflexive approach to passion,

> one that uses the embodiment of passion as an affective, sensual attachment with political implications as a site for exploring the contradictions and entanglements, the constraints and the possibilities that are part of any activity which is pleasurably intense and fervently desired, yet unsettling and perhaps even profoundly disturbing.
>
> (Davis 2015b: 17)

This theoretical perspective is particularly useful in order to understand the affective dimensions of the practice of salsa dancing.

As this discussion demonstrates, on the one hand, a perspective informed by postcolonial theory is necessary to dismantle ongoing constructions of "others" in contemporary dance practices, thus perpetuating "colonial appropriation", which variously reinforced "stereotypes of mystical spirituality and excessive sexuality" (Reed 1998: 509). However, on the other hand, such a perspective may be too narrow to grasp the actual experiences of various people and to understand why they engage in passionate (and arguably problematic) practices. Therefore, while taking into account the cited literature on dance practices, this book also sheds light on how dancers negotiate and think about their dancing, hereby taking into account dancers of various nationalities, gender and class backgrounds. In this way, this study shows how dancers themselves engage with and negotiate images of "exotic others" and cultural "authenticity".

Research perspectives

The circulation of people and affects is one of the main lenses through which I approach the salsa circuit. This section briefly revisits the reflections from the field of (transnational) migration studies relevant to this study, namely the development of a transnational perspective as an epistemological stance based on the critique of "methodological nationalism". Second, it also presents recent conceptualisations of (im)mobility in the heterogeneous field of mobility studies, which take into account several forms of human movement in one theoretical framework, a claim also made by the anthropology of dance.

A transnational perspective

The spatial circulation of people has been a topic in social science literature for a long time, and (transnational) migration studies in particular have theorised about the cross-border movement of people. During the 1990s, a new framing of the circulation of persons was introduced into the academic discourse on migration: the notion of transnationalism, which refers to a condition of "multiple ties and interactions linking people or institutions across the borders of nation-states" (Vertovec 1999: 447). Early scholars of transnationalism in migration studies argued that, contrary to classical assumptions in assimilation theory, "transmigrants" became rooted in their new country while maintaining ties to their countries of origin, making home and host society a single arena for social action (Glick Schiller et al. 1995). Concepts such as "transnational social space" (Faist 2000; Pries 2001) and "transnational social field" (Basch et al. 1994) were coined to account for social relationships that are sustained across borders. In my conceptualisation of the salsa circuit, I draw on reflections of these scholars.

The transnational approach challenged many other hitherto unchallenged assumptions about migration. Wimmer and Glick Schiller (2002) criticised the "methodological nationalism" present in much social science research. Their influential article disclosed parallels between nationalist thinking and the conceptualisation of migration in social sciences, arguing that "nationally bounded societies are taken to be the naturally given entities to study" (Wimmer and Glick Schiller 2002: 304). The borders of the nation state are taken as a "natural" unit of analysis, and researchers adopt a "container model of society", equating society with the nation-state. However, such a view naturalises nation states so that "every move across national frontiers becomes an exception to the rule of sedentariness within the boundaries of the nation-state" (Wimmer and Glick Schiller 2002: 310). Migrants thus appear to challenge the isomorphism between people and nation. Studies on transnational migration allowed new perspectives on space and borders, going beyond such idealist visions of a unity between the state and the population located in its territory. In this way, as Wimmer and Glick Schiller (2002) argue, studies examining the connections between transnational migrants and other actors are able to "carry us beyond the static, reified and essentialized concept of community and into the study of migrants and non-migrants within social fields of differential power" (324).

Since the introduction of transnationalism into social science, a vast array of scholarship has blossomed. Some studies emphasise that not every migrant is "transnational" (Portes et al. 2002), while others bring into light the existence of territories of circulation (*"territoires circulatoires"*) that do not follow the borders or logics of nation states but have their own hierarchies and forms of sociality (Tarrius 1993). Contemporary approaches argue for a transnational perspective as an epistemological lens rather than a theoretical framework (see Dahinden 2017; Glick Schiller 2015). Dahinden describes this as

> adopting an explicitly de-nationalized epistemological stance and con-comitant methodologies in order to investigate and theorize cross-border social phenomena by non-state actors. Such cross-border phenomena are understood as the outcome of particular processes which are embedded in multi-layered structures (political, economic, social) at simultaneously local, national and supranational scales and the agency of non-state actors.
>
> (Dahinden 2017: 1482)

Adopting a transnational perspective thus includes the analysis of the importance of the power of nation state categories in shaping actors' identities and their surrounding structures (Dahinden 2016). A transnational perspective is suited to overcome the "nation-state- and ethnicity-centred epistemology" (Dahinden 2017) for which migration and integration research has been criticised (Wimmer 2009; Wimmer and Glick Schiller 2002). At the same time, by including the importance of nation states as "units of governance and governmentality" (Glick Schiller and Meinhof 2011: 25), it goes beyond what has been described as a too naïve understanding of "global flows" in some approaches to cultural "globalization" (Heyman and Campbell 2009). It is in this sense that this study applies a transnational perspective to better understand the formation of the salsa circuit. Accordingly, I use the transnational perspective as a lens, "a way of looking at social reality without remaining trapped within taken-for-granted assumptions" (Moret 2018: 8).

Adopting a transnational perspective has not only epistemological and theoretical but also methodological implications. The "methodological transnationalism" (Amelina and Faist 2012) adopted in this multi-sited study is discussed in the section constructing "the field". In their outline of a transnational approach to study what they call cultural processes (such as musical creation), Glick Schiller and Meinhof argue that such an approach can include within the same analytical framework:

> (1) persons with a history of movement and connection, irrespective of their place of settlement; (2) those who are part of a place but legally

considered as peripheral to it including persons without accepted documentation including short-term labour contract workers, asylum seekers, "expats", retirees and returnees; (3) persons of migrant background, and (…) (4) persons who are classified as "natives" who share social relations with persons in the other three categories. That is to say: a transnational social field analysis of the relationships between migration and cultural production allows most of us to be encompassed within a single analytical lens.

(Glick Schiller and Meinhof 2011: 25)

In line with this reasoning, this study looks at various actors engaged in the production of the salsa circuit. In this way, this study follows the call for a de-migranticisation (Dahinden 2016) of research on people on the move.

Movement on different scales

Another field of study that deals with the movements of people, and also objects and information (Sheller 2011), is the vast and diverse field of mobility studies, which aims to bring together different types of movement into a single analysis. Similar to the transnational perspective discussed above, it challenges the tendency of the social sciences to treat stability as normal and mobility as problematic (Urry 2007), and criticises the "sedentary bias" (Sheller and Urry 2006). Furthermore, empirical studies from a mobilities perspective question "the taken for granted bonds between people, place, and culture" (Salazar and Smart 2011: ii).

Over recent years, the "mobility turn" or "mobilities paradigm" has entered migration studies (Faist 2013) as well as studies on artists' practices (see e.g. Martiniello et al. 2009). However, the celebratory vision of mobility, emphasising movement and change, has also been criticised (see e.g. Faist 2013). Scholars have pointed out that mobilities need moorings (Hannam et al. 2006) and that "we need to keep notions of fixity, stasis, and immobility in mind" (Cresswell 2010: 29). Cresswell (2010) therefore proposes an approach to study the "politics of mobility", which emphasises how mobilities are both productive of and produced by unequal relations of power. In a similar vein, Glick Schiller and Salazar (2013) develop a "regimes-of-mobility" framework: "The term 'regime' calls attention to the role both of individual states and of changing international regulatory and surveillance administration that affect individual mobility" (189). Drawing on such reflections on the production of mobilities and immobilities, this study not only follows salsa dancers' celebratory narratives of mobility but also looks at the difficulties and experiences of being stuck and the advantages of rootedness.

In a transnational social field, the question of who is able to travel becomes a marker of class. Glick Schiller and Salazar (2013) state that class has often been defined based on differential access to a range of resources: "A regimes-of-mobility approach can challenge us to expand this understanding so the ability and legal right to travel become one of the criteria by which class is defined and class privilege upheld" (196). In this way, class is defined not only by an individual's access to economic means but also in terms of legal status and ability to travel.

Taking up a second important argument of mobility studies, this study brings together different forms of mobility: mobility ranging in scale from the micro-movements of dancing bodies to the politics of global travel (cf Cresswell 2006). It approaches questions related to the cross-border mobility of differently positioned people from an entry point of their common bodily practice of salsa dancing. A transnational perspective combined with an understanding of (im) mobilities allows consideration of the usually separated forms of cross-border mobility of "migrants", "mobile Europeans" and "tourists" as well as a micro-analysis of moving bodies in gendered and (at times) ethnicised/racialised dancing.

Focusing on the movement of human bodies is nothing new for the anthropological study of dance, although it is a relatively recent field of study. As dance scholars often argue, the study of dance had long been neglected by academia, wherein the "mind-body dichotomy inherited from the Platonic-Cartesian tradition, as well as a long-standing bias towards the verbal as a key to human thought" (Neveu Kringelbach and Skinner 2012: 5) may have played a key role. Similarly, scholarship in line with what has been termed the "affective turn" in the humanities and social sciences (Bakko and Merz 2015; Clough 2007) has argued for the importance of (bodily) experiences instead of representation in the analysis of the social. As Clough (2008) observes, "the turn to affect did propose a substantive shift in that it returned critical theory and cultural criticism to bodily matter which had been treated in terms of various constructionisms under the influence of post-structuralism and deconstruction" (1).

Over the last few years, several scholars in the fields of the anthropology of dance and dance studies as well as sociology have addressed topics at the intersections of the two forms of human movement: travel in geographical space and micro-movements on dance floors (Bizas 2014; Davis 2015a; Farnell 2012; Marion 2012; Wilcox 2012). In their introduction to an edited book entitled *Dancing Cultures: Globalization, Tourism and Identity in the Anthropology of Dance*, Neveu Kringelbach and Skinner (2012: 9) state the particularly anthropological perspective on dance practices: "As anthropologists, we are interested in tracing the flows and movements of dance, its social significance as well as its carriers such as migrants and tourists". This book links the study of the embodied meaning with the study of carriers of salsa's "transnational moves" (Pietrobruno 2006). Hereby it also draws on the "turn to affect" (Clough 2008) to account for the importance of emotions.

Scholarship in the field of "affect studies" has theorised processes of the circulation of emotions, such as Ahmed (2004), who delivers a fine "analysis of affective economies, where feelings do not reside in subjects or objects, but are produced as effects of circulation" (8). Building on the work of philosophers Deleuze and Guattari (1980), affect is often defined as referring "generally to bodily capacities to affect and be affected or the augmentation or diminution of a body's capacity to act, to engage, and to connect" (Clough 2007: 2). Although highly diverse in their understandings of what affect is or can be, theories of affect have attempted "to go beyond the dominant epistemological parameters of the linguistic turn" (Bakko and Merz 2015: 7). In particular, researchers have challenged the scientific superiority of reason over emotion (Pedwell and Whitehead 2012). While some scholars thus position the interest in affect as "novel and groundbreaking", others argue that "feminists have always been engaged with questions of affect, emotion, and feeling" (Davis 2015b: 6). Furthermore, the rhetoric of newness risks omitting "feminist histories of knowledge production" (Pedwell and Whitehead 2012: 117). For example, scholarship on service and care industries has analysed the effects of the commercialisation of the intimate life through concepts such as "emotional labour" (Hochschild 1983) and "affective labour" (Ditmore 2007), as I will further discuss in Chapter 5.

A constructivist understanding of social categories

According to an interpretive, constructivist perspective, lived "reality" is constructed by social actors. As Schwandt (1998) specifies: "That is, particular actors, in particular places, at particular times, fashion meaning out of events and phenomena through prolonged, complex processes of social interaction involving history, language, and action" (222). My research participants often held clear and essentialist ideas regarding "culture" and ethnicity, gender and roles inside the salsa circuit. Building on a constructivist epistemology, as a researcher I was interested in the ways these categories came into being, how individuals participated in creating the categories and in which situations they were mobilised. Contrary to some studies that conceptualise dance as the expression of a specific cultural or "ethnic" group, I started from a vision of salsa dancing as a social practice, and thus the idea that salsa needs to be constantly (re)made as Latin or Cuban (or "global", as we will see). Similarly, gender relations are not as stable as one could think on first sight.

Since the 1980s, in the social sciences in general and anthropology in particular, scholars have criticised the tendency to naturalise the association of culture with place (Appadurai 1990; Baumann 1996; Gupta and Ferguson 1992; Wicker 1997) or, in other words, the idea of an isomorphism between a specific territory, an ethnic community or a nation and a culture (Wimmer and Glick Schiller 2002). Similarly, Brubaker (2002) criticised the prevalent "groupism" in social science: the "tendency to take discrete, sharply differentiated, internally homogeneous and externally bounded groups as basic constituents of social life, chief protagonists of social conflicts, and fundamental units of social analysis" (164).

Taking up these criticisms, and drawing on Barth's (1969) work on ethnicity, scholars have developed a relational, interactive and processual understanding of ethnic groups and group boundaries (e.g. Jenkins 1994; Wimmer 2009), whereby ethnicity is approached as the outcome of specific processes of "boundary-making". In this vision, ethnicity is not a "thing in the world" that explains how people behave but something that has to be explained itself (Wimmer 2009).

Taking into account the risk of "methodological nationalism", Wimmer (2009) criticised the tendency of scholarship on migration to treat ethnicity as a self-evident unit of analysis. Instead of assuming group boundaries are based on ethnicity, scholars should thus look at the ways ethnicity is actually made important – or not. Wimmer (2009) suggests researchers should "de-ethnicize research designs by taking non-ethnic units of observation to see both the emergence of ethnic closure and its absence or dissolution" (262). Similarly, Dahinden (2016) discusses strategies to "de-migranticize" migration research through several approaches, one of them being the "reorientation of the unit of analysis", which entails a focus on larger segments of the population instead of the category of "migrants" (2217).

The present study takes these epistemological (and methodological) reflections as a starting point in the development and implementation of the research interest. Instead of focusing on the circulation of people based on their supposed geographical origin, I chose to "follow" salsa dancers that I met at specific events. Only in a second step did I look at whether (and how) ethnicity is mobilised and made important in salsa dancers' strategies of positioning in the salsa circuit. In this process, ethnicity often intersects with racial classifications and representations.

I approach gender from a similar perspective, viewing it as the result of social interactions and following the idea of "gender as process" (Elliot 2016). As Elliot (2016) clarifies in a discussion of the relationship between gender and mobility: "Gender is not about observing how men and women move differently, but about a theoretical and methodological toolbox able to capture how socially, culturally, historically constructed relations between the sexes inflect the texture of mobility, and vice versa" (76). To analyse the specific negotiations on the salsa dance floor, I draw on West and Zimmerman's (1987, 2009) much-cited approach of "doing gender", as well as some of its developments (Deutsch 2007; Hirschauer 1994; 2001; Nentwich and Kelan 2014; Risman 2009). Addressing the gendered relationships in salsa dancing with a doing gender perspective has the advantage of switching the focus from the supposedly stable gender arrangements on the dance floor to the ongoing negotiations and activities of the gendered dancing, thus going beyond much of the literature dealing with gender in salsa. This constructivist approach to ethnicity and gender leads to a focus on the ways in which actors in the salsa circuit are creating – or doing – salsa together (see Schulze 2015: 58).

While the notion of "authenticity" is not as widely used in the salsa circuit as in other dance contexts (e.g. Bizas 2014 reports that students of Senegalese sabar dance described their motivation to travel to West Africa as a search for authenticity), some research participants referred to "authentic salsa". Lindholm (2008) attributes the quest for the authentic to modernity, bringing along the "erosion of a sacred hierarchy" (4), so that still today different forms of personal and collective authenticity are in great demand. From a constructivist stance, claims for authenticity can be approached as a part of actors' discourse and not an "objective quality of the object" (Reisinger and Steiner 2006). Drawing on this understanding, I will analyse the ways in which salsa dancers mobilise the idea of authenticity related to either salsa's history and a specific national context (in this study mainly Cuba) or a personal relation to salsa.

As mentioned, among my research participants a highly naturalised and essentialist idea of categories was prevalent regarding gender (gendered roles in salsa dancing are usually referred to as "the men" do this, "the women" do that), ethnicity ("Cubans and Latinos are like this, Europeans are like that") and roles inside the salsa circuit as related to status (*stars*, salsa *artists*, beginners, "good" dancers, etc.). These categories were rhetorically constituted by dancers who often referred to themselves and others in these ways. While understanding such categorisations as the result of social processes, in the analysis and written account I used (and thus (re)produced) the categories used by my interlocutors. In this way, I speak not only of male and female dancers; in some parts of the study I use the emic terms of *Latinos/Latinas*, *Cubans* and *Europeans* (or, in some cases *Eastern Europeans*) to analyse the ways actors actually engage in boundary-making between dancers and thus create these groups. However, it is important to keep in mind that these are not my categories; nor are they "objective" articulations of demographic "realities". While the categories were often constructed as relatively stable, individuals moved between them and negotiated their meanings.

Furthermore, I distinguish between what I term "salsa dance professionals" and "salsa students" to describe specific positions inside the salsa circuit, despite the various ways the term "professional" can be defined, particularly in spaces of music and entertainment (see Gibert 2011). In the context of the salsa circuit, I use the status of professional to point to individuals who are able to accumulate considerable salsa capital and often are able to transform it into economic capital: the acknowledged *salsa stars* as well as other dancers who teach and perform in the salsa circuit, often called *travelling artists*. However, the two categories are not always clearly separable: dance students may become remunerated teachers in some contexts, and professionals may take lessons with other dancers; the categorisations and identifications are thus always context-dependent and temporary.

Researching the salsa circuit

This study builds on a qualitative, interpretive and constructivist approach. The research process has been guided by a methodological approach inspired by grounded theory (Charmaz 2006; Glaser and Strauss 1967). This approach "prioritizes the data and the field under study over theoretical assumptions" (Flick 2014: 137). Theories are "discovered" (Glaser and Strauss 1967) or rather "constructed" (Charmaz 2006) in the research process and are grounded in the empirical data. Characteristic of a grounded theory approach is a circular research process, involving a close link between collection and interpretation of data and the selection of empirical material (Flick 2014: 139). As Charmaz (2006) argues: "We construct our grounded theories through our past and present involvements and interactions with people, perspectives, and research practices" (10). In this sense, my experiences as a white, female, Swiss national, trained in social anthropology, working in a research institute on the wider topic of transnational circulation, and with an interest in music and dance, shaped not only the choice of this research topic but also the ways I engaged with theoretical concepts, perspectives and the questions I asked during this process (Davis 2018a). Taking into account that knowledge is always situated in what Haraway (1988) terms "feminist objectivity", the present study encompasses the interpretations I acquired through a thorough reading of the various perspectives contained in my observational notes and interviews, building on extant methodological reflections and established methods.

The field of the salsa circuit necessitated a specific set of methodological moves, between field sites, the virtual world and dance floors, and between participant and observer. This section describes the ways I constructed my field, conducted short-term embodied ethnography of salsa events and carried out semi-structured, problem-centred interviews with dancers. Doing qualitative research always raises ethical questions, which I address throughout the section.

Constructing "the field"

How can people who are in circulation and constant movement be studied? Being interested in salsa dancers who form part of the salsa circuit, I was presented with the challenge of a research "field" in constant circulation. In order to start my fieldwork, I therefore had to make choices in terms of entry points into the circuit as well as the construction of the field itself.

One entry into the field is through events, as proposed as a possible way to overcome the shortcomings of the already discussed "groupist" research designs (see e.g. Bessin et al. 2010; Hertz 2009; Salzbrunn 2017). Salzbrunn (2017: 4) argues that an epistemological and methodological entry through the event allows renewal of social science approaches to migration, as it shifts the focus from an *a priori* defined group to the plural affiliations of present individuals. Similarly, in a discussion of anthropologists' preoccupation with "the local" (as a territorialised notion), Hertz (2009: 219) proposes to focus on the event, which points to a "series of recognisable acts happening in a specific time-space" (my translation). Drawing on such an understanding of the importance of events, I adopted a multi-sited research design and chose several "field sites" – including several of the hubs of the circuit (as defined in Chapter 2), namely salsa congresses, dance studios and an organised salsa holiday.

In anthropology, the idea of researchers following their objects of study and a "move out from the single sites" (Marcus 1995: 96) has been discussed explicitly since the 1980s.[17] Since then, scholars have adopted Appadurai's (1986) proposition to follow "things in motion" and Marcus' (1995) invitation to trace the people, the thing, the metaphor, the plot, story or allegory, the life or biography or the conflict. "Strategies of quite literally following connections, associations, and putative relationships are thus at the very heart of designing multi-sited ethnographic research" (Marcus 1995: 97). In this sense, the connections between the chosen sites are important, as Hannerz (2003) states: "The sites are connected with one another in such ways that the relationships between them are as important for this formulation as the relationships within them; the fields are not some mere collection of local units" (206).

These attempts to conceptualise a methodological approach to grasp the connectivity between geographically distant places (instead of focusing on the classical ethnographic one-sited field) have also been taken up from scholars in studies on the mobility of people (e.g. Mazzucato 2009; Richter 2012; Tarrius 2001). An important point of discussion raised in transnational studies of migration is the question of spatiality (see Faist 2004; Pries 2008). In a relational understanding of spatiality (see Massey 1994), space is considered "a contingent and historically changeable nexus between material artefacts and social actions, which is created, represented and appropriated by social actors" (Amelina and Faist 2012: 1714). Amelina and Faist (2012) therefore suggest that researchers of empirical migration studies should "study actors' strategies of space formation and space appropriation" (1714), through multi-sited ethnography and mobile methods. As they argue, researchers should adopt a "methodological transnationalism" to study "transnational mobilities and transnational formations by avoiding a nation-state-centred methodology" (Amelina and Faist 2012: 1708). As argued above, existing literature on salsa is often focused on local adaptations of the "global" dance and thus studies tend to be based on what can be termed a "methodological localism" (see also Mueller 2016). I therefore considered it particularly insightful to use another approach to study salsa dancers' circulation and meaning making. Adopting a multi-sited approach allowed me to focus on the connections between geographically distant phenomena. Indeed, for the salsa dancers I talked to, the question of where they were dancing (the locality) was far less important than, for example, the quality of the dance floor, the skill of their dance partner or the reputation of the other dancers and invited salsa instructors present (see Hertz 2009: 217 for a similar argument in relation to night clubs). Salsa events take place in strikingly similar formats wherever they happen to take place. Taking the importance of actors' construction of space into consideration, I thus conceptualised my different "field sites" as "one geographically non-contiguous space" (Hage 2005). As Hage (2005) notes: "To do so is to make a choice of emphasizing those global relations and the circulation of goods, communication, money, people and emotions that occurs within them" (467). I thus chose a multi-sited research design because I was interested in the "global relations and circulations", putting my emphasis on previously less researched aspects of salsa, particularly the phenomenon of salsa congresses. Obviously, this choice represents a limitation in terms of the importance of actors' embeddedness in specific localities and the concrete material and social contexts, a point raised by several critics of multi-sited studies (see e.g. Candea 2007; Hage 2005).

Choosing a multi-sited research approach based on a relational understanding of space does not imply a negation of the lasting impacts of nation states and their borders. On the contrary, during the whole research process I observed the ways in which the mobility of salsa dancers (in the circuit highly celebrated and normalised) had to be acquired, particularly by Cuban dancers. Linking the multi-sited research approach with a theoretical regimes-of-mobility framework allowed me to focus on the immobilities and non-granted mobilities as well and thus to integrate some aspects related to local and national contexts into the analysis.

Marcus (1995) calls multi-sited ethnography "an exercise in mapping terrain" (99), and Hannerz (2003) reminds us that "ethnography is an art of the possible" (213). It is in this sense that I constructed my multi-sited "field", gradually developing new insights and following newly arisen opportunities (Hannerz 2003: 207). In line with my research topic, I chose to combine several research strategies, such as tracking dance students and instructors, including different sites as well as the researcher's own body into the research process, as proposed by Skinner (2010).

Starting in 2013 and over a period of three years, I conducted short-term multi-sited fieldwork in several phases at ten salsa festivals in seven European cities (Berlin, St. Gall, Milan, Munich, Rovinj, Warsaw, Zurich). I also interviewed chosen dancers in their dance studios in Zurich, Geneva and London between festivals. In addition, I undertook two research trips to Havana in January 2014 and August 2015 for a total of five weeks. I also included social media and particularly Facebook as a research "site".

An important characteristic of my field sites was their short-term character. Hannerz (2003: 210) points to the importance of temporary and sometimes short-lived sites in much contemporary ethnography (see also Pink and Morgan 2013 on short-term ethnography). In the present study, this was particularly the case of salsa congresses, which Kabir (2013) characterises as "ephemeral, itinerant, and non-local" (266). These events start on Friday in the afternoon and end with all guests departing on Sunday night or Monday morning. I experienced research at these events as extremely intense as I had to switch between various roles and research methods with practically no time to rest. At the same time, this intensity was visible in the collected data. Knoblauch (2005) proposes the concept of "focused ethnography" to account for precisely the intensity of data such short-term ethnography may generate: "The short time period covered is compensated for by another type of intensity: focused ethnographies are typically data intensive" (16). My engagement with the salsa circuit encompassed more than just the short-term fieldwork, as I continued to take classes in my home town, maintained contact with other dancers and followed salsa debates not least through social media, particularly Facebook, over an extended period of three years (for a similar point see also Pink and Morgan 2013).

The field of study hence included salsa events in several European cities, salsa studios, a dance holiday in Havana and, to a lesser degree, the internet. It also included my own body as the next section specifies, addressing the ways I conducted research at these events.

Dancing through the field

To better understand the workings of the salsa circuit and the practices of dance professionals and salsa students during such events, I conducted short-term ethnography at salsa events in European cities and Havana. I did not confine myself to observing practices but also participated in various degrees in the field and included aspects of embodied research. These methodological moves, a combination of different degrees of participation and observation, allowed me to have access to different embodied, verbalised and observed experiences and interactions (such as doing gender and ethnicity) and to gain a broader perspective of the ways salsa dance is commercialised and taught in the transnational salsa circuit.

Participant observation is a prominent method in qualitative research to gain access to "what people do". It is defined as "the process of learning through exposure to or involvement in the day-to-day or routine activities of participants in the researcher setting" (Schensul and LeCompte 1999: 91). Debates on the degree of the researcher's participation in a given field (and particularly in the anthropology of dance) have led to scholars arguing for a position of "observant participation" (Daniel 1995) rather than anthropology's more classic "participant observation" (see also Skinner 2010: 111). In this study, my position oscillated between the two poles, at moments pointing more towards the observation and at others more towards the participation, particularly in moments of dancing.

Paralleling the "affective turn", a growing number of scholars in dance (Apprill 2005; Crosby 1997; Ness 1992; Sklar 2001), martial arts (Robitaille 2013) and sports (Wacquant 2004) have argued for a reintroduction of the researcher's own body into the research process. This recognition of the researcher's body as a tool in the research process is discussed in the literature as "dance ethnography" (Crosby 1997; Sklar 2000), "carnal sociology" (Wacquant 2004) or "embodied ethnography" (Wade 2011). These approaches vary considerably in their focus, ranging from the study of the senses to the experiences of movement as part of a wider cultural context. Phenomenology-inspired approaches are interested in studying sensation itself (see e.g. Ness 1992; Novack 1990). Sklar (2000), for example, writes:

> While it has been traditional practice to erase the researcher's body from the ethnographic text, 'subjective' bodily engagement is tacit in the

process of trying to make sense of another's somatic knowledge. There is no other way to approach the felt dimensions of movement experience than through the researcher's own body.

(71)

Other dance ethnographers propose a research methodology that uses the researcher's "embodied knowledge" as a key research tool, awarding it equal standing with theoretical knowledge (Crosby 1997: 75). Crosby (1997) states that a "unique ethnographic voice" can "arise from a dancer's way of knowing and meaning-making" (67). Similarly, the sociology of the body à la Wacquant (2015) emphasises the researcher's apprenticeship of or involvement in a bodily practice in order to generate data and acquire another type of knowledge. In his discussion of "enactive ethnography", Wacquant (2015) states: "Methodically deploying one's body as an intelligent instrument of practical knowledge production speeds up the acquisition of basic social competency – the operant capacity to feel, think, and act like a Whatever among the Whatevers" (7). While some dance ethnographers, phenomenology-inspired approaches and the cited "enactive ethnography" are convinced of the necessity of researchers' embodied experiences to write a meaningful ethnography of the bodily practice in question, this approach has also been questioned as resulting "in too limited a personal view, running the risk of becoming self-indulgent" (Buckland 2010: 340).

Therefore, in this study, I used a combination of an embodied research strategy with participant observation/observant participation and semi-structured interviews, which proved particularly fruitful, as a single focus on either the dancing or the interviews would not have allowed me to generate the insights required for this research. Hutchinson (2009) makes a similar point, arguing that "the subjective experience of the dancer often throws the objective observation of the ethnographer into question, though taking the two views together is necessary for understanding dance as both a visual art and a corporeal sensation" (385).

Taking part in dancing activities (mainly workshops and parties) and acquiring a certain skill level in different salsa dance styles was a helpful research strategy in several ways. First, it allowed me to understand the effects of different pedagogical techniques and to experience "how it feels" to dance salsa, or in other words, to learn "a dancer's way of knowing" (Crosby 1997). In her discussion of dance ethnography, Crosby (1997) reports how she developed shared meanings with her fellow dancers through her own bodily movements. Similar to the process of apprenticeship Crosby describes, I developed a sense of what many dancers had told me: that connection between dance partners and improvisation were key aspects of competence in (social) salsa dancing. As I developed an understanding of these concepts through my own moving body, it contrasted clearly with some theoretical arguments, particularly in terms of the gendered roles. For some of my research questions, I therefore used my own embodied experiences as a critical departure point for further exploration with other dancers during the interviews (for a similar strategy, see Törnqvist 2013: 248; see also McClure 2015). My personal experience thus necessarily informed my understanding of the salsa circuit, but this specific and highly subjective experience was not the focus of this study. Instead, my embodied experiences and emotional engagement were mobilised as a mode of inquiry, which helped me to gain new insights and develop my theoretical reflection.

A second advantage of my dancing was that I could use it as a methodological tool: it proved a successful strategy in approaching interview participants, particularly festival participants at events but also salsa holiday participants and teachers during my two stays in Havana. In this way, the shared dancing experience not only offered a convenient and conventional mode of getting in contact with research participants, but the dancing, a form of "embodied collaboration" (Chrysagis and Karampampas 2017: 11), was also helpful in building rapport and creating a sense of connection. As Skinner (2010) argues in a methodological discussion of what he terms "dance interview": "Because we had danced, there was a commonly shared notion – or assumption – between us that we knew each other" (118). Obviously, salsa's gendered roles proved to be a limitation to this approach, as I mostly danced with male dancers during salsa workshops and parties.[18] Despite this limitation, participating in workshops and at parties as a salsa dancer enabled me to meet and have discussions with female dancers between dances.

As anthropological debates on the researcher's positioning and reflexivity have highlighted, doing participant and embodied research demands enforced reflexivity. As the researcher is inevitably part of what is being studied, she is involved in the production of knowledge. The researcher's social positioning thereby influences the access to specific insights but less to others.

Therefore, the last point I wish to discuss here is what feminist activist Rich (1986) termed the "politics of location". Explaining this now popular concept in gender studies and beyond, Davis (2018a) remarks: "Everyone is located somewhere and our locations invariably shape not only how we view the world, but how the world views us" (641). In a research encounter between the researcher and the research participants, both parts are located socially. The literature suggests discussions of asymmetries in research encounters along the lines of gender, class, ethnicity or race, as well as nationality, sexuality, age, ability or religion. Accordingly, in feminist studies, the power relations are usually seen to be asymmetrical in favour of the researcher. However, as Ryen (2004) notes, in some interview settings, it can be the inverse, in her case when doing "elite interviews with businessmen in big companies" (233). Doing research in the salsa circuit required the navigation and acknowledgement of a complex set of locations: in addition to the positioning asymmetries, there is a specific status hierarchy inside the salsa circuit that proved influential in the ways I was perceived by my interviewees.

Dancers reacted differently when they perceived me as a (female) salsa student, a member of an event organisation or a researcher. These different roles also provided me access to different groups of actors. The prevalent distinction between salsa *artist* and salsa *student* also influenced the ways I could (or could not) access salsa dance professionals who are often endowed with high symbolic capital and presented as *stars*. In the context of a salsa congress, this meant that in interview situations, these individuals perceived me as one of their students, a status position endowed with low symbolic value, reminiscent of Ryen's (2004) "elite interviews".

Acknowledging my location also entailed critically reflecting on the ways my own (privileged) position influenced the research project as a whole and the relationships I built during the study. As Davis (2018a) states, it is important to acknowledge how "identifications and affiliations come into play in a particular research context" (641). As a white Swiss national working at a university, I had access to travel in ways some of my research participants never could. The Swiss passport allows for visa-free travelling to almost any country, and I was able to obtain funding for parts of the travel and accommodation costs.

As a young, blond, female European, I was approached in specific ways in the salsa circuit, which granted access to certain insights (such as the follower role in dancing) and limited access to others. In Havana, for instance, I was seen and approached as one of the affluent, female European (salsa) tourists (for a similar point, see Törnqvist 2013: 250). I was approached several times on the street and invited to take salsa lessons; I also discussed the role of "taxi-dancers" and the way they engaged with tourists with other salsa tourists. These experiences allowed for insights I would not have made without my embodied engagement in salsa during the research. In contrast, the experiences of dance professionals in Cuba were harder to access, not only due to my limited knowledge of Spanish, but also due to our unequal access to mobility and economic capital, which further accentuated the "local/tourist" divide. This "encompassing and resilient identification of any foreigner as tourist" (Simoni 2016: 23) informed the kind of access I had to Cuban dancers based in Havana. On my second research stay, I therefore chose another strategy, by "following" a ten-day organised holiday group, during which I was able to build up rapport with a small number of dance teachers – through my embodied participation in the group – and later ask for an interview, a strategy that was more adapted to the field in Havana.

As this discussion illustrates, the researcher's (privileged) multiple and embodied locations shape the encounters during the research and the project as a whole. My fieldwork notes therefore contain observations of and emotional responses to specific encounters during the research process, which I incorporated in the analysis by treating them as data for my research. In this way, I included a reflexive stance about my position during the research process and the analysis and in the writing of this text.

Interviewing salsa dancers

This study builds on observation notes as well as different types of interviews, ranging from the already mentioned open ethnographic interviews to semi-structured, "problem-centred interviews" inspired by Witzel (2000). To better understand dancers' own viewpoints on their careers, the strategies they employed to improve their situation and the ways actors in the salsa circuit make sense of and give meaning to their doings, I conducted qualitative, semi-structured interviews. While Parts I and II of this book are based on the observational notes and interview material, Part III on salsa dance professionals' careers builds exclusively on the transcribed interview material.

Before I met the research participants, I prepared an interview guide for semi-structured, problem-centred interviews (Witzel 2000), an interview type featuring an open question in the beginning with ad-hoc questions to elaborate on mentioned topics followed by a set of pre-established, more specific questions focusing on a topic. This interview type was best suited to my field with its time restrictions, as it allowed me to combine a less structured part, in which interviewees could develop their "salsa biography" with pre-formulated questions regarding their own perspectives on certain aspects of salsa.

I developed two different interview guides, one for what I came to term "salsa dance professionals", focusing on questions around their career, and another for salsa event participants ("the students"), focusing on their involvement in salsa and questions of gender and ethnicity, with some overlapping parts and additional questions for event organisers. I adapted the interview questions to the interviewee and circumstances of the interview, including for example observations I had made during an earlier workshop with that individual. I used the guide during the interviews as a reminder of important topics and the themes I wished to cover, what Witzel (2000) calls a "background film", while allowing new topics and questions to emerge. After every interview, I wrote a postscript, including new insights that occurred during the interview and observations regarding the interview situation. These postscripts were later used as memos, and they thus formed part of the analysis.

Implementing the theoretical reflections presented before, I chose the research participants for this study based on an entry through salsa events. Through this sampling strategy, I was able to include a range of situations and diverse people in terms of origin, ethnicity and dance style and thus avoid "groupist" (Brubaker 2002) interpretations. However, I did not aim to generate a representative sample. Instead, the interview participants for this study were selected step by step, drawing on a theoretical sampling approach (Glaser and Strauss 1967). Following this approach, cases were chosen based on their relevance rather than their representativeness (Flick 2014: 173). I thus selected research participants "according to their (expected) level of new insights for the developing theory" (Flick 2014: 171) during the process of collecting and interpreting the material. Cases were selected considering the criteria of maximal variation in the sample (Becker 1998), in terms of different positions in the salsa circuit, including salsa dance professionals at different levels of their career, dance students and, to a lesser extent, event organisers. Furthermore, cases were varied concerning gender and nationality/ origin country. As is true with all qualitative research projects, practical issues and convenience played into the sampling strategy, notably in the first phase of interviewing.

In later phases of the project the choices were more theoretically informed, as I tried to maximise the variation and include individuals that were usually presented as outside the salsa circuit: the tendency of "groupism" is not only present in studies on migration or "ethnic groups" as discussed above, but also in studies on so-called "subcultures". As Schulze (2015: 53) has demonstrated, there is a risk of a "methodological subculturalism" in research on subcultures. Taking a supposed "transnational community" of salsa dancers as a starting point for research opens the possibility of a reification of group boundaries and homogenisation of the group. I tried to counter this risk by including dancers based in Cuba, who had fewer possibilities to participate in the salsa circuit.

In total, 36 interviews were recorded, transcribed and analysed. The languages I speak also influenced the sampling, as I decided to conduct all the interviews myself, and thus focused on dancers speaking English (15 interviews), German (14), and to a lesser extent Spanish (6) and French (1). Therefore, English- and German-speaking dancers are overrepresented among the interviewees. Table 1.1 specifies the interviewed dancers' positions inside the salsa circuit.

The salsa dance professionals include full-time dancers and instructors at different stages of their career, with a range of educational backgrounds (some with a professional dance education, others without) and based in Europe and/or Cuba. Additionally, some of them teach in their own salsa schools and are thus also studio owners, while others are freelancers. The festival and holiday attendees were experienced salsa dancers, some of whom teach and perform salsa occasionally. Dancers ranged in age from their twenties to their mid-fifties. The interviewees' origin countries included Austria (1 interviewee), a Caribbean Island (1), Costa Rica (1), Cuba (7), Cyprus (2), France (1), Germany (2), Greece (1), Hungary (1), India (1), Mexico (1), Nicaragua (1), Nigeria (1), Poland (1), Romania (2), Spain (1), Sweden (1), Switzerland (8), Uruguay (1) and the USA (1). At the time of the interview, they were based in Cuba (5 interviewees), Cyprus (2), Germany (5), Greece (2), Italy (1), Norway (1), Singapore (1), Sweden (2), Switzerland (12), UK (5) and the USA (1).

The interviews were transcribed in their original language, and I translated the quotations after I had chosen them for further exploration in the text. All names are pseudonyms and throughout the analysis, I changed personal details as well as places and countries to preserve anonymity.

Table 1.1 Interview participants' position in the salsa circuit.

	Salsa professional	Holiday or festival participant	Organiser
Female	12	5	2
Male	11	5	1
Total	23	10	3

The field notes together with the transcribed interviews formed the basis of the data for this study. To organise, analyse and interpret this material, I chose an approach inspired by grounded theory analysis (Charmaz 2006; Glaser and Strauss 1967) and "thematic coding" (Flick 2014), extended with a theoretically driven reading of the emerging codes. I thus combined a first, data-driven inductive analysis with a second, more deductive approach to my empirical data (see Moret 2018 for a similar discussion of a "two-step hybrid approach" to data analysis). This multi-step analysis, including several methods of coding, inductive and deductive logics, computer software and colourful sticky notes as well as different writing techniques at different stages, led to the interpretations presented in this book.

Notes

1 Throughout this book I will use the notion salsa dancer to include all people dancing salsa, regardless of their status in the salsa circuit. When a distinction between professionals and non-professionals is made, I use the term salsa dance professionals or instructors for actors of the first category, salsa students or festival participants for the latter.

2 I here refer to dancers' emic use of the term dance *scene*, which may differ greatly in number of participants and dance offer. The notion of emic categories is used in anthropology to designate a perspective from within the social group studied (Headland et al. 1990). Throughout this book, emic terms are highlighted with italics.

3 For a thorough analysis of gendered aspects of salsa music and its development, see Aparicio (1998); for an analysis of salsa as Puerto Rican, see Quintero Rivera (1998); Waxer (2002a) gathers several authors on the topics of the origins and newer places of salsa music production; Fuentes (2003) collects interviews with founding salsa musicians.

4 An example of *salsa dura* is Willie Colon's *El Malo*: rebrand.ly/salsa-1. A contemporary band that plays the salsa style of the 1970s is Italy-based *La Maxima 79*: rebrand.ly/salsa-2.

5 An often played *salsa romantica* song during my research was Luis Enrique's *Yo no se mañana*: rebrand.ly/salsa-3.

6 An example of a timba song is NG La Banda's El Tragico: rebrand.ly/salsa-4; a song musicologist Klette Bøhler (2013) classifies as timba, while stating that "*Salsa Cubana* has now become an established term in Cuba for a successor genre to timba" (8).

7 For this reason, Boulila (2015) argues that contrary to images prevalent in the salsa circuit of salsa as a "foreign" and "exotic" practice, the "gender and sexual stereotypes at work in salsa should therefore be placed within a genealogy of European dance conventions and exoticising scripts" (134).

8 The government institutionalised rumba and other Afro-Cuban practices in an attempt to serve its egalitarian agenda and erase racial inequalities (Daniel 1995), an agenda that has not been met yet, as studies of racism in Cuba amply demonstrate (see e.g. Clealand 2013).

9 They are certainly not the first Cuban artists to travel to Europe to perform Afro-Cuban dance, as the literature on rumba performers in Paris in the 1920s demonstrates (see, for instance, Fernandez-Selier 2013 for an exploration of the rumba craze in 1927; see also Blanco Borelli 2016, who offers accounts of several Cuban dancers performing in other countries in the 1950s).

10 See, for example, Renta (2014) on salsa in Puerto Rico, Balbuena Gutiérrez (2014) on casino in Cuba, Waxer (2002b) on salsa in Colombia.

11 Like other partner dances with a similar history, for example tango, salsa is not only performed as *social dance* but also on stages and in competitions. In order to judge dancers, specific aspects of salsa dancing have been codified, often relying on established criteria in ballroom competition. Dancers and scholars have criticised these codification processes as being based on "Europeanist aesthetic values" (Renta 2014: 129) and in particular the canon of ballet that influenced ballroom dance (see Pietrobruno 2006). In contrast to these findings, during my research at salsa events and in salsa studios, Afro-Cuban dance forms were highly admired among salsa dancers.

12 In the following video, a New York-based dance instructor explains the difference between the salsa styles called Cuban, LA and New York. While his account is rather male-centred, it nevertheless gives an impression of the different dance styles: rebrand.ly/salsa-5.

13 For the purpose of this study, this simplified presentation of the different salsa dance styles suffices. For a discussion of this classification system, see Hutchinson (2014a: 9) who argues (among others) that it risks obscuring historical connections between locations. See also McMains' (2015) analysis of how the different locally developed salsa styles merged into one "global congress-style salsa".

14 For an example of salsa fusion, see rebrand.ly/salsa-6.

15 See Romàn-Velazquez (2002b) on London; Puccio (2000) on Toulouse; Wieschiolek (2003) on Hamburg; Papadopoulos (2003) on Frankfurt; Pušnik and Sicherl (2010) on Ljubljana; Schneider (2010) on Sydney; Bock and Borland (2011) on New Jersey; Gagné (2014) and Iwanaga (2014) on Tokyo; Llano (2014) on Barcelona; Escalona (2014) on Paris; Quayson (2014) and Carwile (2017) on Accra.

16 Ballroom dancing can be traced back to professional dance associations established in the UK and the USA in the 1870s (Pietrobruno 2006: 117).

17 Nonetheless, earlier ethnographies often included "multi-sited" research (e.g. the famous example of Malinowski's *Argonauts of the Western Pacific* (see Salazar et al. 2017)).

18 I had taken several salsa classes and acquired an intermediate level of salsa dancing (as a follower) before I started the research for this project. I was therefore able to participate in most of the workshops in the role of the follower. However, my skills in leading were too basic to invite other (female or male) followers to dance with me.

2 The salsa circuit

This chapter offers a theoretical, contextual and empirically grounded introduction to the salsa circuit. I will first conceptualise the salsa circuit as consisting of several hubs, related through the circulation of people, imaginaries, dance movements, conventions and affects. Second, drawing on my data as well as the available literature, this chapter introduces the formation of the salsa circuit from a European perspective, which is often glossed over in studies on salsa. Third, this chapter delivers a descriptive account of two of salsa's hubs – the salsa congresses and the space of salsa tourism in Havana – both of which formed important entry points into the salsa circuit during the empirical research for this study. The fourth part of this chapter builds on the empirical data, to analyse the circulation of people and a specific imaginary of salsa. It describes one group of the circulating actors, whose interest and economic capital keep the salsa circuit going: the self-declared *salsa addicts* (salsa students and festival participants). It analyses the imaginary of salsa as the *Esperanto of the body*, which builds the common ground for today's salsa dancers and forms part of salsa's "affective economy".

Conceptualising the salsa circuit

Since anthropology started to research topics such as circulation and "global flows" (Appadurai 1990), it has been "struggling to bridge the gap between localized, situational inquiry and the study of large-scale systems" (Mueller 2016: 103). Similarly to Mueller (2016), I was presented with the challenge of observing salsa dancers at a micro-level and developing a broader understanding of the transnational networks salsa dancers are engaged in. Based on the emic notion of the *circuit*, and building on Mueller (2016) and Kiwan and Meinhof (2011), I conceptualised salsa as consisting of a circuit with several hubs. I furthermore draw on Becker's (1982) framework of "art worlds" and, complementary, Bourdieu's (1993) theorisation of "fields of cultural production", including Bourdieu's theorisation of different forms of capital.

Bridging theories of localised scenes and global flows

Literature interested in salsa in terms of its social environment often frames salsa as a localised "scene". Such studies focus on salsa's local adaptations, a perspective that often builds on a dichotomy between "global cultural flows" and "local culture" and risks reifying singular geographic locations. This clear distinction between "the global" and "the local" as well as the related view of "culture" as clearly associated with "place" has several theoretical limitations, which this study wishes to address. As anthropologists have argued for decades, the discipline's focus on the local builds on a supposed isomorphism between ethnic groups and place (Barth 1969) as well as between culture and place (Appadurai 1996). Early globalisation scholars argued that the emergence of a "transnational public sphere" has "rendered any strictly bounded sense of community or locality obsolete" (Gupta and Ferguson 1992: 9).

How, then, can we think of salsa if not in terms of localised scenes or as a "global flow" with no anchor in any local social, economic or political realities? And how are the different localised scenes connected? To describe salsa on a "global" scale, my interview partners used terms such as *scene, family, world, industry* and *circuit*. I opted for the emic notion[1] of the *circuit* to underline the importance of circulation in my conceptualisation of salsa: the circulation of people, the circulation of imaginaries, dance movements, conventions and affects. People travel to take salsa lessons, participate in salsa events or teach and perform at numerous events. In their encounters they build on and (re)produce a set of shared understandings of why they do what they do (imaginaries) and how it best should be done and felt (the conventions and affects). This book looks closely at the circulation of people, dance movements, imaginaries and affects, whereby I do not conceive of circulation as an abstract idea of flows but rather as inextricably and inseparably linked to local situations (cf Mueller 2016: 110).

As Urry (2003) argues, "social life is full of multiple and extended connections often across long distances, organised through certain nodes or hubs within which social life is formed and reformed" (157). In the case of the salsa circuit, these extended connections come together in hubs. The salsa hubs should not be understood as physical geographical places but rather as the material actualisation of salsa, the moment salsa happens in a specific space.[2] Hubs can take various forms, such as a salsa event, a festival, a class at a salsa studio or a party at a salsa club, thus temporarily territorialising in specific places. Furthermore, situations such as an online discussion between salsa dancers on the topic of a convention can also be considered a hub. In this sense, the different situations studied in this research project can be conceptualised as highly connected (see also Mueller 2016), reminiscent of post-structuralist philosophers Deleuze and Guattari's (1998 (1980)) notion of rhizome. The model of the rhizome points to a non-hierarchical organisation and is characterised as follows: "unlike trees or their roots, the rhizome connects any point to any other point" (23). This conceptualisation of the salsa circuit consisting of hubs highly connected through circulation is helpful in overcoming ideas of either localised scenes or global flows, as it allows for a relational perspective.

At the same time, the critics of some enthusiast depictions of global cultural flows have argued that there are limits to idealist, non-hierarchical perspectives of social relations. Tsing (2000: 337) warns that a focus on circulation as the defining characteristic of the global mistakenly turns the attention to what circulates instead of to the conditions that allow circulation to take place. Mueller (2016: 120) argues that such a non-hierarchical vision of the social world (in this case the salsa circuit) is insufficient when it comes to understanding hierarchies and unequal access to various resources (in short, power relations). Therefore, the hubs and circulations constituting the salsa circuit have to be understood as being embedded in broader, globe-spanning political, economic and cultural power relations. Scholars of transnationalism argue that "the political borders of states do not delimit the world of the social, although the role of states is one important element in the analysis of power relations" (Glick Schiller 2015: 2277). Particularly when it comes to the circulation of people, current "migration regimes" (Amelina 2017) have to be taken into account when analysing the salsa circuit. The European migration system considerably shapes actors' access to the salsa circuit, as I will demonstrate for the case of salsa hubs based in European countries. From the perspective of some dancers in this study, the salsa circuit is therefore separated into a specific European circuit or North American circuit, which they can only enter under specific circumstances (such as obtaining a visa). To account for these limitations, in some parts of this study I narrow the focus down to a specific European salsa circuit, whose boundaries align with Europe's borders, thus rendering visible the structural difficulties salsa dance professionals of different origin countries have to overcome in order to participate in the European salsa circuit.

Art worlds and artistic fields

To understand specific aspects of the salsa circuit, I found certain theoretical frameworks more useful than others: Becker's notion of "art worlds" (1982) was particularly helpful in analysing salsa dancers' organising of collective action in regards to specific conventions (see also Schulze 2015). His analytical framework allowed me to focus on people "doing things together" (Becker 1986) in Part II of this study. However, to account for the power relations and struggles in the salsa circuit, aspects of Bourdieu's framework of "artistic fields" (1993) and his theorisation of different forms of capital (Bourdieu 1986) were more helpful (see Part III). While Becker's (1982) notion of "art worlds" and Bourdieu's (1993) conceptualisation of "artistic fields" are often seen as complementary in terms of their strengths and weaknesses (Bottero and Crossley 2011), they differ considerably in their theoretical outlook. The resulting tensions between different levels of analysis point to the limits of a sole analytical lens, which I wanted to overcome by approaching the salsa circuit from different perspectives.

To summarise Becker's framework, the term "art worlds" denotes "the network of people whose cooperative activity, organized via their joint knowledge of conventional means of doing things, produce the kind of art works that art world is noted for" (1982: x). Drawing on this understanding, I included not just one specific category of actors into my analysis, such as the self-described *salsa artists*; I also included some of the other actors such as festival participants, DJs and event organisers. Furthermore, I draw on Becker's understanding of cooperation and look closely at some conventions of the salsa circuit, particularly conventions in pedagogical techniques and "gender conventions" (Schulze 2015) in dancing as well as what I coined the "convention of tangible salsa *stars*".

While Becker's analytical framework has the advantage of stressing the importance of collaboration between all the participants of an art world over widespread popular beliefs of artists as individual creators, it has been criticised for its emphasis on consensus rather than conflict among artists and actors who control material and symbolic resources (see Crane 2015). In other words, the main criticism of Becker and interactionism more generally suggests that its focus on people doing things overlooks structural issues of power and resources (Bottero and Crossley 2011). Indeed, conceptualising salsa as an art world did not adequately address the question of power relations inside and outside the specific realm of salsa.

In a second analytical step, I therefore opted to include some aspects of Bourdieu's (1993) framework of "fields" to be able to analyse the specific strategies of actors in terms of the resources and capital at their disposal. Bourdieu's theoretical framework lays the groundwork to analyse the reproduction of social hierarchies. His notion of "field of cultural production" adds a focus on inequalities: "The literary or artistic field is a *field of forces*, but it is also a *field of struggles* tending to transform or conserve this field of forces" (Bourdieu 1993: 30, italics in original). In Bourdieu's analytical framework, cultural products and producers are located within a space of positions and position-takings. Actors struggle to defend or improve their positions, adopting "strategies which depend for their force and form on the position each agent occupies in the power relations [rapports de force]" (Bourdieu 1993: 30). Actors thus develop strategies, consciously or not, that permit them to ameliorate their situation. The analysis of the artistic field is part of Bourdieu's wider theorisation of distinct social fields, in which a social field is defined as "a space of objective relations between positions defined by their rank in the distribution of competing powers or species of capital" (Bourdieu and Wacquant 1992: 114). In Bourdieu's view, numerous discrete and relatively autonomous social fields make up social space, such as the economic, artistic, intellectual and juridical fields (in his case in a national frame). As each field has its own logics, the actors' struggles and capital are differently valued in different contexts (Bourdieu and Wacquant 1992). However, Bourdieu's notion of distinct fields has been criticised for its narrowness (Lahire

2001, see also Moret 2018). I therefore do not restrict my analysis to "social fields" but also include other contexts, which encompass "less strictly bounded and defined social environments and hierarchies" (Moret 2018: 101). Accordingly, I do not analyse the salsa circuit in terms of a national bounded field.

Bourdieu's theorisation of capital

Bourdieu's theoretical framework is based on the assumption that social inequalities are a product of the accumulation of several forms of unequally distributed resources. Enlarging the Marxian understanding of economic capital, Bourdieu conceptualises economic, cultural, social and symbolic capital as related (and sometimes convertible) forms of capital (Bourdieu 1986). In this study I build on Bourdieu's capital approach, taking into account its limits and adding a discussion of a specific salsa capital.

Following Bourdieu, economic capital can be immediately and directly converted into money and may be institutionalised in the form of property rights. In the salsa circuit, economic capital is highly important and at the same time downplayed by most actors. Although often being a prerequisite for access to the salsa circuit (in form of dance lessons, travel costs and entry tickets), as well as the return for dance professionals' work, dancers and organisers often insist on doing what they do only "out of passion for salsa, not for the money". According to Bourdieu (1983), this "inversion of the logic of the larger economy of the society" (311) is specific to the field of cultural production.

Bourdieu distinguishes three states of cultural capital, of which one is of particular interest for this study: institutionalised cultural capital. Cultural capital in its institutionalised state corresponds to academic qualifications such as formal degrees and certificates. This objectification of cultural capital "makes the difference between the capital of the autodidact, which may be called into question at any time, [...] and the cultural capital academically sanctioned by legally guaranteed qualifications, formally independent of the person of their bearer" (Bourdieu 1986: 247). Many of today's salsa dance professionals have degrees in various dance forms, such as "contemporary", "folkloric" or "urban" dance, which may be important in some circumstances. However, contrary to Bourdieu's statement above, in the salsa circuit a dancer's authority may be called into question despite formal qualifications, as the construction of "salsa capital" relies on qualifications only in specific circumstances.

The third form of capital Bourdieu defines is social capital:

> the aggregate of the actual or potential resources which are linked to pos-
> session of a durable network of more or less institutionalized relationships
> of mutual acquaintance and recognition – or in other words, to member-
> ship in a group – which provides each of its members with the backing
> of the collectivity-owned capital, a "credential" which entitles them to
> credit, in the various senses of the word.
>
> (Bourdieu 1986: 248)

The understanding of resources embedded in social networks as a form of capital is particularly helpful in the analysis of salsa dance professionals' careers. A dance professional with close ties to many event organisers will have a larger volume of performance and teaching opportunities than dancers with low social capital. Moreover, as Bourdieu states, social capital demands relational efforts; as I will demonstrate in detail in Part III of this book, social capital has to be acquired and maintained through processes of "networking" (Schapendonk 2015), and it is highly relevant in all stages of the career-building process.

Furthermore, as Bourdieu argues, once accepted and valued by others, the three types of capital already described may become symbolic capital. Bourdieu's work (1993) on an economy of symbolic goods also inspired my understanding of the relational field of salsa as an "affective economy". As demonstrated throughout this book, salsa dancers negotiate their positions in the salsa circuit drawing on various resources. The notion of an affective economy points to the importance of the affective experience of salsa dancing as a driving force of the salsa circuit.

While Bourdieu's capital approach has been highly influential in social analysis, it has also generated criticism pointing to its limits in several regards. An important critique states its inability to account for change of the social order (Calhoun 1993; King 2000). In Bourdieu's framework, an actor's chance of challenging the social order is linked to his or her social position. Therefore, instead of negotiating change, actors tend to reproduce the social order. While Bourdieu's perspective focusing on reproduction is insightful in certain aspects, I will also mobilise other theoretical perspectives that allow me to address how salsa dancers are challenging the social structure, notably a doing gender and a boundary-making approach (see Part II).

A second criticism is particularly important for this study: Bourdieu's "blindness" in terms of nation states (Nowicka 2013; Wimmer and Schiller 2002) and particularly "the methodological nationalism and overall neglect of migration and transnational mobility inherent in the original theory" (Dahinden 2017: 1483). Several authors have attempted to "transnationalise" theories of capital (see, for instance, Erel 2010; Meinhof and Triandafyllidou 2006; Moret 2018; Nowicka 2013). As these authors show, particularly in the process of migration and mobility, "the symbolic value of individuals' resources may vary enormously depending on where they are evaluated, i.e. in the place of origin, the place of residence or other national or regional contexts" (Moret 2018: 102). To analyse the transnational practices of cultural actors of migrant background in European capital cities, Meinhof and Triandafyllidou (2006) coined the notion of "transcultural capital" to account for "the strategic use of knowledge, skills and networks acquired by migrants through connections with their country and cultures of origin which are made active at their new places of residence" (202). They suggest a potential link between all three forms of capital, which migrants may mobilise in order to maximise their options. While being more or less sceptical about the ways the symbolic value of individuals' resources is recognised after a migration, all these authors share the assumption of context-dependency of Bourdieu's capital theory and enlarge it respectively. As all these authors have demonstrated, when taking into account the criticisms, elements of Bourdieu's theoretical framework are well suited to analyse many aspects of transnational phenomena.

To sum up, the conceptualisation of salsa as a circuit with specific hubs, including a theoretical framework drawing on Becker's and Bourdieu's approaches, permits the analysis of salsa from a transnational perspective.

The formation of the (European) salsa circuit

As the discussion of the literature on salsa dance in Chapter 1 shows, salsa's "transnational moves" (Pietrobruno 2006) have led it to become an urban phenomenon with the establishment of salsa dance studios, dancing nights and congresses in many cities in North and South America, Europe and parts of Asia. Most literature discusses the development of salsa dance in North America, leaving aside alternative routes and circulations of salsa and its dancers. This chapter considers the salsa circuit from a European perspective, as one possible alternative. As it argues, the European salsa circuit is of major importance for many of the new salsa dance professionals, or *travelling artists*, and especially Cuban dancers.

Wieschiolek (2003: 122) describes a "salsa boom" in Europe during the 1990s and 2000s and suggests that salsa's popularity started in London then proceeded to the continent and later to Eastern Europe. Although salsa's routes are arguably less linear than in this version of its dissemination, the dancers I met often mentioned a similar timescale for the early establishment of salsa studios in Western Europe during the 1990s and in Eastern Europe during the 2000s. Similarly, Pušnik and Sicherl (2010: 111) state that salsa arrived in Slovenia in the early 2000s.

In the dissemination of salsa, individual dancers played an important role, some of them contributing to building up localised salsa dance *scenes* in various European cities during the 1990s and 2000s. Early salsa teachers in European cities in the 1990s had often migrated from Cuba, Colombia or Venezuela, as my interview partners told me when asked about their first salsa experiences. According to Llano (2014), Cubans were the first to teach salsa in Spain: "Most of them had professional dance training, had participated in dance companies, and had toured in Europe, principally Italy, and then remained in Europe" (Llano 2014: 189). Others had no professional dance training but taught the steps they had learned in family contexts or with teachers they met in Europe. A dancer who danced in London during the 1990s and early 2000s remembers how he started to dance *Cuban salsa* taught by Latin Americans:

> I think way back in 1998 when it was Cuban, we didn't even think Americans did salsa. Most people didn't think Americans did salsa [...]

which is strange: even though a lot of the music we were listening to was out of America. [...] As we knew it's Cuban, [...] because of all the Cuban or South American people that lived in London, mainly Cubans, that's what we learned.

(Abod)

While the debate over ownership of salsa in the US was conducted mainly between Cubans and Puerto Ricans (see Manuel 1994; Singer 1983), in Europe salsa was generally seen as Cuban. The strong presence of Cuban and other Latin American salsa teachers at that time in Europe (and the absence of Puerto Rican salsa teachers) thus led to a very different image of salsa dancing from the political identity project of mainly Puerto Rican immigrants in the US and particularly New York. The different vision of salsa's origins seems to have led to an expansion of *Cuban salsa* in Europe.

It was only in the early 2000s, with the emergence of salsa congresses, that dancers based in the USA, who had already formed dance companies and built up dance studios, started to be invited to Europe to teach workshops and perform. As McMains (2015: 268) argues, in the early days of professional salsa dancers' travelling from the USA to Europe, the web-presence of a few salsa dance professionals played a crucial role for their success among European dancers, who already followed them on their websites and now invited them to teach their "new" styles of salsa dancing (New York, LA, distinguished in On1 and On2). According to McMains (2015: 290), particularly female dancers were able to capitalise on the new possibilities the internet offered, as they were the first to sell instructional salsa videos online and use online journalism (even before blogs existed), thus building their reputations.

The individual entrepreneurship, sometimes related to migratory trajectories, also led to different regional trends in salsa dancing in Europe. Thus there are cities where only one salsa style is danced, due to the local salsa studios' offerings. In other cities, salsa studios of different styles compete for their share of students, thereby developing individual stylistic variations as the different salsa dance styles are open to reinterpretation and influences of other dance movements. The picture of "local" salsa *scenes* and the importance of individuals working as driving forces is thus highly diverse – a fact that clearly distinguishes salsa dance commerce from other dance worlds, for example standardised ballroom with its regulations and governing organisations such as the Imperial Society of Teachers of Dancing. In addition, the otherwise common practice of dance franchising, including specific teaching procedures and manuals to regulate teachers, has less been pursued in salsa. The informal character of the salsa circuit thus leaves room for individual strategies of economic entrepreneurship, as discussed throughout this book.

Nowadays many of the numerous salsa studios are connected to the salsa congresses and dance styles taught and performed at congresses, either through the travelling of the teachers (and sometimes students) to congresses, the invitation of guest teachers to schools or the circulation of dance instruction DVDs and YouTube videos to learn the latest moves.

With the formation of the salsa circuit, a new group of salsa dance professionals came into being, travelling to events to teach and perform. Some of the US-based dancers moved permanently to a European country as they soon realised that there existed a gap in the market. Besides the aforementioned exchange between dance schools in London and New York, Milan became an important salsa hub. Milan-based dance school owners worked with teachers formerly based in the US, which, as Borland (2009: 470) notes, "resulted in the development of a migratory stream of instructors from New Jersey to Italy". Marcos, a salsa dance professional who travels worldwide (his story will be introduced further in Part III), was convinced that European festivals are highly relevant for salsa dance professionals previously based in the US or elsewhere:

> Marcos: You can see there are so many [salsa] artists moving away from the United States or any other places and coming to Europe. Because somehow, Europe is a place where … Europeans value art more […] And it's very important in general, because if it wasn't for many festivals, here in Europe, many artists would have to work in McDonald's or something, you know? It is like that. […] I mean, some of the best artists are here.

Most of my interview partners agreed on the importance of the European salsa "market" for the establishment of their careers as salsa dance professionals in the circuit. The establishment of new salsa routes is due to individual contacts; organisers of large events travel to other events to promote their own congress via flyers and personal contacts. Suzana, who works for a big salsa event in Europe, told me about their marketing strategies:

> Suzana: I mean, lately we also started to travel to Asia, that's why we had many people from India last year, we had from Singapore, we are very well connected with the Middle East. And we had many people from Dubai, from Abu Dhabi, also from Qatar we have, from Oman and so on. Well, it is because of the travelling.

Suzana is part of a transnational network of salsa congress organisers, usually themselves salsa dancers, some of whom run their own dance schools. The event she co-organises applies a marketing strategy that includes "newer" salsa countries in the Middle East, Asia and South Africa.

In sum, the dissemination and commercialisation of salsa dancing has led to numerous individuals building their professional careers on its performance and instruction, so that "the new salsa dance industry may constitute the largest percentage of social dance commerce worldwide" (McMains 2009: 311). From the perspective of dancers in European countries, salsa dancing has traditionally been perceived as a Latin American practice, and despite its new routes, salsa continues to be associated with its Caribbean and Latin American origins. Compared to other regions in the world, the European salsa market is said to be important in terms of its size and is particularly interesting in economic terms, as some dance professionals are able to make a living out of dancing, mainly through teaching salsa. Male and female salsa dance professionals of different nationalities and socio-economic backgrounds thus compete for their share in the salsa circuit. As a result, salsa congresses are particularly important meeting places for salsa dance professionals.

Salsa hubs

As argued above, salsa hubs can best be understood as a specific time-space constellation, in which circulating salsa dancers meet. This study builds on salsa congresses as one entry point into the salsa circuit. I will therefore contextualise the development and some organisational aspects of salsa congresses. However, concentrating solely on hubs located in Europe would have limited the understanding of the salsa circuit. Furthermore, the salsa dance tourism space in Havana turned out to be an important hub of the salsa circuit, and it will thus be introduced in more detail.

Salsa congresses

In salsa dancers' narratives as well as in the literature, the salsa congress held in Puerto Rico in 1997 is credited as being the first salsa event attracting dancers living in different countries. A Puerto Rican journalist who wanted to bring together salsa dancers from different locations launched this event, which united participating dancers from 19 countries, dancing various salsa dance styles to the same music (McMains 2015: 260–263). Some of my interviewees also mentioned similar events with a more regional outreach in the UK and Italy being organised as early as the 1990s.

The commercially successful format of the Puerto Rican salsa congress, uniting dancers of different salsa styles, was soon copied in cities throughout North America, Europe and Asia by local organisers, whereby individual entrepreneurship was once more decisive. Some individuals were highly influential in promoting salsa congresses and competitions, as Fraser Delgado (2014: 109) notes in reference to Miami as a particularly important node in what she calls "the global studio salsa network". McMains (2015: 263) mentions "Torino (Italy), Tokyo, Los Angeles, and Washington (DC)" among the first cities to host salsa congresses after the one in Puerto Rico. Almost 20 years later, several salsa congresses are held every weekend somewhere in the world, mostly in North America and Europe, with lesser events in Asian and South American countries and a few in African countries. An online calendar of dance festivals lists between 10 and 20 salsa events per month for every month of the year 2016.[3] Some of the congresses have been running annually for two decades, others started more recently. The two terms congress and festival are used interchangeably in the salsa circuit, which I will do throughout this book.

Scholarship on festivals has noted an increase in the number of newly created festivals all over the world since the 1960s (Picard and Robinson

2006: 2). MacLeod (2006) argues that the promotion of many festivals depends for its appeal "on a new type of transnationalised festivity rather than local meanings, traditions and social practice" (235). In this context, "festival formats may now be replicated in a series of international venues throughout the world" (MacLeod 2006: 235). This certainly holds true for salsa festivals, which take place in conference venues or in hotels, locations usually used for business gatherings or holidays. They provide the facilities required to host several hundred to several thousand participants, travelling in from other cities and countries. Some festivals have grown out of a local salsa *scene*, while others take place in holiday resorts where practically no dancers live as I observed in the case of the salsa festival in the Croatian coastal town Rovinj.[4] As Kabir (2013) writes,

> there is no logic to the location chosen other than that of it being the domicile of a salsa entrepreneur who has both local and international connections, ambition, together with the advantage of selling the location in question as having some intrinsic attractions to tempt an international salsa crowd, as well as infrastructure for their board, lodging, and dancing.
>
> (Kabir 2013: 265)

I would add to this list the importance of the transport infrastructure, such as a nearby airport, a point one congress organiser particularly highlighted during the interview.

The entry fee for salsa congresses ranges from 80 to 200 Euro (a "full pass", including entry to all parties and workshops), wherein accommodation and travel are not included. The large salsa congresses attract up to 5,000 attendees, some of them with a high percentage of participants travelling in from other countries (reaching up to 80% in the case of the Berlin Salsacongress in 2015, according to its organisers). Salsa congress organisers structure their events in similar ways around the globe: with instruction (salsa workshops, see Figure 2.1) during the day and choreographed shows and social dancing during the night (see also Borland 2009). The workshop programmes include different salsa *dance styles* to choose from, often separated into three different competence levels (beginner, intermediate, advanced). Other Caribbean dances such as bachata are included in the workshop offerings, and since around 2010 other dance forms like kizomba (originating in Angola and Cape Verde, see Beljaars 2016) have been integrated and are taught and danced at salsa events as well. Often, festivals offer several workshops in parallel sessions; for example, the festival in Rovinj 2014 offered nine hour-long workshops each hour, for five slots between 10am and 6pm, over two and a half days, while the festival in Berlin 2013 offered over 100 scheduled workshops between Thursday and Sunday (according to the printed festival programmes available at the event). The festival nights are spent dancing, often to different types of salsa music on several dance floors.

Figure 2.1 Warm-up at a salsa workshop.
Source: © Valentin Behringer.

Around the standard programme of dancing during day and night, in recent years event organisers have created special offers to make their festival more attractive: paying participants can now take part in challenging workshops (known as *bootcamps*) spanning several days taught by recognised salsa *stars*, beach parties, boat trips, safari tours and holidays around the festival.

Some of the bigger events hold championships, where ambitious professional salsa dancers compete and can gain in status by winning titles. No single organisation is generally approved as a regulating body for competitive salsa dancing, and several competitions claim to be world championships of salsa. Renta (2014: 117) lists three world salsa championships in 2014: the World Salsa Federation in Miami, the Puerto Rico Salsa Congress in Puerto Rico and the World Latin Dance Cup in Las Vegas. Some events also offer internal competitions called *stargate shows* during the day, where amateur groups and dance couples perform. The dancers are judged by a jury as well as the public's applause, and the winners perform on stage at the night's shows. Amateur dancers thus can hope to perform on stage or be discovered by one of the attending promoters in order to get invited to another festival.

The spread of salsa festivals thus proceeded hand in hand with the professionalisation of salsa dancing and the emergence of a new type of salsa business, including dance professionals who make a living by travelling in the salsa circuit and teaching workshops.

The space of salsa tourism in Havana

In their discussion of spatial hubs, Kiwan and Meinhof (2011: 5) point to the importance of capital and metropolitan cities (such as Paris, London and Berlin) as "key nodes for migration flows and migrant cultures". In their research with African musicians, they found that not only the metropolitan cities in the global North, but also the ones in the global South such as Antananarivo, Casablanca or Dakar, are pivotal for networking (Kiwan and Meinhof 2011). Although Cuban musicians and dancers played a key part in salsa's early development, and some Cuban dancers were highly influential in its dissemination abroad, it is only recently and not least through foreigners' increasing interest in Cuban dances, that what I call "salsa tourism space" has developed in Havana. I will first address the ways (cultural) tourism developed in Cuba, and then describe the space of salsa tourism in Havana, which has the potential to become a hub of the salsa circuit.

Besides salsa's development and increasing popularity abroad, the establishment of a salsa tourism space in Havana also needs to be understood against the backdrop of the development of tourism in Cuba. As Simoni (2016) notes, following Cuba's independence from Spain in 1902, the Caribbean island became an ever more attractive recreational destination for North Americans, which led to Cuba becoming "the tourist hub of the Caribbean region (Hall 1992: 109)" by the 1920s. The next decades saw the development in Cuba of an entertainment industry with manifold opportunities for gambling and prostitution, nourished by Cuba's representation as "Pleasure Island" (Skinner 2011). With the Cuban revolution in 1959, the number of tourists started to decline, particularly as of 1961, when US residents were prevented from visiting the island by the US economic blockade against Cuba (Simoni 2016: 37). The new government promoted forms of internal tourism and launched programmes to eradicate gambling and prostitution. Since the 1990s, the number of foreign tourists in Cuba has increased again, as a result of the authorities' efforts to develop international tourism as a path out of the economic crisis following the collapse of the Soviet Union. Over the 1970s and 1980s, the Soviet Union heavily subsidised Cuba's export products; Cuba depended on the communist bloc for 80% of its trade and with its collapse the nation confronted a massive economic crisis (Simoni 2016: 39). "In the new economic context of crisis, the Cuban government attached all the more urgency to the development of international tourism as a privileged path to draw much-needed hard currency into the country" (Simoni 2016: 39). At the same time, the Cuban government restricted forms of informal encounters, often understood as sex tourism, between Cubans and foreign tourists.

As scholars of tourism have noted, the Cuban government encouraged the development of special types of tourism, among them beach, heritage and health tourism (Babb 2011: 26). In tourism promotional materials of the 1990s, Cubans were portrayed as "living out of smiles, dances, and music" (Simoni 2016: 41), a representation many of the salsa tourists

I interviewed shared. Contemporary travel guides also acknowledge "the presence of music and dance as unquestionable components of Cuban daily life" (Ana 2017: 177).

The often informal tourist economy around folkloric dances and salsa represents a small share of the gross tourist economy.[5] Nevertheless, cultural tourism has opened up access to tourists bringing in hard currency to a new group of musicians and dancers who were formerly excluded from tourist places (see also Ana 2017; Bodenheimer 2013). Furthermore, the development of the private sector over the past years has led to new opportunities for opening up private businesses (Ana and Lubiński 2018). Many musicians and dancers try to take their share in the financial opportunities the growing cultural tourism offers.

During my research trips to Havana I listened to numerous bands playing the standard repertoire of *son* music pieces (made world famous by the success of the Buena Vista Social Club) and observed young dance couples performing in and around the restaurants in touristic *Havana vieja*. During my visit in August 2015, several young men approached me on the street and invited me to learn salsa with them. Although some of my Cuban interviewees rejected the label salsa as "only a marketing tool" and preferred to call their dance *casino*, these young Cubans in the streets labelled their dancing salsa as a way to (re)inscribe Cuban dance in the history of salsa, being well aware of the transnational salsa craze and tourists' hunger for "authentic experiences" such as salsa lessons in Havana.

Davis (2015a) reports a similar phenomenon of dance tourism, though of larger dimensions, in the case of Buenos Aires, where tango tourism became "a booming industry with thousands of Europeans, North Americans, and Japanese and Koreans heeding to Buenos Aires each year to dance tango" (23) by the 21st century. She describes the tango scene of Buenos Aires as offering more than 300 tango events a week, plus tango shows and performances in the streets.

In Havana, the infrastructure for salsa dancing is smaller and tends not to be as specialised, so that on my first research trip in 2014 a visiting dancer complained about the lack of opportunities to go out and "dance with good Cuban dancers". During my research visits in 2014 and 2015, dance tourists tried their luck at dance and concert venues such as the *casa de la música*, the outdoor club 1830 or the weekly dancing night in the Hotel Florida. Alongside these dance venues, over the last several years, dance schools exclusively aimed at visitors have become popular in Havana, teaching salsa, son, rumba and so-called Afro-Cuban folkloric dances as well as new (European) dance trends such as kizomba. The schools often work together with salsa teachers in other countries, who organise salsa holidays and bring groups of students to take classes in the schools in Havana; others cater to individual travellers' needs. Until recently, Cuban laws allowed only certain forms of private entrepreneurship. Due to these regulations of tourism and private enterprise, Cuban nationals were not allowed to be owners of dance schools catering to tourists. Juli, a dance professional who taught salsa lessons despite this legal prohibition, told me about the problems she had with the authorities and the ways she tried to convince them that "it is not my fault that tourists like me to show them how to dance" (for an analysis of her story, see Chapter 6).

With the changes in the Cuban political landscape, including plans to expand private enterprise since 2010, small private enterprises are now allowed (although in restricted numbers). The government issued licenses for self-employment, which has led to more salsa teachers offering their services and studios opening up, as interviewees told me during my second visit in Havana in August 2015 (see also Ana and Lubiński 2018).

Organisers advertise dance holiday packages using slogans such as "learn to dance with Cuban dance partners", thus drawing on essentialist ideas of Cubans as good dancers and catering to the visitors' wish to dance with Cubans once in the country. Based on my observations, the phenomenon of salsa teaching in Havana is highly gendered, as most of the incoming tourists are female dancers, looking for (Cuban) male dance partners. This imbalance in the demand leads to more opportunities in salsa teaching for male dancers.[6]

While dance studios engage the common tourist imaginary, they are also linked to the specificities of the salsa circuit, as the example of the new kizomba trend in Havana's dance studio offer demonstrates. Recently, the festival format has been introduced to Cuba. During the time of my research in Havana, there were some dance and music festivals for salsa dancers, but I did not come across events that also invited guest teachers (as at the European congresses described above). However, from 2016 (after my final research trip), a new salsa congress started in Havana, which invited the most sought-after teachers of *Cuban salsa*, all of Cuban origin, and mainly based in Europe.[7] The establishment of such events in Cuba highlights the importance of the salsa circuit outside of Cuba and the (recent) attempts of Cuban actors based in Cuba to participate in the global salsa commerce without having to leave the country (as the dance professionals I interviewed mostly had, see Part III).

As this introduction to the space of salsa tourism in Havana, including some historical context information, has demonstrated, salsa events in Cuba have the potential to become a hub of the salsa circuit. However, as will be analysed more in detail in Chapter 7, actors in the assumed birthplace of salsa are sometimes unsuccessful in their attempts to participate in the salsa circuit, as they lack the necessary resources to access the mobility of other salsa dancers and thus remain stuck at the edge of the circuit. The example of Havana's tourist salsa space points to the global power inequalities affecting the salsa circuit, as it draws attention to the highly unequal access to some hubs for differently positioned individuals. This will become particularly clear when compared to the European salsa students' mobile trajectories, discussed in the next section.

Circulating people and imaginaries in an affective economy

This section addresses the circulation of people, affects and a specific imaginary of salsa as a "global" *Esperanto of the body*. I here loosely draw on

Törnqvist (2013) and her analysis of tango tourism in Buenos Aires, building on Bourdieu's understanding of symbolic economies. However, I add the importance of dancers' affective experiences to the picture, thus extending this suggestion. My main goal is to demonstrate that the salsa circuit can be understood as an affective economy, based on not only the shared beliefs but also the embodied experiences of salsa as a pleasurable, addictive, transnationally uniting practice. To do this, I also draw on recent theorisations of affect (Ahmed 2004; Bakko and Merz 2015; Clough 2007; Davis 2015b). The affective economy is grounded on a "'refusal' of the 'commercial'" (Bourdieu 1980b: 261), in which economic interests and profits are downplayed, while symbolic values and the importance of emotions are stressed.

This section first focuses on one particular group of people, the festival participants and salsa students. As these individuals strive to learn ever-changing moves and dance the night away, they lay the ground on which dance professionals build their careers. Drawing on the "affective turn" in social sciences, the main goal of this section is to better understand salsa students' motivations and experiences. I will introduce Karl, whose story will be analysed as an example of a "mobile salsa trajectory", which shares some similarities with the transnational salsa careers of salsa dance professionals.[8]

In the second part of this section, I discuss the idea of salsa as a common language, including the discursive construction and embodied experience of salsa as an "open space for anybody". By applying a transnational perspective to the practices of salsa dance students and by including the affects and imaginaries that dancers share regarding salsa, this section demonstrates that a transnational perspective can also be fruitfully mobilised in the analysis of non-migrants, to better understand how individuals develop transnational identifications, networks and practices (see also Dahinden 2009).

Mobile salsa trajectories

Karl's story will serve as the central theme to disentangle some of the elements that keep the salsa circuit alive, by using it as an example of a "mobile salsa trajectory". Davis (2015a) in her study of tango "aficionados" uses the concept of "tango trajectory", building on the work of Strauss and Glaser (1970) and Riemann and Schütze (1991) to describe processes that disorder a person's life and imply a reconstruction of a person's "identity". As she writes, "becoming a tango dancer may [...] evoke the biographical disarray, changes in identity, and altered expectations for the future that are common to any trajectory process" (Davis 2015a: 77). I will not go into the depth of Davis' analysis of passionate dancers' trajectories, but instead highlight the elements that are of most interest in this chapter's discussion, mainly the mobility and surrounding reasoning in what I call mobile salsa trajectories of salsa students. It is important to keep in mind that the serious salsa students I portray in this chapter are not representative of all salsa students. Many serious salsa students stay in their local *scene* and never develop mobile salsa trajectories; other dancers keep taking a weekly class in a local studio or quit salsa dancing altogether after a while.

Karl, at the time of the interview 30 years old, lives in a small Swiss town and works as managing director of his own IT business. He started to dance salsa when his then-girlfriend suggested taking lessons together. They found a nearby salsa studio and, though after a year their relationship ended, he continued taking lessons in the school. After five years, he felt that he wanted to develop his dancing further so he decided to take private lessons.

> At that time, it was my most intensive time; I went out dancing five times a week, for more than two years, really all the time! So I wanted to improve my dancing, and went to [name of a salsa instructor] before I did my round-the-world trip, which actually was a salsa round-the-world trip.

Karl wanted to learn Spanish and improve his dancing, so once he had completed his Bachelor's degree in economics he went travelling; starting in Brazil, he then went to Buenos Aires, Sydney (to take the above-mentioned lessons with a *salsa star*), Bangkok, Tel Aviv, Moscow, Riga, Stockholm and London. As he proudly told me, he found people to dance with in all of these cities. Once back in Switzerland, he continued short travels to about eight salsa congresses a year, while building up his IT business. When I asked him if something had changed in his life due to his intense hobby, he said:

> I think about almost everything has changed. [...] Once you enter the scene [...] you get to know so many people. And somehow your life goes there. [...] All of a sudden, all your friends are there and your private life is in that environment. It's not just a hobby, it's different. Also, the worldwide connections, it got so extreme.

Karl clearly feels that his life has changed due to salsa, an experience often shared by serious salsa students as well as the interviewed salsa dance professionals (further theorised as "conversion narrative" in Chapter 5).

Following the lines of Karl's story, I will now look at three elements of the mobile salsa trajectories: the intense phase of addiction, the importance of training with acknowledged *salsa stars* and transnational connections.

The summary of Karl's mobile salsa trajectory reveals the ways salsa dance students get into dancing, sometimes following an experience with other dances, often involuntarily through a friend or a partner. After a while, dancers "get hooked" and start to invest more of their time and money into salsa dance lessons and parties, the moment Karl describes as the "most intensive phase" in his salsa learning. Iannis, a salsa dance professional who teaches in his own studio, observed a similar tendency in his students during that phase:

> I see from our students, when, after a while, some months or a year, I think people are at work during the day and they are thinking, "OK,

in five hours I'll go dancing". And it's like, what they think about for the whole day. When they're gonna finish work and go dancing. [...] they get into it and then it's like an addiction, really. I don't know if addiction is a good thing, generally, but it happens to many people, they are addicted to salsa.

As Iannis observes, once introduced to the dance form, certain salsa students become quite obsessive about dancing salsa: the interviewed dancers used metaphors relating to addiction ("You need your weekly fix") or illness such as "virus" ("I caught the salsa virus"). Religious metaphors were used as well; as one dancer put it: "Since I've started I've converted two friends of mine, they are now dancing as well". In the above quotation, Iannis raises the question of addiction that has been discussed in several studies on dance (e.g. McMains 2006 on "glamour addiction" in the ballroom dance industry or Davis 2015a on tango dancers). Self-confessed salsa "addicts" rarely complain about their "addiction" but are happy with the changes that salsa dancing has brought to their life. Candice, a regular festival-goer and self-defined salsa addict, told me at length about her "intense phase", thereby proving Iannis' assumption right:

> And all I could think about was salsa, and all I wanted to do is dance. And so I was in the office and I was like, oh my god, I wanna dance, I wanna go dancing. I'd wake up in the morning [...] and think: I wanna dance today. And then I'm gonna take my shoes with me to the office, take an extra pair of clothes and I spend the whole morning: today I wanna dance, today I wanna dance, today I'm going dancing. [...] And then, you know, sometimes it doesn't work out, or I go, and then I feel so happy.

The above quotation points to the importance of the affective experience of salsa dancing as a driving force of the salsa circuit: as dancers univocally stated, the experience of "being in the moment" (McClure 2015) of the dance may generate strong feelings of happiness. This also became clear in the interview with Suzana, while discussing why she considers salsa "the best hobby ever":

> It is because you just lose yourself, you know, during let's say that song 5 minutes, you don't care about anything else, you're just you and your partner, the dance floor, the music, the lights, and it's like a dream. I would rather do this than playing chess, I think [laughs].

To account for such intense experiences of complete absorption in what one does, Csikszentmihalyi (1990: 4) has developed the concept of "flow", describing a state of "optimal experience", "in which people are so involved in an activity that nothing else seems to matter". In this sense, the activity of salsa dancing becomes important for no other reason than the experience of doing it: "dancing is like magic", as Suzana put it. However, to achieve the state of being able to "lose" themselves in the dance, salsa students have to invest time and money in their dancing skills.[9]

As McClure (2015) found in her study with salsa dancers, the level of competence in dance skills is an important criterion in salsa dancers' affective experience of pleasure. The often-used expression "to train" instead of "going out" also reveals salsa dancers' goal to improve in their dancing. Karl therefore progressed from going dancing five times a week, to taking private lessons. Later, Karl travelled to Sydney for a month to take lessons with a well-recognised dancer of the salsa circuit, whom he considers the best in quick footwork (the rhythmical improvised dancing of the lower body). Though Australia would not be the first-choice destination for all European salsa students wishing to improve their dancing, his choice reflects the importance of individuals attracting students – despite the geographical location of their studio.

Salsa dance professionals are often called artists, and many of them have star-status among salsa students. Academic scholarship on stardom and fandom has analysed the construction of stars and celebrities as related processes (Holmes and Redmond 2006). However, in the salsa circuit the construction of *stars* works differently than in many other social worlds: *salsa stars* are accessible and tangible. The salsa artists are tangible insofar as they not only perform on salsa festivals' stages (like other *stars* of the world of entertainment) but also teach workshops and, particularly important, they dance with salsa students during the parties. For many of the salsa students I met, their dances with one of the salsa artists were the highlight of their festival experience, as exemplified by the following observation. At one festival evening, I noticed a familiar male dancer standing near the DJ desk, the preferred dancing spot of the artists, for several hours before finally daring to ask the artist of his choice to dance with him. The next day, he proudly told me how nice the dancer was and that she had even recognised him that day! I also observed several female dancers queuing in long lines on the dance floor to wait for their turn to dance with a specific male artist. In workshop breaks on the following day or during the waiting time at airports on their way home, dancers engage in enthusiastic discussions about every detail of their dance with one of the *stars*, sometimes boasting in front of their friends about a dance with a particularly prestigious *star*. (I will discuss the implications of this "convention of tangible *salsa stars*" for the dance professionals in Chapter 5.)

Karl's trajectory reveals not only the importance of learning with a specific teacher, but also the weight dancers give to the experience of learning with new teachers. Salsa dancers often wish to improve their dancing and learn new turn patterns and body moves, which is possible in attending a salsa congress with its large offer of salsa dance workshops.

Karl not only felt the need to improve his dance skills, he also wanted to learn Spanish to better understand the lyrics of salsa songs and "because culturally it's got a lot to do with salsa, South America. Almost all the music comes from there". He therefore chose to spend three months in Buenos Aires (again, not a typical salsa destination), the second stop on his salsa world-trip. The other cities he mentions were either destinations in which he had already established contacts with salsa dancers he had met at salsa congresses or cities where a salsa festival took place. The "worldwide" connections salsa dancers develop are an important element of their trajectories. Salsa dancers feel part of a *community* or *familia* of salsa dancers. During the intense phase, salsa dance students start calling themselves *salseros* or *salseras*. They develop new relationships and sometimes meet future partners (Karl met his fiancée) and for some, their whole social life revolves around salsa. The regular attendance of local salsa nights as well as the bi-monthly or sometimes even monthly attendance of salsa congresses in another country form part of this.

Rephrasing Reed (1998), who describes dance as a "tool in shaping nationalist ideologies", we could say that salsa here helps to shape "transnationalist ideologies". Of course, this development of transnational subjectivities and networks is the result not of a political project but rather of a dancer's investment in salsa as a bodily practice, and arguably a market-driven one. Pushing this argument further, Davis (2018b: 665) states that the biographies even of tango dancers staying in one place should be considered as transnational, as they actively engage in what she calls a "transnational cultural space". Indeed, as other literature argues, transnational identifications and practices do not require migration or cross-border mobility. In an article entitled "Are we all transnationals now?" Dahinden (2009) argues that when studying transnational phenomena, non-migrants should be taken into account too, as they might also be involved in transnational activities. She thus sets out to study transnational social relations as well as "transnational subjectivities". Building on her findings, Dahinden (2009) argues for a differentiated position and concludes that "even if almost everybody is nowadays to some degree transnational, this should not hinder us from distinguishing different transnationalisms as they reflect varying social positioning in this globalised world" (1382). In this way, the transnational relations and subjectivities developed by Karl and other salsa students have to be analysed as related to their favourable situation.

Clearly, the participation in salsa festivals and the development of transnational connections has to be analysed in regards to socio-demographic backgrounds: salsa festival-goers are often individuals with higher education, stable jobs and enough leisure time to allow spending time and money for their salsa "passion" (cf Skinner 2007).[10] As I have shown, salsa dancers at festivals invest a considerable amount of time and money in order to learn this shared bodily practice. They need to afford the festival price as well as the journey (often a flight) and the hotel room. Global economic inequalities shape the experiences of the "transnational encounters" (Davis 2015a) on the dance floor to a considerable degree, not only in what is usually perceived as tourism (for example in Cuba) but also in the congress circuit in Europe. Hutchinson (2014a: 13) points to the importance of class in an analysis of salsa congresses, stating that although the dance floors of salsa festivals "may create an ethnically inclusive community, it is one with little class diversity".

To sum up, as Karl's story and the other dancers' quotations demonstrate, some *salseras* and *salseros* develop mobile salsa trajectories in the salsa circuit alongside their regular jobs, fuelled by their strong wish to dance, to improve their dance skills and to connect to people outside their place of residence. Salsa students also develop transnational networks and subjectivities, and salsa dancing is perceived as a mobile skill that is transferable to many places while travelling to or working in other cities (cf Skinner 2007).

The *Esperanto of the body*

The last section of this chapter deals with the circulating idea of salsa dancing as a "global" language, predominant among dancers at salsa festivals. I examine how salsa is discursively and emotionally produced as a kind of universal leisure practice through two related arguments: the emphasis on diversity and the shared bodily practice as a common language. In his analysis of the economy of symbolic goods, Bourdieu (1980b) describes artistic fields as "universes of belief" (168) and stresses the significance of the "collective belief" (267) in the "game". Similarly, Becker (1982) insists on the importance of conventions. My analysis further reveals the importance of affects as common ground in salsa's affective economy.

The first argument suggests that salsa's universality stems from its appreciation of diversity. As several studies of salsa have observed, there is a strong belief in salsa as an "open space for anybody" among salsa dancers (e.g. Skinner 2007, see also Boulila 2018). Indeed, as my research shows, one of salsa's attractions lies in its alleged ability to overcome the usual social markers of difference such as class, age and race. I was astonished by the consistency with which my interview partners of diverse backgrounds and with sometimes diverging interests repeated the idea of salsa's openness and described salsa as a space of equal differences in several aspects. In the words of Nara, a US-based travelling *salsa artist*:

> In fact, I think the beauty of salsa is its diversity and how accepting it is to all demographics, all different cultures, age groups, income levels, education levels, whatever. And that's the beauty. And I think that the range of what ... or the range of people actually contributes to what this dance is. It's nice to have different cultures represented, they make it richer.

Nara's account of salsa reads like a description of political "multiculturalism", including the idea of the equal value of each "cultural group" (see Taylor 1992). As discussed in Chapter 1, in constructivist scholarship such an essentialist understanding of people as part of clearly distinguishable and homogenised "cultures" has been criticised (Schwandt 1998: 236). Nonetheless, the representation of salsa as a leisure activity that allows diversity and equality, serving as a unifying element, forms a constitutive part of the actual salsa imaginary at salsa congresses. A prominent salsa festival promoter describes his event's goal as "creating unity through salsa". Salsa dancers in Europe reproduce this romantic vision of salsa as a unifying element. A number of studies have argued that dancing could be understood as a form of "cultural democracy", investigating the ways "the space of the dance floor has been used to assert black, feminised and gay identities" (Wall 2013: 264). Gilroy (1991) suggests that the dance floor could be viewed as a cultural space in which the usual hierarchies of society are inverted and where competences in dance are more important than skills that dominate outside.

Asked why salsa appeals to them, many of my interview partners referred to similar examples of diversity, for instance in terms of diverse class backgrounds, as Isabelle explains:

> In salsa dancing you have got young and older ones, from student to construction worker to the doctor and lawyer, you have everything! That's what I find interesting, you meet people you wouldn't otherwise … Usually you always move in your … in the same environment.

Isabelle, a regular festival participant and salsa teacher in her hometown, here refers to different professional groups participating in salsa. For dancers in Europe, salsa is thus a meeting place, which allows them to connect to differently positioned people than themselves in ways they do not perceive as possible in other circumstances. Abod, a UK-based amateur dancer and regular festival-goer in his early fifties, perceives salsa as a space with no age limit:

> If I just go to a nightclub I probably would stop dancing because many nightclubs … it's all right when you are young … when you get to a certain age, then you think [he stretches out his hands in a sign that supposedly means "stop"]. Whereas salsa, the good thing about salsa is the fact that there's no age, typical age limit, in England anyway. There's no age, there's no colour, it's just completely mixed.

Indeed, age seems to be less exclusionary in salsa than in other dance spaces; nevertheless, it is important to keep in mind that Abod has a certain level of competence in dancing and that this might be an important element in understanding his experience. Furthermore, like many other dancers, Abod, who was born in Nigeria and later moved to the UK, sees salsa dancing as less discriminatory not only in terms of age but also in terms of skin colour. In this way, salsa is often presented as a "multiracial utopia" (Hutchinson 2014b: 30). In a similar vein, Juan, a professional dancer from Cuba, living in Italy for more than 20 years while dancing and teaching, explained:

> I saw European society change for good thanks to music from Cuba, music from New York, thanks to salsa, thanks to all that is happening.

People now are more friendly, more communicating and less racist. They see a person how she is, not for her colour, not for where she comes from. And when you go dancing, the most exciting thing, when you go to an event like this or to any disco, you can see the black [man] with the blonde, the blonde with the mulatto or the white with the white ... But you never have racial prohibition. And when I go dancing with you, I don't ask you what religion you are. You can be a Catholic, apostolic, a Muslim, you can be a Buddhist, I don't care! Nobody cares who you are for dancing. And this is a very serious thing. It's serious and important for the whole of humanity. [...] I'm only interested to meet you again at another festival, to embrace you. And to dance with you because I like the way you dance.

Relating to a broader societal change and referring to current political debates on religious difference, Juan underlines his perception of salsa's potential as a unifying force.

As demonstrated, my interview participants agree about salsa's inclusionary aspect and the irrelevance of usual social distinctions such as class, age, race and religion in salsa spaces – at least for the duration of a dance, in what Kabir (2013) calls a "momentary transnational utopia" (274). The shared value of "passion for salsa dancing" unites dancers, pointing to the importance of the salsa circuit as an affective economy, which entails the moral obligation to ascribe to this imaginary.

The second element of salsa's understanding as a universal practice is its understanding as a form of bodily communication. This experience allows for encounters with "others", but not necessarily racialised or exoticised others, as argued in the discussed literature on salsa. Valentina, a dancer involved in congress organisation, expressed this as follows:

And in the end, we all speak the same language. I can go to Japan without speaking a word of Japanese but once on the dance floor we understand each other. I can go to Miami and just dance, the man leads and I join in. Even though every human does it differently in their individuality, the basics are always the same, that's the beauty of our dance.

Salsa dancers thus feel connected to other dancers far away through their common dance practice, independent of their ability to talk to each other. Ernesto, a dance professional who makes a living out of his worldwide teaching activities, told me that salsa, for him, is the *Esperanto of the body*, referring to the global endeavour of this constructed language. Its founders and adepts wished to create a language that is quick to learn and thus does not privilege speakers of one language over others. The idea of a language of the body is also enhanced by the downplaying of other verbal communication in dancers' salsa experience, adhering to the common saying that in salsa people do not talk: "You don't have to say a lot, don't have to talk about your problems, can just forget everything and just dance, you don't even have to talk, that's not part of it" (Patric).

In *salseros'* and *salseras'* discursive production of the salsa space as open and non-hierarchic, other elements that could separate them are thus downplayed (see also Gagné 2014: 449). Furthermore, for dancers, salsa dancing is attractive precisely for its affective dimension and the possibility to connect with strangers on another level than language: the body (see Figure 2.2). In a similar way, Hamilton and Hewer (2009) state that salsa "can be seen as a medium of expression through the communicative body, that is, a body in process of creating itself" (505). Abod describes this experience:

> The thing that I get the most pleasure out is coming up to somebody I never ever met in my life, spending four minutes and thinking: wow, that was an awesome dance! And that to me, that is what salsa is about. You go to somebody, a salsa dancer, you've never ever met before and have a beautiful dance. And you have to have a partner in order to do it. And that's what I like, and that's my attraction to congresses, just to go there and just dance. […] So that's my socialising now, it's salsa travel.

In salsa dancers' accounts, the pleasure gained from the affective, embodied experience of the moment of dancing is even increased when dancing with

Figure 2.2 Enjoying a dance at a festival.
Source: © Valentin Behringer.

somebody "never ever met before". Ajay, an internationally touring salsa instructor, summed it up in the following words:

> Since it's a social dance where you dance with different partners, a festival is a perfect place to dance with a hundred unknown people who've come from God knows where and enjoy that. You can't get that back in your own city where you live, so festivals are a great meeting place for social dancers because there's a certain excitement about being able to do all those beautiful turn patterns and all that stuff with someone you'd never danced [with] before. And the first time you hit a song in your life, wow, this works like magic.

Following a similar logic, Karl told me about his active search to dance with partners from as many different countries of origin as possible.

> I still remember very well, Athens was my first congress abroad, and I tried to dance with as many nationalities as possible. [...] It was so cool, I mean, where else do you have so many cultures in one room, elsewhere you don't find this. So I thought I want to experience it, how they dance in Russia and so on. So I tried it for the whole evening, one after the other, and hoped to have another country. [...] So you ask, "where are you from", and when it is the wrong country, you continue. But it was really cool.

On my questioning, Karl acknowledged that, in the end, the dances were not that different, and the experience on the festival dance floor rather depended on individual characteristics and levels of competence in dance than on the country of origin. However, like all the other quoted dancers, he understood difference in terms of origin country as a value in itself. The dancers' discursive construction of "others" thus relied on the value-free, but highly essentialist discourse of difference in cultural or national terms.

The various origin countries of dancers were seen as enhancing the congress experience, and sometimes hierarchies were negotiated between groups of dancers. Interestingly, salsa ownership and affinity were not only claimed by *Latinos/Latinas*, but also negotiated among *Europeans*: during my observations at European festivals, I was often told that Eastern European dancers were particularly "good dancers". Maria, a Polish salsa artist, while talking about the emerging salsa countries in Eastern Europe, told me that *Eastern Europeans* "are catching up very quickly" in terms of salsa dancing because they have a "temper more similar to [the] Latin temper, so the dancing feels more natural" for them. New actors appear and draw a new picture of the imaginary salsa geography. In her article about transnationalism at the Berlin Salsa congress, Kabir (2013) makes a similar observation and indicates the presence of sizable contingents of Polish, Czech, Romanian, Bulgarian, Latvian and Lithuanian dancers. "Clearly, salsa has given post-communist European subjectivities an entry point into a hitherto denied world of expressivity, flamboyance, and fun" (Kabir 2013: 270). The numerous salsa congresses held in the Baltics, Eastern Europe and even Russia attest to salsa's success among people living in these countries; this development is not unnoticed by salsa dancers living in Western European countries, who have socialised with salsa for many years. For instance, London-based touring salsa dance professional Andy was convinced that Russian female dancers are the best: "There that's the best social dancers. [...] I think Russia has in percentage 95% of the best dancers in the world, in terms of social dancing. They are beautiful dancers, very good dancers". In this quote, social dancing is contrasted with competitive and show dancing, and the argument put forward is that Russian followers have great dance skills.

Another Swiss-based male dancer told me at length about his travels to Moscow because of the great female dancers there. Dancers meeting at festivals in Europe were thus not only categorised according to their nationality but also gendered: Eastern European and Russian dancers were said to be particularly good followers (usually women), while Western European dancers were said to be good leaders (usually men). In this respect I found a discussion between festival organisers revealing that during a meeting of salsa congress organisers at one of the festivals, the organiser of a large and successful event in Vienna told the others that the previous year he had had to kick out 40 party dancers at 9 in the morning, "because in Eastern Europe it is like this, the party goes from 1am to 9am, they are used to doing it like that". Proudly, he added: "And at my congress I have the girls from the East and the guys from the West". His statement was met with laughter; the other organisers cheered and one of them asked how he did it. He explained that he had travelled a lot over the last three years promoting the festival. Vienna thus found itself at the crossroads of European integration.

As these examples demonstrate, salsa in the European circuit is often promoted with a focus on its inclusionary aspect, not its supposed Latinness. The salsa dancers and event promoters (re)produce the imaginary of salsa as a unifying practice, minimising references to salsa's historic associations with Latin America, the Caribbean or New York, thus making it available to an interested public all over the world.

To summarise, through the two interrelated arguments of the appreciation of diversity and the shared bodily practice as a common language, salsa is discursively and affectively constructed as a unifying practice. Salsa congresses are imagined as spaces of diversity and equality in terms of nationality, class, age, race and religion, thus echoing debates about political multiculturalism (Taylor 1992). This shared representation is pushed by promoters who market salsa thus and serves as common ground in the affective economy of the salsa circuit.

However, although salsa dancers see their practice as a "global" language of the body, which unites people of various backgrounds, they completely gloss over the highly heteronormative and gendered character of these salsa spaces (see Part II), as well as questions of class (the ones mentioned above but also in terms of mobility capital, see Part III) or age and physical (dis)ability. While on an individual level, the salsa dance floor may be experienced as a meeting place of "different" people, it is nevertheless embedded in larger power relations that structure the experience of "transnational encounters". Furthermore, as Boulila (2018) points out in her analysis of the salsa dance industry in Europe, there are "racial underpinnings of cosmopolitan consumption": "Although salsa as an individual movement can be interpreted and performed by *any body*, not all bodies have the same access to symbolic and material systems of power" (6). The following chapters will demonstrate the other side of the narrative of salsa as unifying practice by disentangling some of the elements that structure the transnational salsa circuit hierarchically, along the axes of gender, ethnicity, race, class and mobility capital.

Conclusion

In this chapter, I laid the groundwork for the analysis of the following chapters, by conceptualising salsa as a circuit with hubs. The latter can take the form of a salsa event or an online discussion between salsa dancers; all situations being highly connected (see Mueller 2016). The metaphor of a rhizomatic network is particularly fruitful when combined with Becker's notion of art worlds (1982) and Bourdieu's framework of artistic fields (1993) with different forms of capital (1986).

Building on the model of the salsa circuit, I described two salsa hubs: festivals and salsa tourism in Havana. The description of the salsa congresses as hubs demonstrated their significance in terms of a meeting point and job opportunities for salsa dance professionals, who started to construct transnational careers travelling from event to event (as analysed in Part III of this study). The contextualisation of the space of salsa tourism in Havana as a potential salsa hub pointed to the global power relations between countries, affecting individuals' possibilities to participate in the salsa circuit. As I have argued, despite Cuban musicians and dancers having played a key role in salsa's early development, the salsa tourism space in Havana is a relatively new phenomenon. Several factors influenced its development, among them the Cuban authorities' marketing of tourism, as well as dancers' activities abroad, which fuelled Europeans' interest in travelling to Cuba to dance salsa.

The last section of this chapter empirically approached the circulation of salsa students and imaginaries in the salsa circuit. By focusing on three stages of the "mobile trajectories" of serious salsa students, I demonstrated that they engage in the time- and cost-intensive activity of salsa dancing due to their strong affective relation to the dancing experience, whereby they also develop transnational networks and subjectivities. As shown, dancers engage in salsa dancing out of their wish to engage in transnational encounters with "others" but not necessarily with exoticised "others", as critical studies on Latin dances have argued. Furthermore, the interviewed dancers were more driven by their wish for self-cultivation than a desire to perform what have been called "traditional" gender identities (for a similar argument see also McClure 2015: 28), a point I will elaborate in Chapter 4.

According to the literature, tourism, festivals and dance all contain an escapist element. Drawing on Turner's conceptualisation of liminality as the midpoint of transition in ritual, tourism is often analysed as a state of "in between-ness"; "a time and place of withdrawal from normal modes of social action" (Turner 1969: 167). Numerous studies point to the liminal activities the tourist experience offers as escape from everyday work lives (see e.g. Cohen 2010). Picard and Robinson (2006) argue that the metaphor of escape, often used in contexts of tourism, also reflects the festival experience, "as participants find themselves in a different time and space" (17). Due to their specific time and space frame, festivals are thus interpreted as "ritualised transgressions" (Picard and Robinson 2006: 11). Similarly, dance has been analysed as a temporary escape from everyday suffering (Spencer 1986). Following this discussion, the described mobile salsa trajectories, salsa dancers' stay in Havana as well the dancing experience itself, in which dancers claim to "lose" themselves share commonalities. Likely, the sensual and "existential pleasure" (Törnqvist 2013: 102), also reflected in salsa dancers' description of their dancing experience, leads to salsa being perceived as a uniting *Esperanto of the body*. The values circulating in the affective economy of the salsa circuit are based on the dancers' beliefs as much as their affective experiences and a sense of (bodily) communication with others.

However, despite dancers' celebratory accounts of the emancipatory promises of the dance floor, like any other social space the salsa circuit is structured by internal and external hierarchies, particularly along the lines of gender, ethnicity, race, class and mobility capital – as the following chapters will demonstrate.

Notes

1 My conceptualisation of the salsa circuit should thus not be confused with the theorisation of "cultural circuits" by Stuart Hall and his colleagues at the British Centre for Contemporary Cultural Studies (CCCS) (see for instance du Gay et al. 1997). Nor does it refer to another CCCS concept: the highly influential but also criticised notion of subcultures (for a review of the concept's history and critique, see Schulze 2015).

2 In their study on African musicians, Kiwan and Meinhof (2011) also propose a "transnational and translocal network model" with several "key parameters", which they call hubs. However, my model differs in the conceptualisation of hubs as temporary rather than their more static notion of human or spatial hubs.

3 Several websites collect information on salsa and other dance festivals; one of the most comprehensive is festivalsero.com (accessed 14 March 2018).

4 See crosalsafestival.com (accessed 14 March 2018).

5 While some of today's foreign visitors may be inclined to visit a show at the Tropicana, Havana's famous Cabaret, others may be interested in watching a rumba performance at the *Callejón de Hamel* or listening to one of the timba bands in a *casa de la música*.

6 Similarly, Aterianus-Owanga (forthcoming) describes highly gendered dance tourism in Senegal, mainly built on female European students travelling to Senegal to learn sabar.

7 See dancefestivalincuba.com (accessed 14 March 2018).

8 Some salsa dance professionals start with such a "mobile salsa trajectory" and later develop a professional career in the salsa circuit. Mobile salsa trajectories thus may develop into transnational salsa careers.

9 As McClure (2015) has demonstrated in detail, the possibility to "be in the moment" in social salsa dancing is also determined by the gendered roles, which can be interpreted differently depending on the theoretical framework.

10 This also distinguishes salsa congresses from local salsa *scenes* where dancers' socio-economic backgrounds can be highly diverse (see, for example, García 2013 on salsa dance places in Los Angeles).

Part II

Negotiating ethnicity and gender

Introduction – Conceptual notes on conventions, ethnicity and gender

Part II of this study focuses on the ways in which actors in the salsa circuit (re) produce the circulating representations of ethnicity and gender. From the discussion in the last chapter and following the cited dancers' representations, the salsa circuit could be viewed as a space in which ethnicity and race are made less relevant than gender. However, the analysis actually shows the opposite: while ethnicity constitutes an important frame for many of the interviewed dancers, gender is more playfully negotiated and its structuring effects more openly contested. Furthermore, the two categories intersect: as the sociological analysis of bodies has demonstrated, embodiment is always intersectional and transcends categorical boundaries (Villa 2010: 216). However, for analytical reasons the next two chapters analyse the negotiations of several of the gendered and ethnicised conventions of the salsa circuit separately.

As already discussed, Becker (1982) analyses art worlds in terms of cooperation, networks and conventions. He particularly demonstrates that collaboration between many different people is needed to produce any form of artwork, and he looks at all the different tasks that must be performed in order to do so. To exemplify this division of labour in the production of art, he refers to Hollywood films: "The list of credits which ends the typical Hollywood feature film gives explicit recognition to such a finely divided set of activities" (Becker 1982: 7). As Becker (1982) argues, in order to cooperate, people "rely on earlier agreements now become customary, agreements that have become part of the conventional way of doing things in that art" (29). These conventions concern the decisions necessary to organise some of the cooperation between some of its participants (Becker 1982: 42).

Schulze (2015) draws on Becker's (1982) ideas to demonstrate how "hardcore kids" organise their collective activities with regard to gender around "gender conventions". As she argues, the world of hardcore only exists due to the collective activities of its members who work to bring it into existence (Schulze 2015: 21). Following her approach, the production of gender (and ethnicity) can be understood as part of this work or collective activity. Relating to West and Zimmerman's (1987) "doing gender" approach, Schulze (2015) states that gender is a "product of social doings of some sort" (21). This framework is easily transferable into the context of salsa and the ways dancers organise based on gender conventions.

The theoretical framework of "doing gender" (West and Zimmerman 1987, 2009) conceptualises gender as a routine accomplishment in social interactions. From a "doing gender" perspective, "gender is not something we are but something we do" (Deutsch 2007: 106). Gender is understood as universally relevant and important in producing societal hierarchies. West and Zimmerman (1987) build their approach on the analytic distinction between sex, sex category and gender. They understand sex as "a determination made through the application of socially agreed upon biological criteria for classifying persons as females or males" (127). Placement in the sex category is achieved through the application of sex criteria, sustained by "identificatory displays" in everyday life. Gender "is the activity of managing situated conduct in light of normative conceptions of attitudes and activities appropriate for one's sex category" (West and Zimmerman 1987: 127). Building on Garfinkel (1967), West and Zimmerman (2009) propose to perceive of gender as an achieved status, "moving masculinity and femininity from natural, essential properties of individuals to interactional, that is to say, social, properties of a system of relationships" (114). This ethnomethodological inspired approach is thus interested in the specific doings of gender or, in other words, the "work" involved in producing gender (Schulze 2015).

I use similar theoretical assumptions to analyse ethnicity, framed as "doing being ethnic" (see also Brubaker 2002: 163), combined with an approach focusing on the upholding of group boundaries (Barth 1969). Lamont and Molnár (2002) define symbolic boundaries as

> conceptual distinctions made by social actors to categorize objects, people, practices [...]. They are tools by which individuals and groups struggle over and come to agree upon definitions of reality. Examining them allows us to capture the dynamic dimensions of social relations, as groups compete in the production, diffusion, and institutionalization of alternative systems and principles of classifications. Symbolic boundaries also separate people into groups and generate feelings of similarity and group membership [...]. They are an essential medium through which people acquire status and monopolize resources.
>
> (168)

As this definition makes clear, symbolic boundaries (for an overview see Pachucki et al. 2007) are used to categorise social actors and negotiate status.[1] The concept, therefore, is helpful to analyse the ways in which salsa dancers talk about others. In this way, it becomes apparent that different interest groups struggle for symbolic and economic capital: processes of categorisation are not neutral, but power relations enter through a hierarchization of one of the created groups (Jenkins 1994). I will exemplify this process with the negotiations around "Latinness" and the convention of pedagogical techniques ("teaching convention") among dance instructors perceived as *non-Latino* and *Latino/Latina* (or, more specifically, *Cuban*) in Chapter 3. In Chapter 4 I address the negotiations of two gender conventions of the salsa circuit: the leader and follower structure and the gendered moves in the dance.

Note

1 While scholarship on boundaries generally acknowledges the importance of symbolic and social boundaries, this chapter mainly focuses on the (re)production of symbolic boundaries. However, the symbolic boundaries have social consequences in the affective economy of the salsa circuit, particularly regarding the accumulation of salsa capital and economic capital.

3   Negotiating salsa's "Latinness"

This chapter addresses the ongoing negotiations of salsa's "Latinness" between salsa dancers. Dancers with different countries of origin develop various strategies and claim different positions to legitimate their authority as salsa dancers. In this process, they mobilise arguments of "authenticity" and ethnicity, which also intersect with gender.

Although most dancers I talked to adhere to the idea of salsa as *Esperanto of the body* and a space for anybody, a closer look reveals that internal struggles are also carried out on the battleground of cultural "authenticity", origins and "roots". However, ideas of salsa as associated with Latin American or Caribbean "roots" have to be nurtured and "authenticity" related to ethnicity is constructed in interactive ways, as the second part of this chapter demonstrates.

Actors in the European salsa circuit often distinguish between the categories of *Latinos/Latinas* and *Europeans*, or just *non-Latinos*. Furthermore, they often distinguish between *Latinos* and *Cubans*, the latter being sometimes included in the larger category of *Latinos/Latinas* and sometimes set apart as an extra category of dancers. The prevalence of these categories has to be interpreted against the backdrop of the historical dissemination of salsa music in the US political context, where the category of *Latino* is highly relevant (McMains 2015). This chapter follows the actors' logic and presents the boundary-making of the two thus distinguished groups.

This chapter loosely draws on Urquía's (2005) analysis of London's salsa scene as well as Pietrobruno's (2006) ethnographic study on Montreal's Latin dance schools. Pietrobruno analysed salsa teachers' quest for legitimation in several salsa dance studios in this North American city. The salsa teachers in Montreal used the rhetoric of authenticity to "sell" different salsa dance styles, whereby they either invoked or rejected the discourse of authenticity and origins (Pietrobruno 2006: 112). The salsa teachers in Pietrobruno's study constructed authenticity in terms of salsa's supposed origins (the Caribbean or New York). On the contrary, Urquía's description of salsa's development in London during the 1990s demonstrates that salsa became "de-ethnicised" and other aspects were valued more in the context of London's clubs. Urquía (2005) argues:

As dance lessons increased in importance as the main way to learn Salsa, dance teachers became the source of the most authoritative salsa regardless of their own ethnicity or cultural background. In this way locals could become more authoritative than Latin Americans and the ethnic dimension of Salsa as cultural capital began to be eroded.

(390)

Other forms of knowledge and not ethnicised qualities such as technical excellence and pedagogical techniques are important skills in today's teaching business. Indeed, Latin Americans are not automatically seen as good salsa teachers. However, as my findings show, in the struggle for reputation among different dance professionals in the salsa circuit, some dancers do attempt to build on ethnicity to construct their career by emphasising the idea of cultural authenticity, and Urquía's observation has to be nuanced. Furthermore, salsa dancers also draw on other resources to construct authenticity, and as Lindholm (2008) argues, "there are two overlapping modes for characterizing any entity as authentic: genealogical or historical (*origin*) and identity or correspondence (*content*)" (2).

This chapter considers the negotiations of authenticity in several sites: at European salsa festivals and in salsa tourism spaces in Havana. It explores the boundary-making processes and position strategies individual dancers develop in order to create and maintain their reputation as artists in the salsa circuit. To do this, it first examines the boundary-making strategies of non-Latin salsa dance professionals and then focuses on the positioning strategies of Latin American salsa dance professionals. I analyse the performed ethnicised practices as part of symbolic conflicts and strategies of entrepreneurship in the competitive field of the salsa circuit. The last part of this chapter addresses the negotiations of authenticity in the space of salsa tourism in Havana.

Non-*Latin* salsa dancers' generalising salsa

This section focuses on the negotiations of salsa's definition and the ways perceived non-Latin dance professionals position themselves as legitimate dance teachers. I demonstrate actors' boundary-making processes to distinguish themselves from other dance professionals. I will particularly analyse the ways in which actors in the salsa circuit negotiate salsa's "Latinness" and the boundary-making strategies mobilising the convention of correct pedagogical techniques, the "teaching convention".

"Anyone can learn about its roots": undoing salsa's "Latinness"

As argued in Chapter 2, in the salsa circuit, salsa dance is promoted as open for anyone, and its historical associations to places in the Americas are downplayed. Salsa dance professionals who cannot lay claim to Latin "roots" engage in negotiations of salsa's "Latinness" to legitimate their dancing. They follow a strategy of universalising salsa by insisting on a definition of salsa dancing as an acquirable skill. This strategy exists in two variations: while the first understands salsa's Latinness as acquirable for non-Latin people, the second denies any importance of this Latinness. Both variations finally lead to the legitimation of non-Latin salsa teachers, as the following discussion demonstrates.

Ajay, an Indian-born salsa performer and instructor who became interested in salsa dancing during his studies in the USA, explained to me during the interview:

> Of course if you're coming from Latin America, you're born and brought up with that culture, with the dance, with the music, especially with the music, and you speak the language, you understand the lyrics of a song, all of that does help and all of that does make their dancing experience more authentic. But it's like saying, "if you're not an Indian you can't do Yoga" [...]. It's not like this, it's pretty like anyone can dance and anyone can learn Spanish and anyone can educate themselves about Latin America and its roots and all that stuff. So it's easier for those who grow up with it because they don't need to go through certain things of learning just because of where they have been and how they have grown up.

In the above quotation, Ajay reiterates the tension between salsa as a specific dance tied to an idealised and essentialised origin in Latin America and an activity that may be learned by anyone today. The elements he mentions are the ones mostly negotiated when salsa dancers invoke ideas of salsa's "authenticity" (see also Urquía 2005). They include knowledge of what Ajay calls "the roots" of salsa as well as mastery of the Spanish language and an embodied vocabulary (the movements). Using the term "authentic" to describe the experience of *Latinos* and *Latinas*, he indicates the dance's origins and images of a homogeneous place of origin. Nevertheless, Ajay insists that non-Latinos can learn all of the above-mentioned elements, thus confirming the discourse of salsa as a universal leisure practice and *Esperanto of the body*.

Salsa dancers do often insist that they can learn the (bodily) language of salsa, but some believe this learning process can include a mental transformation, as German salsa dance professional Anna recalls during the interview:

> Salsa had a huge effect on me, psychologically, yes, so that I got a lot of self-esteem and self-affirmation. Suddenly I realised that out of a shy, young girl full of complexes, I developed into a, how can I say, while dancing I felt myself, sensed myself, felt an energy in myself that no one would ever have thought I have [...]. And I didn't feel as German, I never felt as German, yes. And suddenly I had found my destiny, in dancing, in passion.

As this dancer describes, salsa dancing becomes a space for and source of self-esteem and empowerment. Anna also draws a connection to the supposed non-German origin of salsa in order to identify with a more emotional character. When I asked what she meant by not feeling as German, she answered:

> For me, Germans are quiet, introverted people. And I am not like this, I think. I am very emotional and very passionate, in the dance and elsewhere. And I can't identify with German people and always try to transmit something of my energy to them during the dance lessons, so they can feel themselves. And they all think I'm a *Latina* or Spanish, that's nice.

Anna here describes herself as emotional, passionate and energetic and associates these traits with a non-German origin, thus ethnicising the practice of salsa dancing. Through her dancing, Anna constructs "an alternative sense of self" (Bosse 2008: 60) that she perceives as more vibrant, similar to the dancers Bosse (2008) studied (as discussed in Chapter 1). The reference to the cultural otherness of the dance allows some dancers to embody specific types of femininity (and masculinity), which are described as liberating and empowering. By constructing salsa, its history and the feelings it generates as something learnable, non-Latin salsa dancers represent and experience the practice as a leisure activity, though with its own history.

By contrast, the second way to claim a legitimate status as salsa instructor consists of a redefinition of salsa as not particularly related to Latinness, instead focusing on the individual expression of a dancer. This is demonstrated in the following discussion drawn from an interview with Nara:

JOANNA: And is history important? Like all these historical "roots" you were referring to? For your dancing?

NARA: So my knowledge of the roots is really limited, I don't actually know that much, I will admit that, 'cause I haven't studied it in that way. My expression to it has all been pretty spontaneous, in the moment, whatever the music is calling to. Not sure what they're saying necessarily, or the historical background, or who's singing, I don't know all of these details half the time, but I do know what the music makes me feel. So I just follow that.

Nara, a female salsa professional with high reputation as a solo artist, who grew up in North America as the child of Asian parents, here downplays the importance of the "Latin" elements: neither an understanding of Spanish, knowledge of the singer nor any "historical background" is important to her dancing. Nara defines her dancing as a direct response to the music and the ways the music makes her feel (a position she also defends in regard to salsa's gendered structure, as elaborated in Chapter 4).

This insistence on the kinaesthetic response puts the affect of the individual dancer at the centre of the dancing experience and de-centres the practice of salsa dancing from its focus on an essentialised origin. Musicality has become a key concept in the salsa circuit over recent years, and dance instructors as well as students insist on the importance of a musical understanding of the dancing and direct response on a kinaesthetic level.

I observed several musicality workshops, during which salsa dance professionals discussed the instruments and rhythms played in salsa songs. Salsa students were asked to imitate the rhythm pattern of the *clave* and the main rhythmical instruments of salsa bands, by clapping their hands or speaking them: pa pa, paa, paa, paa, pa pa, paa, paa, paa. Once the complex musical patterns were integrated, salsa dancers tried to move one particular body part – the feet, the shoulders, the hips – on a specific beat to accentuate the heard rhythm in the dance. Experienced dancers are able to thus interpret the music, which is understood as an individual expression and look to dancing. Other musicality workshops consisted of the teaching of a structured choreography, where students learned to synchronise their dance steps to a specific song, following the moves showed by the workshop teacher. As becomes clear from this discussion, salsa dancers have different understandings of how they wish to relate to the music during a dance and despite its importance, the concept of musicality remains vague. Nevertheless through the increasing mentioning and teaching of musicality at salsa events, it is framed as a skill that individual dancers can claim to master.

Musicality is partnered by the insistence on the connection between two dance partners, an important concept in tango dancing as well, described as "becoming one body with their partner, one organism moving in synchrony to the music" (see Davis 2015a: 65). In salsa dancing, on the contrary, during workshops instructors insisted on eye contact between dance partners, particularly during moments of individual dancing where the couple's hold is suspended briefly. Further, salsa students learn how to communicate through the touch of the hands or fingers, whereby a certain tension in the arms is necessary in order to communicate quickly when necessary (see Figure 3.1).

This interpretation of the concepts of musicality and connection de-centre the focus of salsa teaching from a discourse of cultural or "ethnic" authenticity (linked to an imagined past or elsewhere) to individual authenticity and technical aspects, whereby the immediate dancing experience stands at the centre. In this perspective, an individual's personal relationship to salsa dancing is deemed more important than the person's supposed relation to the dance through his or her upbringing or origin. In a discussion with Candice, a regular congress participant, this became very clear:

> When you dance with someone you always just wanna know, "how long have you been dancing?" But even that doesn't matter, because after two years it doesn't, you know. Everyone can dance, it's just a question of how much you love it and how much you do it, rather than anything else.

Candice insists on the importance of the time factor as well as the passion an individual demonstrates for learning the practice. As this discussion shows, the interviewed non-Latin salsa dancers constructed salsa-related "authenticity" as a property of individuals, with no reference to "cultural" or ethnicised "authenticity".

Figure 3.1 A couple demonstrating the taught sequence at the end of a workshop.
Source: © Valentin Behringer.

"Latinos teach badly": boundary-making

During my research, the "teaching convention" proved to be an important element in the boundary-making process between dance professionals perceived as *Latin* or *Cuban* and those perceived as *non-Latin*. With the spread of salsa events in Europe (including workshops for differently experienced salsa students) as well as the proliferation of dance studios, such formalised teaching situations became more important. The ways the dance is taught therefore became an important issue in negotiations about the legitimacy of salsa teachers.

Anna, a German salsa dance professional who became a studio owner after 20 years of travelling to and teaching at salsa events, distinguished her teaching methods from others, qualifying them as "German":

> They teach very badly, the *Latinos*. Yes, Cubans are great dancers but they don't have any idea how to teach Germans. I know the way the German thinks and I can get a feel for them and I developed a method so they can learn and feel themselves better. And I guess that is the secret of my success, so that after 22 years I am still in this hotly contested market, even though there are many rivals.

Here Anna portrays *Latinos/Latinas* and Cubans as good dancers, repeating a common discourse that assumes people of Latin American origin are naturally endowed with dance skills. Although she acknowledges their competence as dancers, she constructs them as lacking the "teaching concept" to teach Germans. Therefore, she draws the picture of an essentialised German way of learning, one that she is able to understand through her own Germanness. In stressing her own pedagogical techniques, she is able to draw on something the Cubans, better positioned in terms of dance (and the authenticity value attached to their dancing), are supposedly unavailable to achieve. While this teacher speaks about the German context, where she has her own salsa studio with several employed teachers, another dance professional, Ernesto, uses a similar argument for the festival circuit, explaining why certain festivals invite him and others do not. Ernesto perceives the "newly arriving" Cubans as a threat to his own teaching activities, as they better fit racialised stereotypes.

> I don't know why some countries invite me and others no more. [...] There are thousands of teachers, millions! Soon we'll have more teachers than students. My goodness ... it's incredible! And for example, we should not forget that salsa transmits many clichés and organisers and most of the public too, are open for these clichés. There's nothing I can do, it's like this. For example in *Cuban salsa*, the big stereotype is as a boy: young black Cuban, if possible the shirt a bit open... look at me, I am not this Cuban stereotype. As nowadays there are many Cubans coming over from Cuba, who are like this, they'll probably rather take them at a festival. But afterwards they will maybe realise that the teaching isn't as good [and they say]: "what was his name, Ernesto? Come on, let's call Ernesto again!"

Ernesto, who has been teaching Cuban-style salsa for a long time, also developed a specific teaching method, as he told me at the beginning of the interview. Again, in order to distinguish himself from the young, racialised Cubans whose "authenticity" might grant them a higher reputation, he presents himself as a better teacher with clearly structured pedagogical techniques.

These teaching techniques focus particularly on the way the dance relates to the music: in practically all workshops at salsa congresses, salsa dance is taught by demonstrating the steps while counting eight beats, with steps on the counts (1, 2, 3, [pause] 5, 6, 7 [pause] or [pause] 2, 3, 4, [pause] 6, 7, 8), thus "breaking down" complex movement patterns into smaller segments and relating them to specific steps.[1] This teaching vocabulary includes both counting to eight, and explaining where the weight of the body lies while stepping on the right or the left foot as well as other technical terms. During my observation in dance studio settings as well as festivals, I found that it is not uncommon to have a full one-hour class without any music. The teachers concentrate on the counting and demonstration of steps and body movements on the counts. This way of learning strongly contrasts with ways of music-related learning, in which the rhythmical instruments of the music guide the steps and the body movements are learned through imitation (McMains 2009).

Dance instructors like Anna or Ernesto, whose legitimacy as salsa instructors might be challenged (in both cases due to age, as well as ethnicity/race for Ernesto as a non-Cuban and in terms of gender for Anna as a female dancer), draw on images of Cuban teachers as less adapted to European dance students. In this vision, salsa dancing is constructed as a series of steps on counts that have to be acquired in the specific context of a dance lesson (see Urquía 2005). It is related to the claim to possess a specific teaching technique, and the argument is used to distinguish one's teaching from other dance teachers in the salsa circuit.

A somewhat related assertion against dancers of *Cuban salsa*, and sometimes Cuban dancers per se, is the argument of the "educated dancer". At salsa congresses, the boundaries between *Cuban salsa* and other salsa styles are spatially institutionalised in different rooms with different DJs. Dancers heatedly discuss which style is better and thus mobilise various aesthetic arguments. These arguments intersect with ethnicised, racialised and class-based boundaries, and for salsa dance professionals the struggles over styles may, in certain situations, be related to performing and teaching opportunities. This was made explicit in the interview with Suzana, an employed co-organiser and promoter of an important salsa event in Europe. She explained why she does not wish to invite instructors of *Cuban salsa* to her event, based on a boundary between "educated dancers" of New York-style or On2 and dancers of *Cuban salsa*:

JOANNA: Maybe a bit for the artists, like, where are they coming from? How do you choose them?

SUZANA: [...]. We promote New York-style, we like New York-style, and our friends are *cross-body* ... line dancers, let's say. And I don't like so much Cuban, it's not ... I don't like timba [music] very much [...] And I don't like the people from the Cuban [style]. I'm very honest. [...] it's because of the teachers. [...] Because once I saw [dancers of a famous company] dancing socially, Cuban, it was amazing! But usually people dancing Cuban they are very disrespectful on the dance floor. [...]

JOANNA: And in what way are they another community, the Cuban? [...]

SUZANA: [...] I don't know, we just share different things, we are totally in the ... You know, to dance New York-style is more complicated, but it's better. [...] Honestly if it's a mixed party, I don't like it. It happened to me, I was dancing *cross-body*, they were dancing Cuban, extremely, I got hit many times, they don't even say sorry, anything. I think it's that us, On1 or On2 dancers, in many schools we are also educated. So I was the same in my school, like: "you dance on the dance floor, it's not all yours. You have your part, you have to protect your partner, you have to look around, you have to respect the people around!" The Cubans they proved me that they don't do that.

Suzana marks the boundary between dancers of Cuban style salsa and other styles through her discursive strategy, mobilising several arguments: the music, the alleged disrespect and the lack of education on the dance floor. Furthermore, she constructs Cuban-style salsa as less technical (and hers as "more complicated"). Although she acknowledges the skills of some chosen dancers of *Cuban salsa*, her statement clearly positions New York style as better. She thus creates a hierarchy between Cuban and other styles of salsa.

Nevertheless, one element Suzana mentions is the importance of Afro-Cuban dances and rumba, dances that contemporary salsa dancers of all styles include in their performances on festival stages as well as on dance floors. Over the last few years, movements from these dances have become markers of "authenticity" – cleverly marketed by dancers originating in Cuba. Suzana, in her position as a congress organiser, thus acknowledges the importance of salsa artists of Cuban style, as she is interested in what the paying festival participants want.

To summarise, while European and other non-Latin (or in some cases non-Cuban) salsa dance professionals attempt to enhance their reputation through the emphasis on qualities such as technical ability, teaching methods and individual response to music, they represent Latin American and particularly Cuban dance professionals as lacking precisely these qualities.

Latin American salsa dancers' reclaiming salsa

I will now discuss the ways dance professionals of Latin American and more specifically Cuban origin in the European salsa circuit deal with these accusations of a lack of a teaching method by demonstrating their teaching skills, and by claiming a cultural authenticity that is place- and origin-related, thus engaging in what has been described as "authenticity work" (Peterson 2005: 1086).

"In Europe I have to count exactly on eight beats": learning the teaching convention

Dance professionals of Cuban origin are well aware of the image of "good dancers but bad teachers" in the salsa circuit, and newly arrived dancers quickly learn about the importance of the teaching convention in the (European) salsa circuit and include it in their repertoire. In an interview in Havana, Germany-based Cuban salsa dance professional Yaimara told me: "In Europe people learn differently than here, so in Europe I have to count exactly on eight beats so that the others can learn". London-based Cuban dance professional Reinaldo agrees: "I have friends [in Cuba] they don't know 'one, two, three', for example. I didn't know 'one two three'!" To perform their status as salsa teachers or, in other words, to be a salsa teacher entails learning the appropriate teaching vocabulary.

Instructors of the salsa circuit all had to learn this teaching method to use it in their classes. As McMains (2009: 311) argues: "Salsa dancers who acquired their skills by growing up in a culture in which salsa music and dance are part of everyday life cannot rely on the methods by which they learned as the basis of a successful teaching business". Yaimara explained:

> And I am still learning. As well for my teaching, my methodology. [...] In Cuba we learn differently. Many people just watch, then they copy and one day they do it, that is part of the culture. Even just walking, women in Cuba are walking totally different. But as I realised, here it is not the same, not only for German people, for the whole of Europe, it's logical, it's not your culture.

Teachers of *Cuban salsa* who have learned to dance in lived contexts and without standardised teaching techniques have to adapt their approach to transmit the knowledge of dances. They therefore learn how to translate the body movements they know into a specific form of teaching vocabulary – counting on the beat and breaking down movements into their components.[2] In this way, they demonstrate their ability and skills in teaching students, thus adapting to the teaching convention.

Furthermore, Cuban dancers often need to include quicker turns and complex figures (what is generally referred to as "technical" dancing) for their European students. Several dance professionals told me about the different ways of dancing in Cuba and the European salsa circuit. Reinaldo put the differences as follows:

> But in Cuba no one dances salsa, there are rappers, there is rock, there is romantic music, you know. There is nothing [...] salsa. Even they are in shock with me, they are: "wow, how you dance man? Because we never saw you dance like that!" And before, we [were] dancing in a small group like a Rueda de Casino [several couples dance in a circle and switch partners], and now when I go, these girls who used to dance with me, they are like: "no no, you complicate too much now, you do too many things now", and this and that. Because they don't do, the dance is not what they do in here, people take [classes] like every week, everyone trains to get better.

Reinaldo here describes a paradox several of my interview partners reflected upon: "the way we dance here is not the way they use to dance there". *Cuban salsa* as defined in the (European) festival circuit is not exactly the same as the ways people dance in informal contexts (in Cuba or other countries). What is called *Cuban salsa* at festivals reveals itself as influenced by salsa's transnationalisation and mixing in the festival circuit – rather than a carbon copy of what is or was danced on Cuban territory. Despite the common understanding of *Salsa Cubana* presented in the European salsa circuit as being a direct Cuban "product", so to speak, and the construction of authenticity as place-related, Cuban dance professionals have to go through a process of adapting their teaching and dancing to the salsa circuit.

This gap in different learning and teaching techniques has historical reasons: at the beginning of the 2000s, when different salsa dance styles became more popular in Europe, dance teachers from North America, and particularly New York and Los Angeles, started to be invited to teach at events in Western European cities (see also McMains 2015: 269). Abod, who lived in the UK at that time, remembered the different teaching methods these US teachers used compared to those of the Cuban (and other Latin American) teachers living in the UK:

> And the thing with the LA [Los Angeles] guys was they brought time discipline. Improved teaching technique in dancing. And because a lot of teachers came from a ballroom background, they brought improved teaching techniques. And a lot of the Cuban dancers at that time, people might disagree with me, were teachers just because they were Cuban. And everybody expects the Cubans are going to dance, so they taught. There were a few good Cuban dancers but there weren't good teachers in that structured syllabus. [...] So the LA people brought that [...] One thing that did happen in England, [...] is when LA came, a group of Cuban teachers, they saw a threat to their livelihood, suddenly somebody tried to do accreditation.

McMains' (2015) historical analysis of salsa dancing in LA and New York shows that successful dance teachers implemented teaching techniques they had learned in ballroom dancing. "Because there was no tradition of teaching Latin dances in formal classes in Latin America, when a demand for Latin dance classes among Latinos began to grow in the 1990s, salsa dancers turned to the ballroom dance industry for models" (McMains 2015: 230). Today, ballroom and competition-oriented dancesport organisations are often organised on a national level and, with salsa's arrival in Europe, they became interested in doing accreditation for salsa dancers. As Abod recalls, the British ballroom dance organisation UKA (United Kingdom Alliance of Professional Teachers of Dancing and Kindred Arts) became involved with salsa. Urquía (2005: 391) notes in his study on salsa's re-branding in London that the UKA started to issue diplomas, claiming to wish to improve salsa teaching. This bolstered the status of accredited teachers but at the same time excluded several of the so-far successful salsa teachers of Latin American origin who were thus threatened in their status as legitimate teachers of salsa. As Urquía (2005) writes, "The examinations, certificates, medals and a book (in English) of dance steps also intimidated those Latin American teachers whose visas did not allow them to work officially and who were wary of the official sounding UKA" (391). The attempts at codification were therefore contested and, to counterbalance, the argument of "cultural authenticity" was put forward. As Urquía's (2005) study further shows, in the symbolic conflict over salsa in London, claims of (ethnic or cultural) authenticity stood against claims of technical excellence, in ways very similar to those of today.

Taking up the example of the institutionalisation of salsa in London through the ballroom dance organisation UKA in her critical analysis of "salsa cosmopolitanism" in Britain, Boulila (2018: 10) states that "claims to authenticity or cultural property can act as a strategy against the commodification of salsa by organisations like the UKA". Extending the same line of argument, "doing being ethnic" (see the next section) can be understood as a tool to counter the processes of exclusion at work in the (European) salsa circuit, particularly regarding the participation of non-European salsa dancers; in terms of access to the circuit, this includes material struggles such as institutionalisation by European national dance organisations and the above-described symbolic struggles among dance professionals inside the salsa circuit. In the context of the salsa circuit, a specific form of "Cuban authenticity" becomes a resource that dance professionals can mobilise to construct salsa capital (see Chapter 7).

"Move your body! that's the Cuban style!": doing being Cuban

One strategy to deal with the trope of the "bad teacher but good dancer" for teachers of *Cuban salsa* is to engage with it by embodying and representing Cubanness, by "doing being Cuban". While most salsa dance professionals choose and concentrate on one or several of the salsa dance styles, dancers of Cuban origin told me that other people look at them as mere representatives of *Cuban salsa* and that they often hear phrases like: "oh, you're Cuban, so you don't dance New York-style salsa". Dancers of Cuban origin in the salsa circuit reinforce this naturalising argument, when choosing *Cuban salsa* as their only field of expertise and performance. I identify three entangled elements of doing being Cuban: the construction of Cuban salsa as originating in Cuba, the performance of knowledge about how things are done in Cuba and a specific embodied vocabulary marking Cubanness.

When talking about salsa, Cuban dancers often use the roots metaphor, mobilising a strong image of ancestry. Reinaldo told me: "But many people know that salsa, the roots, are from Cuba". Thus, these dancers actively try to reinscribe Cuba into the "origin myth" circulating in the salsa circuit. They push this argument forward against the dancers who do not know about salsa's history. In this way, Cuban dance professionals are able to present themselves as more authoritative in terms of teaching *Cuban salsa*. As Yaimara explains:

> It is very clear, actually many people have wrong information. I don't blame anybody, but Cuba was totally closed with the *bloqueo* [the US embargo] and many people left Cuba and went for example to the US and took the music with them, like Celia Cruz for example or other musicians and they played the music there. But the music is the same that was in Cuba for a long time. And then they gave it the commercial name of salsa, the name was commercial but what they played was the same music as in Cuba. And after that, salsa made an evolution, with the New York-style, the Puerto Rico-style, nice style as well.

Yaimara here refers to the US embargo against Cuba and the many musicians who left Cuba during the 1960s. In these ways, dancers of Cuban origin draw on the argument of salsa's history to enhance their own legitimacy as salsa teachers. The following field note demonstrates the ways in which Cuban dance professionals perform and embody Cubanness.

> I participate in the rueda[3] workshop led by Juan, a well-known Cuban dancer performing and teaching in Europe for over 20 years now. The room is huge, a sports hall with a stage at the front of the hall, the DJ desk next to it and pictures on the wall, showing the common clichés of colourful street scenes of Havana, mainly historic cars in front of colonial style houses. Juan steps into the middle of the big room, wearing a skin-tight sleeveless shirt in white with the Cuban flag on it, black trousers and sport shoes. [...] At the end of the workshop, after much applause, Juan shows the patterns taught during the class and the participants film him with their mobile phones or cameras. Afterwards, several people approach him and ask him to take their picture with him. He agrees and poses with one after the other in front of the colourful posters on the wall. A person asks me to take their picture and hands me over her cell phone. [...] Juan now says, he wants a picture of him in front of the flag: he stretches his arms over his head and shouts: "mi Cuba, mio!" Smiling, he asks if the whole flag is in the photo. People are now leaving and Juan walks back to the DJ desk and changes his sweat-soaked shirt.
>
> (Edited field note, salsa festival Rovinj, 2014)

As becomes clear in this field note, teachers of *Cuban salsa* engage in a playful way with the imaginaries of Cuba, positioning themselves as ambassadors and authorities of Cubanness. T-shirts or baseball caps in the colours of the Cuban flag are popular accessories among Cuban dance teachers during the workshops. In a similar vein, I observed several times how Cuban dancers demonstratively showed a Cuban flag on stage after their dance performances – the only national references on salsa festivals' stages. By using national symbols, the dancers defined their dancing as Cuban and were able to capitalise on their perceived "cultural authenticity". Through such performances of the national identity, Cuban dancers "authenticate" their dancing. These dancers thus actively participate in the upholding of the Cuban clichés and participate in the construction of *Cuban salsa* as something essentially Cuban. In other words, they are doing salsa's Cubanness. The following field note of an observation at a workshop demonstrates some more elements used in this process.

> Although it's only 11am the festival location is already crowded. There are ten different workshops taking place at this time and I choose one of the rare Cuban-style classes (this festival is basically addressing *cross-body* style dancers), the workshop programme announces it as *Salsa Cubana*. When I arrive in the room (one of the smaller festival rooms), the

teachers are already standing on a small stage in front of the room where the workshop participants can see them. Both of them wear white t-shirts and white trainers, combined with jeans (hers tight, his looser), he wears a small necklace of coloured beads, a symbol of the Afro-Cuban Santería religion. He is putting on a headset microphone and welcomes us all in Spanish. He then switches to English with a strong Spanish accent and presents himself and his dance partner: "I'm from Cuba, she's from Hungary. So guys, never think, 'oh, I'm not Cuban so I can't dance Cuban-style', that's wrong! She is Hungarian and she dances Cuban-style!" He continues praising his partner while she smiles and tries to stop him. He continues: "the most important thing is to have fun while dancing, to laugh, to stop thinking".

He then starts teaching basic steps, but soon interrupts: "we in Cuba, we bend the knees, that is really important, otherwise the hips can't move". In order to show us what he means, he completely straightens his legs and walks backwards and forwards with stiff hips – "that's like hula hoop, we in Cuba call it the European style". People around me laugh at his joke, he is a great entertainer. The room is now packed with people; a woman in front of me looks around and leaves the room saying it is too crowded.

After several repetitions of the steps, the teacher puts on some music and the rhythm gets faster. I have to be careful not to bump into the people around me, as the teachers show quick turns and large arm movements. "Men macho! Ladies sexy!" he reminds us and explains the way men should stretch out their right arm just before the turn: "it's just natural, like when you say hi to someone". He stretches out his right arm and at a final movement, turns his wrist for a quick move of the hand. I try to do it, and for me this is not an easy movement, I never say hi to someone like this, the men around me try to do it but the movement doesn't look like the teachers'.

Later he reminds us about the bent knees: "it's about quality, not quantity of steps! In Cuba, when we are dancing, we don't think, 'how many moves I have'. The most important is el sabor (flavour); you need to bend your knees". And while he talks he shows what he means by it, bends his knees and moves the whole body, his torso and arms move in constant flow. "You've got the steps, yeah, now move your body! That's the Cuban style!"

(Edited field note, salsa congress Berlin, 2014)

This field note stems from a large salsa congress offering predominantly cross-body style salsa workshops. The context of this observation is important insofar as the instructor here presents himself as Cuban and advertises explicitly for *Cuban salsa* as a fun practice for non-Cubans, particularly Europeans. Such explicit advertising is rare at events with more dance students of *Cuban salsa*.

I will discuss two revealing elements of doing being Cuban from the above workshop situation: first, the ways teachers explain "Cuban culture" and thus distinguish themselves from non-Cuban teachers through the performance of their particular knowledge; second, the importance of bodily movements as a specific type of embodied vocabulary to mark authenticity.

The instructor above puts forward his own being Cuban explicitly and through mentioning several times the way dancing is done in Cuba ("we in Cuba" do it like this). At the same time, he uses his status as teacher to make fun of "the Europeans", whom he portrays as dancers with stiff hips, straight legs and no *sabor*. The concept of *sabor* is related to salsa dancing and is often translated with the English notion of swing or flavour; Renta (2014: 118) describes *sabor* as "the heart and soul of salsa dancing, an aesthetic tradition involving improvisation, creativity, and a corporeal response to the polyrhythmic quality of salsa music that stems from its African heritage". In critiques of salsa's commercialisation, the concept of *sabor* holds a special weight, as performers of stylised and choreographed salsa are often accused of lacking *sabor* (for a detailed analysis of *sabor* in the context of Puerto Rican nationhood and salsa's global commercialisation, see Renta 2014). The dance professional invites the dance students to learn the ways dancing is done in Cuba, taking the role of a teacher not only of dancing but also of "Cuban culture", thus becoming a sort of "cultural broker" (Szasz 1994).

The teacher in the above field note also describes some movements in *Salsa Cubana* as "natural", which is often used to describe *Cuban salsa*.[4] This dancing style is often classified as coming "from the street" in contrast to other, more ballet- or acrobatics-inspired styles. In discussions of salsa dancing, ideas of "naturalness" and "street dancing" are often opposed to ballet-inspired aesthetics (McMains 2015). New York (On2) style salsa is sometimes accused of being transformed into ballet. In this way, Cuban-style salsa is presented as genuinely different from the other salsa dance styles, a dancing where *sabor* and fun are the most important ingredients, and dancers are invited to "stop thinking".

The instructor in the above-described situation performs a balancing act between presenting the cultural knowledge he transmits and his Cubanness as exclusive and using the argument of salsa's learnable character to make the dance accessible for non-Cubans. In such ways, Cuban dance professionals reinforce and perform their status as "authentic" Cuban dancers and accumulate and sustain symbolic capital.

A third way salsa dance professionals are doing being Cuban is through the execution of complex movements of the whole body. This is what the instructor performs while exclaiming "that's the Cuban style". Such movements are created through the isolated movement of different parts of the body, such as the hips, the spine, the arms and the upper body. They rely on mastering the muscles and movement of different body parts at the same time, "sensuous polyrhythms within the body" (Daniel 1995: 3). Such movements borrow from rumba and other so-called Afro-Cuban dances, and they consist of a specific embodied vocabulary, which has come to signify authentic Cubanness in the salsa circuit, since salsa congresses have started to schedule workshops in rumba (and dances for *Yoruban orichas*, deities of African-derived

Cuban religion, see also McMains 2015: 305). Dancers of all salsa styles take up elements of these dances and include them in their dancing, "to spice it up", as one teacher put it.[5]

During my observations of performances at salsa festivals between 2013 and 2015, it was quite common to use elements of rumba, besides elements of ballet, contemporary dance, urban dance and hip-hop.[6] Even dancers who would otherwise disparage *Cuban salsa*, such as Suzana, the congress organiser quoted above, consider so-called Afro-Cuban dances an important part of salsa festivals. Ana (2017) observes an increase in rumba workshops at European salsa events "that can enrich one's style of dancing casino, making its overall appearance more 'authentic'" (178). Steps and movements of so-called Afro-Cuban dances have thus come to signify a specific authenticity, and Cuban teachers are sought-after to teach it (see Figure 3.2). For dance professionals of Cuban origin, stressing their dancing as authentically Cuban may therefore prove an effective marketing strategy.

In her "genealogy of the mulata body", Blanco Borelli (2016: 13) coins the term "hip(g)nosis" as a "feminist response to the mere objectification of the dancing mulata". She argues that female dancers in Cuba were not only objectified but that they also powerfully used their hips in reaction to such representation. Drawing on her interpretative framework, I would argue that in the salsa circuit, objectification (and reappropriation), including sexualised and

Figure 3.2 Salsa Cubana men's styling workshop.
Source: © Valentin Behringer.

racialised representations of dancers' bodies, concern not only female but also male dancers. In the next chapter, the salsa-specific sexualised body parts will be discussed, whereby the female hips figure centrally. For men, the movement of the torso and isolation of the chest and shoulders hold as signifiers of a salsa-specific masculinity, often sexualised and racialised as well. Enlarging Blanco Borelli's (2016) analysis, I would argue that (Cuban) male salsa dance professionals powerfully use their chests to engage with objectification (by their numerous female European students).[7] As has been argued for the world music market, there exist multiple pressures for "authenticity", to which musicians have to respond (Glick Schiller and Meinhof 2011). In a similar vein, Cuban salsa dance professionals respond to calls for sexualised and racialised representations of "authenticity" in the salsa circuit.

To summarise, I identified three key ways of doing being Cuban: through the verbal and visual repetition of one's teaching as specifically Cuban, through the self-representation as cultural broker and, powerfully, through the performance of a specific embodied vocabulary. As Peterson (2005) notices: "If authenticity is constructed and subject to continual change, then it clearly takes an effort to appear authentic" (1086). Through such "authenticity work", Cubanness is constantly performed and the legitimisation as "better" is nurtured.

Expectations of authenticity in salsa tourism in Havana

I will now turn to the encounters between European salsa students and their Cuban salsa teachers in spaces of salsa tourism in Havana. The logics of the affective economy of the salsa circuit are at work in these encounters, but under slightly different circumstances from those of their European equivalents, as they are usually framed as interactions between tourists and Cubans and draw on different expectations from both sides. The interactions therefore entailed manifold negotiations of the issues at stake.

"My goal is to dance like a Cuban": European students' expectations

Scholarship on tourism has underlined the importance of tourist imaginaries and expectations both in the holiday experience (Skinner 2011) and in shaping the choices made (Ana 2017). Similarly, Davis (2015a) underlines the importance of dancers' "fantasies" in the "passionate encounter across many different borders" (181) between tango dancers. Urry (1995) states that expectations are constructed "through a variety of nontourist practices" (132) and distributed through media, which construct the gaze. "Such practices provide the signs in terms of which the holiday experiences are understood, so that what is then seen is interpreted in terms of these pre-given categories" (Urry 1995: 132). During the salsa dance holiday I observed in Havana, I asked the participating students about their expectations before their travel to Cuba. The responses of male and female salsa students included arguments related to their imaginaries of Cuba as a travel destination as well as arguments specifically linked to the dance holiday as a way to witness "authentic Cubanness".

Salsa students' imaginaries of Cuba as a travel destination included representations of Cuba as a "tropical paradise". The announcement of the renewing of diplomatic ties between Cuba and the USA at the end of 2014, and thus between my two fieldwork stays in Havana, was also a topic among some salsa students. They wanted to see Cuba "before it changes", an argument Ana (2017) analyses as the response to a "shattering" of a fantasy. As she argues,

> the quest for the authentic had been doubled and supported by one of the most common assumptions that were still functional among tourists: that Cuba remained unchanged, 'frozen' in time and isolated from the rest of the world for more than half a century.
>
> (Ana 2017: 176)

However, with the media coverage about the likely future changes, tourists felt the urge to travel to Cuba as soon as possible. This was exactly the discourse of some of the salsa dance holiday participants: one of them told me that she had heard that one should travel to Cuba now (in 2015 and 2016), because "afterwards it will be over". She was not interested in seeing a branch of H&M in the Obispo [a central street in Havana], so she had decided to come to Cuba before it changed. Such a "perpetual quest for unspoiled experiences and local colour" (Ana 2017: 176) builds on romanticised and nostalgic visions of Cuba.

In the search of "authentic experiences", cultural tourism and particularly dance classes figure high in tourists' imaginaries. Taking dance classes and dancing with Cubans was therefore perceived as privileged access to "the real Cuba". Furthermore, for many European salsa students, a trip to Cuba is a rite of passage in an individual's salsa trajectory (cf Puccio 2000). Paradoxically, as the Cuban interviewees insisted, among the island population other dance forms such as reguetón are more widespread than casino or salsa. Nevertheless, the visitors are looking for a genuine experience of taking dance classes and dancing with Cubans in Cuba. In this process, the rumba and other Cuban folkloric dances were seen as particularly difficult ("the most difficult dances in the world", as one salsa student put it).

Roberto, a salsa student whom I met in Havana, explained exactly what he was looking for in the lessons in Cuba:

> The basic step is one thing, but the other thing is how to move. There's much more to it than just six basic steps and a wiggle of the hips. But it's shoulder, arm, head, chest, exactly that's it, I watch the details; how is he holding his knee, how is the foot, is he on his heel or the point. That's what I try to imitate. If I like his style. I will never be able to do this and I will not compare with a Cuban, but my goal is at least to look like a Cuban, or try to look like this. That's what I wish to take with me, dance wise.

Dance lessons in Cuba include the promise to "look like a Cuban". Ana (2017) has described rumba's function "as an embodied souvenir that makes 'Cubanness' available and, in a way, portable, through the body that experienced it" (178). Taking lessons with Cubans in Cuba for many salsa students entailed the promise of "authenticity", a Cubanness that could be embodied and then be integrated in their salsa dancing. In a similar vein, Manuela, another dance holiday participant, told me about her expectations:

> I wanted to find out how people here move, where the movement comes from. I find it difficult to put this into words, but people here move their bodies beautifully. [...] Of course I also hoped to be able to take the movements with me, so that I can learn to move in this way, at least a little bit.

Salsa students travelling to Cuba thus hoped to have access to an embodied experience of Cubanness, accessible through dance lessons with Cubans, which is often a gendered phenomenon. The encounters between European students and their Cuban salsa teachers and dance partners were also shaped by the huge economic disparities between them: for Cuban dancers and dance professionals, dance tourism in Havana allowed privileged access to tourists. These interactions were not only used to access the European salsa circuit (as argued in Chapter 6), they also have the potential to provide Cuban dancers with foreign currency and gifts such as rum, clothes or other products that are hard to get in Cuba (e.g. cosmetic articles, digital cameras or smartphones) (cf Bodenheimer 2013). At the time of my visit, a single dance lesson (usually about one hour) with one of the Cuban dancers cost 12–15 CUC (equivalent to 12–15 USD); thus, two hour-long lessons were equivalent to the average monthly income of 25–30 CUC provided to workers in state jobs.

For Cuban dancers, engaging in the salsa tourism space therefore meant privileged access to a lifestyle and opportunities they otherwise would barely have.[8] Huge economic disparities led people with diplomas in folklore or contemporary dance to work as dance teachers with tourists. One dancer I met during the organised salsa holiday was Olorun, who teaches tourists while being part of the Cuban National Folkloric Company. He told me during an interview after a dance lesson: "We professional dancers from the [*Conjunto*] *Folklórico*, like many dancers, we make a living from the classes with you. From classes with foreigners, I mean this is the economic income that brings more".

The encounters between salsa students and teachers were founded on highly diverging mutual expectations, which led to manifold negotiations, as I will discuss in the next section.

"For them it's just a job": conciliating an "authentic experience"

The main point of discussions among the European dancers participating in the dance holiday in Havana was the ambiguous relationship built up with the Cuban dance teachers and dance partners. Manuela, who had come to

Cuba "to learn more about Cuban people and their lives", observed an ever-present "tourist–Cuban template", which did not allow tourists "to meet them on equal footing". Additionally, European dance students constantly asked themselves whether to trust their Cuban dance partners and believe their stories (e.g. of poverty), a feeling that Simoni (2016) describes in his study on informal encounters in Cuba. As he found, "avoiding cheating and deception tended to be among tourists' major concerns" (Simoni 2016: 50). The salsa students' romanticised quest for an "authentic experience" was disrupted by their feeling of "just being a tourist". The disappointment was particularly present regarding the dancing experience.

Daniela, a holiday participant who had come to Cuba to improve her dancing through practice with experienced dancers, told me:

> To be honest, I find it a bit disappointing. I mean I really hoped to be able to dance freely with them. And now I find that they [...] don't make any effort. I mean, you can tell that this is a job. [...] sometimes I feel that for them it's just a job.

The salsa students who were looking for intense emotional dance experiences were disappointed by the Cuban realities. The gap between visitors' expectations and their experiences also appeared when salsa students wished to go out dancing at parties. Most dance schools in Havana offer the services of Cuban dance partners not only during dance lessons but also for an evening at a party. Yaimara, who had organised the dance holiday, explained her view:

> I find this means respect, and I find it is normal, when you wish to invite your dance partner, that you pay the entry fee, drinks and a salary of 10 CUC. [...] Because it is the time they take for you and they are with you 100%, you still learn a lot, even though it is not a dance lesson, you learn because you repeat the movements you learned in the class. And on the other hand, for Cubans here with the situation, they don't have the chance to go to a *casa de la música* every day. With the problems and all, they prefer to give the money to their family, for food.

However, paying a dancer to accompany them to a salsa party generated unease among some of the female holiday participants. Exchanging money for a dance seemed at odds with the expected authentic and gendered experience of a salsa night out.[9]

Over dinner in the hotel, the topic was discussed in length. While some of the group found it "OK" to follow the rule of 10 CUC plus entry fee, drinks and the taxi, someone found it "too expensive". One woman said this reminded her of an escort service, and said she would never invite a dance partner for dinner so that he comes dancing with her. Another woman found it "not authentic anymore" to pay for an evening with her dance partner. Despite these discussions, holiday participants managed to go out with their dance partners several times and usually expected their dance partners to join them whenever they suggested going out dancing.

As these discussions among female salsa holiday participants demonstrate, their gendered expectations entailed in the promise of salsa dancing in Cuba were complicated by the economic disparities between them and their Cuban dance partners. Instead of the expected emotional encounters, dancers had to deal with the concept of dance as a paid-for service. The conventions of the affective economy of the salsa circuit frame the exchange on the dance floor in non-economic terms. This convention is clearly disrupted in Cuba's current space of salsa tourism. While salsa tourists looked for an encounter framed as "authentic" in terms of dancers' mutual wish to dance together, the Cuban salsa dance professionals had to meet the tourists' gendered expectations. In the salsa tourist dance spaces, salsa was usually performed as a heteronormative encounter, which entailed the idea of men being in charge of flirting (see Törnqvist 2012 for the same observation in tango tourism). The economic inequality between the students and the teachers reversed the "classical" role-play of the men treating the women. Unable to perform economic agency, the male dancers usually insisted on seeing their dance students home to the hotel, even though they lived far from the city centre themselves. In this way, they negotiated the gendered expectations around dancing.

Some of the Cuban salsa dance professionals also had to navigate their own working (and everyday life) schedule. Olorun, who is employed in a dance company and teaches foreigners, put it like this:

> I mean, I teach classes with you in the morning but when I finish the class I need to go to work, you know? When I finish work I come with you to go out at night at the *casa de la música*. This means there are days that I work for the whole day.

When I asked him about the salsa parties, he told me that he did not like them at all due to the presence of *jineteros*:

> *Jinetero* is the person who is with a foreigner. At these places there are many of these people. I don't go to these places, I mean I never go, except for working. For example when you [the group] invite me to dance I go to this place because you invited me to go out dancing. [...] I go to this place because I work with you and because I go dancing with you specifically. [...] I don't like to go to these places, at all. I don't know, we dancers who are dancing all day long, for us dancing is not a way of having fun. I don't like the place, nor do I go there because I enjoy dancing, I only go there when I have to, for work. I am working with a student, with a group and they pay me to go there.

The 24-year-old Olorun distances himself from the practices of so-called *jineteros*. He understands his work with tourists as a job and necessity due to the economic situation. As a graduate dance professional working in an internationally touring dance company, he is able to access mobility and lead the life he dreams of without the help of a European girlfriend.[10]

The misunderstandings and negotiations of the encounters on the Cuban dance floor were thus shaped by the diverging interests and expectations of the Cuban dance teachers and the European students. At the same time, such encounters allowed both parties to fulfil their fantasies – of an "authentic experience" as well as "a better life", an argument Davis (2015a: 168) makes for the encounters between Argentinean and visiting tango dancers in Buenos Aires.

Conclusion

This chapter focused on the constructions of "authenticity" of differently positioned actors in the salsa circuit. As it has demonstrated, "authenticity" is negotiated and filled with different meanings in the salsa circuit. *Non-Latin* salsa dancers are undoing salsa's supposed Latinness through their insistence on the learnable character of salsa. They construct a dancer's "authenticity" as the property of an individual in relation to the dancing, stressing their mastery of musicality and connection. They thus construct what Lindholm (2008) classifies as a specific form of authenticity: one of content. These findings mirror studies of salsa's "globalisation" and adaptations in localised scenes, which have argued that salsa has been "de-ethnicised" (see for instance Urquía 2005). However, this chapter complicates this image: it demonstrates the ongoing strategies of *Latin*, and especially Cuban dancers to "re-ethnicise" salsa by claiming "authenticity" through reference to their country of origin and access to its essence, *sabor*. In this process, salsa dance professionals as well as their students rely on specific bodily movements drawing on rumba and *Afro-Cuban* dances (analysed as an embodied vocabulary) as a signifier of authenticity. This strategy draws on a "historical" authenticity (Lindholm 2008: 2).

In a study of Argentine "tango immigrants" in New York, Viladrich (2013) shows similar mechanisms. Tango practitioners from Argentina represent their dancing as the most authentic, implying that "those who were born and raised in Buenos Aires are the ones best able to understand the tango's untainted spirit" (Viladrich 2013: 82). The tango performers she spoke with argued that "learning to dance tango goes beyond achieving technical mastery, as it requires the ability to grasp the inner spirit that is rooted in deep-seated Argentine sentiments" (Viladrich 2013: 83). The reference to the tango's "real soul" (Viladrich 2013: 83) echoes salsa dancers' conversations about the importance of *sabor*, which is used in the branding of *Cuban salsa* as particularly "authentic".

As this chapter has shown, *non-Latino/Latina* salsa dancers draw a boundary between themselves and *Latinos/Latinas* by claiming a better pedagogical technique, drawing on what I termed "teaching convention". Confronted with these accusations, the Cuban interviewees positioned themselves as knowledgeable in the current ways of teaching salsa. Although adapting their teaching techniques as well as their dance movements, they need to constantly (re)produce *Cuban salsa* as specifically Cuban and thus to engage in "authenticity work" (Peterson 2005) with and through their bodies. "Doing being Cuban" can be understood as a response to the boundary-making processes inside the salsa circuit as well as outside. In this process, for salsa dance professionals of Cuban origin, the performance of "Cuban authenticity" guarantees their participation and reputation in the European salsa circuit.

Notes

1 For a short demonstration of the On2 technique, see rebrand.ly/salsa-8.
2 This process is not specific to the salsa circuit. Bizas (2012) discusses the same difference and adaptation in pedagogical techniques in the case of New York's Senegalese sabar teachers.
3 In the festival circuit, *rueda* is taught as a type of *Cuban salsa* danced in a big circle with constantly changing partners.
4 For a solo show of a male performer of Cuban-style salsa, see rebrand.ly/salsa-9.
5 The two dancers in rumba do not touch each other as in salsa; they look at each other. The male dancer attempts to make contact with or gesture towards the female dancer's intimate area, with his hands, hips or a foot (a movement called *vacunao*). The female dancer moves her hips, while she rejects his attempts. For an example of an improvised rumba performance after a workshop at a salsa congress, see rebrand.ly/salsa-10.
6 In the following video, dancers seen as leading figures of LA-style salsa include such movement in the short choreography they teach at an event: rebrand.ly/salsa-11 (particularly at 0:35).
7 The improvisation by a dance professional after a rumba workshop in front of his students in the following video can be analysed as a performance of the dancer's skills and a demonstration of a specific kind of sexualised (Afro-)Cuban masculinity: rebrand.ly/salsa-12.
8 Meeting tourists in Cuba is complicated by the government's control over *jineterismo* (literally translated as tourism "riding", which includes hustling and prostitution) and its attempts to limit contacts between visitors and residents (see Simoni 2016).
9 The following discussions reveal that issues are at stake similar to those at European festivals. The negotiations around the institution of *taxi-dancers* (see Cressey 1932, also Törnqvist 2012) are analysed in detail in Chapter 5.
10 Insisting on his professionalism, Olorun told me that he was not interested in engaging in a relationship with tourists and "meeting another girl every week". Other Cuban dance partners in the group demonstrated less reservation, and I observed and heard about several romantic relationships between European dance students and Cuban dancers during the dance holiday. In her study on tango dancers, Törnqvist (2013) addresses the "impossible romances" between tango teachers and their students in Buenos Aires, while Davis (2015a) has a more nuanced view of such relationships as a result of visitors' and locals' shared fantasies.

4 Doing, redoing and undoing gender in salsa dancing

This chapter focuses on micro-level interactions on the dance floor to explore how salsa dancers negotiate gender and which gender representations circulate in the salsa circuit.[1] Salsa as a social practice is a site for the (re)production and negotiation of specific gender arrangements. In terms of dancing itself, salsa dancers rely on several "gender conventions" (Schulze 2015), two of which I will explore more deeply in this chapter: the leader and follower structure of the dance and the gendered moves in the dance.

Scholarship on partner dance often regards the gendered dancing as reinforcing restrictive gender roles in society, because the male dancer initiates the dance moves, whereas the female dancer responds to the lead (cf Borland 2009). By contrast, as Borland (2009) summarises, in the cultural studies literature, "the more improvised, internally focused, unisex dancing of the 1960s is often represented as offering a new space for the enactment of alternative, egalitarian gender relations" (476). In literature on salsa, the gendered roles in the partner structure of dancing have also been addressed, often related to the question of public displays of female bodies and sexuality (Bock and Borland 2011; Skinner 2008). The gendered arrangements in salsa are described as "gender hierarchies that characterize the traditional roles of men and women in pre-feminist times" (Pietrobruno 2006: 19) or as "performance of submissive femininity and dominant masculinity" (Schneider 2013: 554). Furthermore, as some scholars argue, representations of gendered arrangements in salsa are often based on Western people's conceptions of gender in Latin American countries (Schneider 2013). By taking gender hierarchies for granted and relating them to the past or to an assumed "Latin culture", these analyses stay silent about how contemporary dancers of both sex categories are involved in doing gender, how they make sense of these roles and how they negotiate them.[2]

A theoretical framework solely focused on fixed structures of dominance and submission not only bears the risk of overlooking the ongoing negotiations of salsa partnerships, but it is also unsuited to address the actual embodied doings and experiences of research participants. Davis (2015b) makes a similar point for taking embodied experiences seriously in the analysis. In discussions of the doing gender approach, the importance of bodies has been highlighted as a resource for creating differences between men and women (e.g. Messerschmidt 2009; Villa 2010).

Focusing on the interactional level, this chapter does not approach the gender arrangements as stable or as the result of salsa dancers' socialisation, but instead is interested in how salsa dancers are "doing gender" (West and Zimmerman 1987) on the dance floor. Some scholars have argued for the introduction of an approach of "undoing gender" (Deutsch 2007; Hirschauer 1994, 2001; Risman 2009). Hirschauer (1994: 679) suggests that, depending on the context, there are different degrees of gender's importance, understood as a continuum of the salience of gender. In his conceptualisation of "undoing gender", the actualisation or neutralisation and even a neglect of gender become possible (Hirschauer 2001: 214). Risman (2009) points in a similar direction: "perhaps a criterion for identifying undoing gender might be when the essentialism of binary distinctions between people based on sex category is challenged" (83). Furthermore, the doing gender approach has been criticised for its "ignoring of the links between social interaction and structural change" (Deutsch 2007: 107). Deutsch proposes that researchers, instead of focusing on the persistence of inequality, should take into account how "the interactional level can also illuminate the possibility of change" (114). She likewise proposes using the notion of "undoing gender" for social interactions that reduce gender difference (Deutsch 2007: 122). West and Zimmerman, in a later article (2009), negate the possibility of an undoing of gender; for them, the term undoing "implies abandonment – that sex category (or race category or class category) is no longer something to which we are accountable (i.e., that it makes no difference)" (117). They thus propose using the notion of "redoing gender" for any interaction in which individuals are held accountable.

While West and Zimmerman's argument in their 2009 article adds an important distinction between "undoing gender" and "redoing gender", Hirschauer's focus on the context in which the interaction happens seems relevant to this chapter's discussion. While analysing salsa dancers' embodied negotiations of gender, it asks if these practices can be considered as a doing, redoing or undoing of gender in the specific analysed interaction. The conclusion takes up the question of structural change and relates the doings on the dance floor to the transnational careers of salsa dance professionals (which will further be theorised in terms of salsa capital in Chapter 7).

In this chapter, I thus explore the ways in which gender is produced in the setting of transnational salsa congresses. How are dancers doing gender and (re)producing the binary, heteronormative partnership? How do they negotiate salsa masculinities and femininities and challenge the routinisation of gender so that we can speak of a redoing or undoing of gender?

Producing the convention of leading and following

The principle of a (heterosexual) couple is the basis of partner dances such as tango and all the standardised ballroom dances (see Davis 2015a on tango; McMains 2009 on ballroom). As already mentioned in Chapter 1, research into salsa has traced the couple formation back to European dance traditions brought to the Caribbean in colonial times (Daniel 2002: 43).

In the salsa circuit, the dance is taught as a partner dance, with one partner indicating the next moves and the other one responding to the lead. Dancers mainly touch hands or the shoulders of their partner (which leaves space for improvisation with the non-touching body parts, particularly for more experienced dancers). The partnership in salsa is commonly framed as one between a man and a woman and between a leader and a follower, both roles being gendered and entailing specific responsibilities.

"Guys and girls are the fundamental basis": forming salsa partners

The second workshop I observe on this Sunday morning is announced as a "partnerwork salsa-tango" for the beginner/intermediate level. The room at the convention centre fills up with people, dressed distinctively: women wearing black leggings, a t-shirt and coloured high heels or flat dance shoes, men in t-shirts, sports trousers and trainers or black jazz shoes [special footwear for dancers with a flexible shoe sole]. A group of six young people approaches the stage, they all wear black shirts (the men's: short-sleeved; the women's: tank-top, tight) with coloured letters: Dubai Latin Fest. Two of them climb onto the stage while a third con- nects her smartphone to the sound system next to me. I tell her about my research and on my question she tells me that she's from Spain but now lives in Dubai where she has joined a salsa dance company. During our short discussion, the room has filled up with more than 80 people, all standing in front of the stage, waiting for the class to start.

The young man on stage grabs the head-mic, puts it on and welcomes the participants. He asks "all the men" to go to the right side of the room, "all the ladies" to the left side of it, still turned to the stage at the front of the room. He then stands in front of the men, with his back turned to them, while his female dance partner does the same in front of the women. He starts counting in English: "one two three; five six seven", and both instructors start doing steps on each count, followed by several turns. He continues, explaining verbally and through his body, what "the men" should do, focusing on the hands and arms. He then stops and explains what "the ladies" have to do, while his partner shows with which leg to do the steps in the turn and kicks the right leg behind her back. They repeat the sequence several times, always counting the steps, until the participants are able to follow their instructions. After several repetitions, the two dancers on stage turn around, now facing each other, and dance the same pattern together: starting in a couple hold, his right hand on her left shoulder blade, her left arm on his right shoulder, their other arms at an angle between their bodies. He steps forward, she backwards, then she steps forward, he back- wards, they turn around, he steps out with his right leg, she is at his right side, now the kick, with pointed toes she kicks between his legs, looks directly in his eyes, and they turn around again. After their energetic, elegant demonstration, the participants applaud. The instructor now asks them to "form couples" and I observe how several people partner up very quickly, taking each other's hands or standing close (I assume they know each other and came to the workshop together), always a woman with a man, while others just stand still and look around, searching for a partner. Now several female participants have no dance partner and the teacher calls them to the front of the room, just next to the stage, where the remaining three female dancers of the group (all three long-haired and wearing tight leggings) take their hands and dance with them for the rest of the class.

(Edited field note, Salsafestival Switzerland, February 2015)

This field note from a workshop at a salsa congress shows in an exemplary way how the gendered arrangement of the partner dance is learned and the (heterosexual) couple constantly reproduced. In all partnerwork workshops (where leaders and followers are taught a sequence in order to dance together) I observed, the teaching couple consisted of a woman and a man and performed set roles: the male dancer performed the leading role, the female dancer the following role. An individual who wishes to learn salsa is thus confronted with this partner structure and the gendering of dance roles (leader and follower) from the very first salsa lesson: there is a clear boundary between the two roles. Aspiring dancers are first placed into two dance-related categories (leader and follower) based on their sex category, often as explicitly as in the above example, where women and men first had to separate spatially. In a second step, they are taught how to enact the complementary set of steps and moves (see Figure 4.1).

Salsa dancing can be regarded as a case of "institutional reflexivity" in Goffman's sense. As he describes, institutional practices transform social situations into scenes of gender performances, in this process affirming beliefs about two different sexes (Goffman 1977: 325). To illustrate this argument, Goffman (1977: 319) describes a number of institutionalised frameworks in which gender can be enacted and that have "the effect of confirming our gender stereotypes and the prevailing arrangement between the sexes" as mechanisms of institutional reflexivity. Different practices or environmental settings, such as toilet segregation, are "presented as a natural consequence of the difference between the sex-classes, when in fact it is rather a means of honoring, if not producing, this difference" (Goffman 1977: 316). Using Goffman's (1977) theoretical framework is helpful as it renders clear that the salsa dancing couple is not a "natural consequence" of biological differences, it is rather the product of these placement practices and the spatial division of two categories as well as the allocation of the leading role to men and the following role to women. The institutional setting, here the salsa class, informs knowledge about how things are done in salsa. Leading and following practices are based on this knowledge, and they in turn help to reproduce the institutional framework.

Figure 4.1 Learning the leader and follower roles.

Source: © Valentin Behringer.

Furthermore, instructors in all the workshops I observed addressed their students as "ladies and men" (or "guys and girls") when they set up to explain the different steps and arm movements of leaders and followers. The vocabulary of leader and follower (used in other partner dance contexts, for example lindy hop) was rare; the different roles were just called "dancing as a woman" or "dancing as a man", thus presenting it as a "natural" thing for a man to lead and for a woman to follow. The use of the gendered language instead of the notions of leader and follower naturalises the binary construction of the leader role as performed by men and the follower role as performed by women. In this way, this gender convention was just a given, for (most of) my interview partners, such as Ajay, an experienced salsa instructor who regularly teaches at festivals.

JOANNA: So you said guys and girls ... is that important in that world? In what ways?

AJAY: Well of course guys and girls are important because you have to dance with people who are from the opposite sex. So it's the fundamental basis, you need to have enough guys and enough girls to make salsa happen.

Ajay explicitly states the imperative to dance with someone of the opposite sex. In this way, salsa in European festival spaces is in most cases constructed as a dance between a male leader and a female follower, based on the convention of heteronormativity.[3] As West and Zimmerman (1987) conclude: "doing gender also renders the social arrangements based on sex category accountable as normal and natural, that is, legitimate ways of organizing social life" (146). Hence, salsa workshops and teaching situations are the sites in which students are placed in two groups – leaders and followers – based on their sex-category: men lead, women follow.

"Ladies, just follow his lead": gendering leader and follower roles

Beginner salsa dancers do not simply learn steps and moves; the leader and follower roles are also imbued with different meanings. When salsa dancers learn how to lead and how to follow, they also learn how to enact salsa masculinity and salsa femininity, as each role is linked to "particular expectations and responsibilities" (McClure 2015: 90).

In most of the festival partnerwork workshops I observed, a huge part of the time was used for explanations and demonstrations of the leading technique, principally steps and arm moves for the leaders. Students were told where to put their feet, how to hold their hands and on which counts to indicate a change of direction for the followers. In this way, the leading role was constructed as very active, whereas the task for followers was often reduced to "just follow his lead" (see Wieschiolek's 2003 article with this title). The followers were sometimes shown a specific step or move of *ladies' styling* as in the field note above, where followers had to do a kick with one leg (a move inspired by tango dance and unknown to most salsa dancers, which thus needed to be demonstrated several times). Otherwise, followers were rarely addressed. Discussing the leader and follower relationship, dance instructor Marcos told me:

> So imagine, guys have huge responsibilities on the shoulders. They have to think about the beat, they have to think about the step, they have to think about what's gonna happen next, they have to think about you, and they have to think about the space around. And it's a lot of tasks to manage in one single thing. And that's the thing, for girls that is very important to learn: how not to think. To turn off autopilot, you know. Once that happens the guys will have the chance to experience what is the feeling of leading, and the girls what is the feeling of being led. And it's a huge pleasure later on.

In Marcos' account, the list of the leader's/men's "responsibilities" is long: the learning process for leaders is complicated by the importance of rhythmical and musical understanding (dancing in time), the execution and coordination of often-unfamiliar movements with the arms and legs and the importance of the interaction with the partner and the dancers around, which is constructed as the leader's responsibility. As salsa social dancing is based on the improvisation of sequences of steps, leaders further have to anticipate the next move they wish their partners or themselves to do. Following, on the contrary, is here constructed as a passive reaction to the signals received. Although following needs a considerable amount of training as well, as followers have to keep balance even when spinning several times and include styling in their dancing, the role is often framed in terms of "no thinking". Followers are furthermore responsible for the working of the connection between the two dancers, meaning that they have to hold up a certain tension in their arms in order to react quickly to the leader's proposition.

The division of labour between the leader and the follower is not simply a technical requirement of the two roles but creates a general "silencing of female instructors" (McClure 2015: 90), which helps to create and maintain what I call "hegemonic male salsa capital" in Chapter 7. In this way, the gendering of the leader and follower practices reflects gendered hierarchies of power, in which male dancers are placed in a "dominant" position and women dancers are placed in a "submissive" position (cf Schneider 2013). As argued above, it is precisely in this way that scholarship often analyses partner dances such as ballroom, tango or salsa. However, when taking into account dancers' affective experiences of the gendered roles, such clear-cut ideas are blurred.

Several dancers complicated the notions of leading and following and the way these practices are gendered when talking about the experience of dancing. Instead of understanding the follower role as defined and restricted by the leader, some of the interviewed dancers spoke about their positive experiences of giving up control or being able to "lose oneself". A female dancer in her early fifties told me that she had started dancing after her divorce and that in contrast to her job where she was the director of a small enterprise, in salsa she could just "drop off" her head at the cloakroom "like a coat" and let herself be led. This desire to give up control was also expressed in a statement in a discussion on Facebook, concerning a "more democratic distribution of deciding how the dance will go and not just the leader totally dominating what happens from start to finish". One answer to these attempts to "democratise" salsa was the following statement:

> [...] The reason I enjoy salsa is because it gives me the opportunity to let go, submit and be swept around the dance floor in the arms of a man (or woman). It's almost meditative that feeling of giving up control. This might make me sound a bit old fashioned but I assure you I'm not! I use so much "male" energy in other parts of my life – taking charge, making decisions, trying to be "successful" – that I relish the experience of some-one else being in charge. I can lead, I'm not a bad leader and it definitely helped my following to learn but it is not where my heart lives in salsa. Sweep me round the dance floor and do with me as you will! However, once the music stops I want equal rights again!!!!
>
> (Facebook discussion)

This quote demonstrates that the follower role in salsa dancing can be experienced as "meditative"; this dancer relates it to the giving up of control – relating this indirectly to "female energy". She draws a boundary between the dance floor and "other parts" of her life, characterising this other part as a place where she uses another type of "energy". She also insists on the temporal and context-specific frame that allows for this experience: the dance floor. The quote stems from an experienced dancer who has also learned to lead, a practice I will analyse in the next section. Here I wish to stress the importance some dancers attach to the follower's position as one of deliberately giving up control, an embodied and affective experience that is placed in contrast to other social situations where gender is done differently.

The leader role, on the contrary, was predominantly described as "powerful", "creative" and active, but it also comes with restrictions, as Karl made clear when talking about his experiences in both roles:

> I think it is different for men and women. [...] I really think it is a completely different feeling, honestly I envy you, 'cause you can just let yourself go in music and the lead. Whereas as man you always have to think about what am I going to do next, what will follow, it's quite technical.

Karl uses the naturalising language of "men and women" in order to speak of the leading and following roles in salsa dancing. He had the experience of dancing as a follower himself and clearly found the two roles different. Like other leaders, he describes leading as "technical" (a highly gendered notion itself) and as a state of mind where one always has to think about what comes next. Like Karl, Patric (a long-term dancer and casual teacher) told me that he would actually like to follow more often because of the different feeling but that in his experience, other men didn't like to dance with him and lead him, which hinders him from doing it more often.

As the discussion demonstrates, a focus on the affective experiences of dancing allows for a nuanced understanding of the leader/follower roles. While the leader/follower structure in salsa may reinforce hierarchies between men and women, the dancing also creates experiences of flow in the role of a follower and a sense of restriction in the role of a leader. This finding parallels McClure's (2015) analysis of social salsa dancing. McClure's detailed study focuses on gender and sexuality in salsa dancing, analysing the bodily practices as a mode of subjectification linked to normativity and as a mode of resistance and self-transformation. Drawing on observations, interview excerpts and her own dancing experiences, her work mainly centres on the "relations between bodies, selves and others" (McClure 2015) and concludes:

> A Foucauldian/Butlerian reading of the power relations in the heteronormative dance partnership suggests that women are constrained by the expectation that they will follow. However, a Deleuzian reading instead

positions the follower as particularly able to operate in a present-centred mode of being and open to the possibilities for unpredictable new becomings, while the leader is constrained by his responsibility to generate and direct the momentum and flow of the dance.

(McClure 2015: 48)

Salsa dancers engage in processes of meaning-making regarding the gendered roles and experience them in different ways. A tension becomes apparent between a liberating experience on an individual level and a reproduction of gendered power relations on the level of the dance structure. While this tension becomes particularly apparent on a theoretical level, some salsa dancers also negotiate it in embodied ways.

The following sections will further analyse how the gender arrangements in salsa dancing are experienced and negotiated in processes of doing, redoing and undoing gender, thus challenging the routinisation of salsa's gender arrangements in specific gender conventions.

Working out the gendered dance partnership

Salsa dancers participating in the salsa circuit position themselves in relation to the gendered arrangements in salsa dancing and their assigned role in different ways. Many interviewed dancers related the leader/follower relationship in the dance in one way or another to gender or a "Latin culture": some believing there are essential differences between men and women and viewing salsa as a natural expression of these differences. Others told me about a tension between salsa dancing and ideas of gender equality. They expressed a similar dilemma to that which Davis (2015b) notes among tango dancers (not least herself), between a feminist stance including "political and normative commitments" and the "passion" generated through gendered practices in partner dancing.

Dancers' views on salsa dancing can be subsumed into three broad practice-related perspectives, varying in their degree of essentialisation: the first reinforcing gendered categories, the second potentially challenging them and the third undoing them. As I will demonstrate, the experiences and perspectives of female dancers appear to vary depending on their level of competence in dancing as well as concerning their positions in the salsa circuit (students or salsa dance professionals). By contrast, male dancers in my sample tend to hold similar views independently of their status in the salsa circuit. I will now explore these three perspectives and discuss some of their implications for the doing, redoing and undoing of gender in an embodied way through salsa dancing.

"A nice role play": reinforcing the gendered categories

The stance that most amateur dancers took was the position that following in dance as a woman and leading as a man was somehow a "nice role play" between two individuals of the opposite sex. This is the case for Manuela, the only novice dancer in my interview sample. She told me why she liked being asked for a dance and being led in salsa:

MANUELA: On the one hand I think it's old fashioned [laughs], but on the other hand it's beautiful, because somehow it is in line with this salsa feeling. Elsewhere we as women are not that feminine anymore, especially in Switzerland, in the job, everywhere we have to function. The difference between men and women is not really made anymore. So I like it that there is a space where this exists, where this … even though it is old fashioned, but it's still beautiful. And somehow I also think it's exciting, precisely the game between man and woman, it is like part of it, it's in dancing, the man leads, and you have to let yourself be led, then you really are the woman. [...] It is part of it.

JOANNA: And how does it feel when you dance like this, as a woman, as you said?

MANUELA: I like it very much. Yes. That you really get the chance in your everyday life to really be a woman, to dress nicely, to move feminine and to let yourself be led. In the beginning that was very difficult for me, to let them lead, because somehow, I also grew up, with my mother, she is a real power woman, she is the boss in the house [laughs]. And she always taught us to take this role ourselves, to be independent, do what I want and don't really be feminine. But I am not really like this. I mean, I am not the type of woman who wants to have a career or to take a somewhat male role. Not at all. I am way too sensitive [laughs]. [...] That's why I like it that there is a place where one can still really be a woman, where it is accepted.

From this account, we learn that salsa dancing can be experienced as a sort of "compensatory space" for young, highly educated women like Manuela, who holds a Master's degree and works in the communications department of a university. In her view, her upbringing as an "independent" and "not feminine" woman initially hindered her ability to learn how to follow in the dance. A potential conflict between independence and the follower role is dissolved in her affirmation that she is not a career-oriented type of woman ("I am not really like this"). She does not completely adhere to what she conceives as a male role in her professional life; instead, she fully embraces the possibility salsa opens up for her to "really be a woman".

This echoes Davis' findings in her study on transnational tango dancing. She writes about a female dancer wherein "performing femininity becomes a way to express part of her self-identity that she has had to keep under wraps in her work situation and everyday life" (Davis 2015a: 108). Similar to these tango dancers, some of the female interviewees actually liked dancing salsa not in spite of but precisely because of its gender arrangements. For them, salsa opens up a space where they can dress up and behave in ways they would not in other social situations, and they clearly mark the context of salsa as specific and different from other social situations in their life. In this way, salsa becomes a "game" (Villa 2003), a point I will further discuss below.

Some male dancers and leaders took a similar stance. In the interview with Patric about the history of salsa and the meaning of the roles, he said:

PATRIC: These roles still exist. Through the dance they are probably more defined or forced. You really have to live it, you can't just ... as a dancer, the one who leads, you really need to be a bit macho. You have to perform this role, even though you might not be like this, you have to assume the role [...] You can express your femininity and as a man you can express your masculinity, by leading her, saying where to go, it is defined by the dance. I believe this is OK, really.

JOANNA: So you're comfortable with this?

PATRIC: Yes I am. You just shouldn't adopt this too much in your own life. You shouldn't believe, once you go out [of salsa] that you can be that decisive besides dancing. But I don't think this could happen. I rather believe that you can't do it enough, or not in this way and in dancing you can experience something that is also healthy, I think. It also fosters self-confidence [...] I believe this is also natural to some extent and should be like this and should stay like this.

Patric interprets the performance of salsa femininity and masculinity as part of the necessary "role play" in salsa dancing. Again, the couple is heteronormatively constructed as consisting of a man and a woman, and both have complementary responsibilities. Referring to salsa femininity and masculinity, Patric reflects on the possibility that individuals "might not be like this", underlying the playful character of the dance situation as a performance of gendered roles. By drawing a clear distinction between dancing and the outside world, he confines the embodiment of a certain type of masculinity to the salsa space as it might potentially lead to conflicts "besides dancing". Like Manuela, he separates the salsa space from other social settings. He also uses the term "natural" to describe leader and follower roles, referring to essential differences between the two categories of men and women, based on a view of two complementary and essentially different gender categories and perceives the role play as a "healthy" compensation.

In salsa, the gendered role play is not only naturalised but, as Patric's reference to salsa masculinity as "macho-like" suggests, constructions of gender in salsa also intersect with specific representations of "Latinness". In the interview, Patric associates salsa with the history of *Latinos* and relates the leader/follower structure to a specific kind of masculinity. While drawing on exoticising projections, he considers the embodiments of this type of salsa masculinity complementary to his everyday life.

In all of the above accounts, the construction of salsa as "different" from other social situations (mainly work) is striking. Villa (2003) analyses a similar phenomenon in tango, which she describes as a relatively autonomous, mimetic world of game, interrelated with other existing worlds. As she argues, to stay in the game, the actors (the amateur tango dancers) consciously distance themselves from their everyday practices (Villa 2003: 136). They engage in playful gendered performances of tango femininity and masculinity precisely because they do lack such clear rules of the game (at the roots of tango passion) in their everyday lives (Villa 2003: 154). Davis similarly argues that

> tango cannot be viewed as a reiteration of traditional gender relations that existed in another time and place. Nor is it simply a reflection of relationships between men and women as they exist in late modernity. Rather, tango provides an opportunity for contemporary individuals to experience something that is missing in their everyday lives. It offers them an escape from the norms of equality that facilitates their desire for passion.
>
> (Davis 2015a: 126)

According to Davis (2015a), tango gender relations can be understood as a compensation for some of the costs of late modernity. In this way, for some salsa students, the gender conventions in salsa are seen as a game with specific rules, taking place outside of their everyday lives and enabling affective experiences they are missing otherwise. However, as I have argued before, the gendered (and exoticised) role play is not the only element that attracts dancers to engage in the salsa circuit, and not all dancers accept the so far described (re) production of gendered roles, as the following two sections demonstrate.

"You can switch the roles": disentangling sex category from gender

The second stance dancers took regarding the gendering of the leader and follower roles was a de-essentialised vision of leader and follower skills, not relating them to sex category. This vision was usually taken by more experienced dancers or salsa dance professionals. Although in salsa the leader role is constantly constructed as masculine and the follower role as feminine, some dancers are experimenting with a role switch and thus potentially challenging the naturalisation of gendered dance roles and sexuality. As West and Zimmerman write, when an individual "identified as a member of one sex category engages in behaviour usually associated with the other category, this routinization is challenged" (West and Zimmerman 1987: 139). The role switch in salsa potentially allows for a disentangling of leader/follower roles from the sex category and the challenging of the heteronormative structure of salsa dancing.

Based on my own experience and observations, it takes anything from several months to several years of practice before an individual is able to dance in a way that is considered advanced. In salsa dancing, actors usually learn one of two roles and must invest a considerable amount of time to improve in this one role. Due to these learning practices, a switch of role requires training (see also McClure 2015). I will now turn to these practices of switching and analyse in which contexts they happen. Here I am interested in the ways they are framed and legitimated and the potential of a role switch as a challenge to the routinisation of gender in salsa partnership. Salsa dance professional Maria (whose story will be introduced in Part III) expressed the potential as follows:

JOANNA: It's about the gender in the dance, so for you, what is a good female dancer like?

MARIA: You know, for me it's not really about gender in this dance, even if of course the dance as salsa has a really, I mean, the genders are really defined in the dancing, yes. [...] But if it's coming about the dancing by itself [...] since the dance is a couple dance, so you enjoy and you communicate with other people, so the joy is together. [...] And for this you have tools, the leader has certain tools, the follower has certain tools. And you use these tools to get simply what you want from dance, which is simply the pleasure and the joy of communicating. So it's hard to say [...] what is a good female dancer, because I know also females that are really good leaders, I was dancing, here is one of them, a friend of mine from Spain, she is just really awesome as a leader so I dance with her as well. So that's what I'm saying, that about the dancing by itself, you can switch the roles as well and it's fine, and it's still dancing.

In this interview extract, I gendered salsa dancers in my initial question about "female dancers", whereupon Maria negated the importance of gender in salsa. She rather set the emphasis on the communication between two individuals, being achieved through differently used tools by leaders and followers. In a next step, she dissociated the leader and follower roles from the sex category. Sometimes dancers switch roles, thus disrupting dominant conventions of who is supposed to lead and who to follow based on sex category. The heteronormative structure of the dance and the standardisation of gender are challenged as the equation between sex category and role is cancelled.

During my research, I observed women leading another woman during a festival party or in the workshops, or a man following another man several times.[4] Drawing on Butler (1993), Schneider (2013) qualifies such non-heteronormative dancing in salsa as "queer performances", as they have the potential to question normative behaviour. However, as in Schneider's study (mirroring McClure's 2015 findings), at the observed events such a partnering was usually framed as a transgression of "normal" salsa behaviour and needed justification or legitimisation in several ways. In this way, the "subversive potential of non-heteronormative performance" (Schneider 2013: 565) in salsa is questionable, as it actually reinforces the binary gender category.

Maria continued her explanations about the role switching, saying that it was something people did "just for fun". She thus framed the situation of a man following or a woman leading as something entertaining that should not be taken seriously. The gender convention is reinforced through the marking of the situation as an exception and thus defining the boundary. In the situation I described in the field note above, three female salsa professionals danced as leaders, constructing a teacher/student relationship. This happened in several classes I observed. In the workshop context and the hierarchical positions these dance instructors (or members of salsa dance companies) had, leading was a skill that more experienced dancers were able to acquire. Nevertheless, the role switching of female dancers becoming leaders was situationally framed as a necessity, the usual argument being that "there are not enough men", so there were not enough leaders available. Female dancers were thus supposed to dance in the leader role only if there were not enough male dancers to lead them. In workshops where female participants outnumbered male participants, the imbalance was either resolved through experienced female dancers switching or by instructors asking male dancers to change partners after several minutes and dance with two female dancers. In this way, the gender convention of men leading and women following was not disrupted. Boulila (2015) analyses how similar situations marginalise lesbian and bisexual women who want to lead.

The need to legitimise a role switch also became clear in the interviews and discussions I had with salsa dancers. I asked several instructors about their experiences in class.

JOANNA: Did you ever have girls who wanted to learn how to lead?

MARCOS: Oh yes. Because you know sometimes you have on average much more girls than guys, and I had been experiencing many girls that are really really good leaders. And I think it's much more, they are much more sensitive, much more smoother as leader, because they know what is the feeling of [...] leading well or badly, you know. And I think, a guy who has experienced how to be led, they become really good leaders, because they have more consciousness you know. They feel, OK this is painful, this is not comfortable, you know. I personally have been dancing as a girl many times, just to check it out how it feels.

Marcos, who is a regular instructor at salsa events and gives classes where he lives, here uses several strategies to legitimise a role switch. Like several other instructors, he proposes that men learn the follower role in order to become better leaders. Likewise, his own dancing "as a girl" is framed as a necessity in order to become a better leader. In a similar way, Karl explained: "There was a time when I actually danced as a woman, for me it was just about improving my lead. So virtually a man led me and I could experience how is it as woman". Through the framing of the role switching as part of enhancing the leader's competence, it is, again, clearly marked as a context of learning and thus not as a "real" salsa dance situation. McClure (2015) had a similar experience during her research, stating: "This interpretation serves to legitimise switching roles in a way that avoids challenging the gendered and heteronormative structure of the dance" (161). By constantly marking women leaders and men followers as exceptions, the binary gender structure of salsa dance is actually validated; in other words, although dancers challenge the routinisation of gender, the heteronormative and gendered structure is upheld.

"A conversation instead of a lecture": undoing gender

The third perspective dancers take complicates the notion of the gendered role play, which was until now understood as a dance between an active leader and a passive follower. As the next quote demonstrates, some followers also try to open up agency for both partners, in their discourse about salsa but also in an embodied way on the dance floor. They thus attempt a blurring of the opposition between the gendered roles of leading and following. Thus, Laura, an experienced dancer and teacher, stated to my question about the gender roles in salsa dancing: "[In my classes] I always say: the man says what one dances and the woman says how. Of course the man is the leader, that's clear, the woman has to follow, but just the way she wants to [laughs]".

By attributing the woman/follower with agency to actually shape the dance, Laura here interprets the relationship between leader and follower in a slightly different way. Several followers described their dancing experiences as actively taking part in and influencing the dance. In this process, the skill level a dancer has acquired seems to be the decisive element, as McClure (2015) argues. Isabelle, an experienced follower and instructor in a local salsa school, explained:

> I mean, as a woman you are restricted. The man leads, decides which moves he wants to dance, if you want or not. So you are very limited. But nevertheless, as a woman it's your job to make the best of it. [...] You can just let yourself be led and that's it or you bring your style into it, so you can express yourself anyway. And that's what I love about it, once you've got this, it's a process and of course you need to have a certain level; before you are concentrating on being led, react etc. But then, when the man lets you go and then I am free. And actually I am a free spirit and that's my moment. And although you are free, the connection has to be there. Cause you have to be able to react when he comes and gets you again. It doesn't matter if you are led or free, it's always this interaction. [...] Yes, and it's my expression [...] what I bring into it and how I interpret the music. And that's me. Independently of whom I dance with.

Isabelle first uses terms like "restriction" and "limitation" but then extends the follower's repertoire, saying she can also bring her "style" into the dance and "express herself". She can especially do this during the moments of the dance where the leader releases her and she dances freely. In social salsa dancing, the moments of breaking up the partner hold are filled with small, quick steps and isolated movements of body parts such as legs, arms, the pelvis or the upper body – which are usually called shines, footwork and/or *ladies' styling*. Although Isabelle loves these moments in dancing, she nevertheless insists on the importance of a partner during them. She understands the male leader as facilitating her expressive performance and the interest of salsa dance lies precisely in the interaction with or "connection" to a partner. She describes herself as a "free spirit" but nevertheless prefers dancing with someone else.

Another important element allowing for the expression and interpretation of the follower is the way the leader conceives of leading. An often-stated argument during workshops concerning leaders is that they should always "adapt" to the follower and not just do whatever they wish to do. Leaders are thus urged to respond to followers. Regular festival-goer Candice talked about "new possibilities" when I asked her to elaborate on the type of dances she liked:

> You know, when you dance with someone, there's lead and follow, he leads you follow. When you get to the next level, then you dance with the music, you're not just doing steps anymore, you're playing with the breaks, you're responding to music. And then there's the whole thing playing with your partner. And for me the most responsive guys are the ones who play with the music, they listen to the music but they also listen to you as a follower. So they are saying OK, you heard something I didn't hear, I'm gonna adjust to that. I'm gonna give you space to do something here, I'm gonna let you influence the dance. And I'm gonna hold you in a way that you've got more freedom and you can do other things. And instead of leading as an order or an instruction, I'm gonna lead as a, I'm opening you up to new possibilities, so it's an attitude thing.

In Candice's account, it becomes clear that dancing with the music is an important part as well as what she calls "playing" with her partner. Like Isabelle before, she links these two processes to a certain level of competence. Candice likes to influence the dance herself, inspired by her own understanding of the music. In order to do this she needs a responsive partner who allows her the space to do it. By redefining the follower role as active and the leader role as responsive, she breaks with the common understanding of the leader/follower relationship. Building on West and Zimmerman's (2009) reformulation of their approach to doing gender, this challenging of the routinisation of the gendered arrangements can be analysed as redoing gender. The basis of salsa – leading and following – is still upheld, but the ways they are embodied differ from the above-mentioned situations. In this way, leaders and followers with a certain skill level are able to redefine their dance relationship as a partnership rather than a hierarchical relation between leader and follower. In her analysis of lindy hop, Wade (2011) argues that more advanced dancers use connection "to create a single dancer that cannot be fragmented into a leader and a follower at all" (237).

There are dancers who not only try to enlarge the follower role but clearly formulate a critique of salsa's leader/follower structure, such as the dancer who initiated the Facebook discussion cited above, asking for a less dominating leader. Negotiations about the leader/follower structure and related salsa masculinity and femininity are taking place between dancers with different experience levels. In this process, female dance professionals play an important role in criticising and sometimes potentially redefining the dance. This became clear in the interview with Lavinia, who was born in Mexico and later moved to Italy to start a transnational career. Asked for her motivations to travel in the salsa circuit, she told me that she wanted to challenge common representations of "Latin culture":

> I want to give a strong and a right way of sharing my culture, my Latin culture. You know, I'm saying: 'I'm Mexican, I'm Latin, I'm a woman' [...]. To be honest, because, I am Mexican right, so the Mexican, some, not everyone, but some of the Mexican people that had been here, had created a particular image of being Mexican. So for me I think not all Latin people are lazy or irresponsible or alcoholics, or these negative situations. And not all women are just sitting and not working by themselves and not strong enough to do their own thing, I think we can work, we can also be strong and say what we think, and feel, yes this is the way I'm feeling, I wanna do it this way. You know, these stereotypes. I want to show that there is no stereotype. That Mexicans and women, we can also be this way.

Lavinia here reclaims an identity as a Mexican woman that challenges discriminatory stereotypes of "Latin people". She also depicts the image of a passive Mexican woman, an image she wants to change through her dancing and choreography work. Lavinia was asked to choreograph a group consisting of only female dancers, and she told me that she wanted "to do something different, instead of a lady, booty, sexy style. You know, that's like a stereotype". Instead, she describes her choreography as a "powerful, energetic" dancing. Nevertheless, Lavinia also dances as a follower with her dance partner, something she describes as one of her "main difficulties". She wishes to have equal standing.

JOANNA: And is this possible in the dance?
LAVINIA: In the dance, physically, no. Because someone needs to follow, if not, it would be a fight. Of course if you have the capacity and the professionality to also learn the figures, it will create more connection, but as a role yes, physically, you have to receive the command.

We did not have time to discuss the question of why she had to be the one who follows in dance (and not her dance partner), but to me it seemed that Lavinia accepted her role in dancing as part of salsa under the condition that she had an equal share in other domains of the professional dance partnership, such as the choreography of the pieces she performed with her dance partner and their dance group.

Other female dancers do try to actively change the gendered structure (which is possible only once they have acquired a certain reputation in the salsa circuit). I will illustrate this with the case of Nara, a salsa instructor and performer. She is one of the few professional female dancers who pursues a solo career and is regularly invited to teach and perform at salsa events worldwide.

> So for the most part, salsa is, like everyone always thinks about the women, oh they are beautiful women and this and this and this. But if you think about the way most of it is structured, like if you think of partner names, most of the time it's the man's name that holds weight. And it's a leader, even though the follower embellishes and creates these beautiful things, it's still the lead determines what's gonna happen, right. So in that sense it's kind of male dominated, given, or leader dominated, let's say instead of male dominated. Because that's even when women are leading we still expect the leader to know what to do for everything.

In Nara's experience, although women are highly visible in salsa, they are not in charge when it comes to dance partners and dancing itself. Here, she links male "dominance" to the ways leader and follower roles are enacted in salsa dancing. In a second step, she revises her statement and explains that the domination is linked to the leader/follower structure of dancing, so that even when a woman takes the lead, the problem stays the same. Nara has thus developed her own discourse about the leader/follower structure; she actively tries to change the perceived male-dominance in the salsa business, on one hand through travelling as a (successful) solo instructor, on the other hand through the way she dances. She thus deliberately tries undoing gender (Hirschauer 2001) in an embodied way. We discussed her views on gender relations in salsa and she mentioned that they were quite controversial and that she needed to have a "thick skin". On my questioning about what was controversial and in what ways she wanted to change things, she explained:

> I mean one of the contested points in my dancing is the lead and follow relationship, which for the longest time, and still, predominantly is viewed as the leader dictates what's happening in the dance, so it's not so much of a conversation as much as it is a lecture. And I think I saw it that way too when I first started dancing, until I got bored with that relationship and was like OK, now that I know more, I have more things to say. I don't wanna just sit here and listen to you speak the whole time. Specially if you think of an entire night of dancing. Maybe one song is five minutes, but if you think of four hours of dancing and just four hours of sitting there and listening to someone speak and not getting a chance to say something, it's one no fun, and two, it's not my personality. Because I always have a thing to say, even if I don't know anything. But now as I got better, I started to learn more, then I had more

questions to ask, more things to suggest. And that view of the relationship between the leader and follower as a conversation instead of
a lecture is still kind of controversial. Because there are a lot of leaders,
especially people that have been around for a long time, that view that:
no, you're breaking it, that's not what you're supposed to do. You
know, you're supposed to embellish what the lead, the spaces that the
lead provides you, not actually take those moments yourself. And in that
way I would say, there are no other females in salsa that do that [...] So
in that way I feel like I've changed that and I know there are other
women dancing now that kind of use what they've seen with my dancing and my approach to it as a doorway, or a gateway for them to
express themselves as well.

Nara uses the metaphor of dancing as a dialogue, proposing that the
relationship between a leader and a follower in salsa dancing should be
reinterpreted as a conversation in which both partners take part.

She is criticised by more established dancers in the salsa circuit, who accuse
her of "breaking it", meaning breaking the connection that the follower is
supposed to maintain. Followers are taught to react to the leaders' signals in
order to establish a "connection" and keep it up for the rest of the dance.
The imperative for a connection in order to enjoy the dance results in an
interpretation of followers' active participation as "bad" dancing.[5] At the
same time, Nara is a successful solo artist and has a large fan base of dancers
who wish to learn from her. Talking to Nara's students after one of her
workshops at a festival, I realised how much they liked her for demonstrating
such "new ways" of dancing to salsa music. She perceives herself as
pioneering a new way of dancing salsa.

Through her critique and changing of the structure of the dancing itself,
Nara is not only undoing gender but also redoing the ways salsa works.[6] This
becomes clear through the negative reactions she gets from established dancers,
whom she overheard talking about her, calling her dancing "no salsa"
anymore. The established dancers try to delegitimise Nara's dancing, engaging
in struggles over the power to define what salsa is and what it is not. (Un)
doing gender and what could be termed "doing salsa" are related processes, as
individuals try out new ways, challenging current salsa conventions. In such
struggles, individuals with higher salsa capital (see Chapter 7) may take the risk
to challenge the organisation of the salsa world.

"I don't shake my hips all the time": from gendered *styling* to body movement

This section addresses a second gender convention of the salsa circuit:
gendered dance movements. In salsa dancing, not only leader and follower
roles are gendered, but also specific movements of certain body parts. Explicit
addressing of the ways men and women are supposed to move in salsa are

frequent. The verbal reminder "ladies: sexy, men: macho!" was expressed during workshops at festivals, and teaching practices involve body movements clearly designated as either female or male.

Ladies' styling and, to a lesser degree, *men's styling* classes form an integral part of salsa festivals' workshop offering. The focus of these classes lies on learning a sequence of steps and movements, including big moves with the hips, isolated movements of the upper torso, caressing of the hair and upper body as well as the all-present arm movements with wrists bent and fingers spread (see Figure 4.2).[7]

Female dancers were often told to practise these movement patterns in order to make their dance look "sexy", highlighting parts of the female body such as hips, buttocks, breasts and arms. In her study on salsa in New Jersey, Borland (2009) analyses the "sexy woman" stereotype as related to the representation of the "hot Latina", circulating in media and popular culture, and which is (re)produced through salsa's *ladies' styling*. There exists a vast literature on the (historical) "fetishization" (Piedra 1997), "exoticization" and "sexualisation" of the Latina body (García 2013: 102), whereby particularly the hips and buttocks are theorised.[8]

On the contrary, looking at salsa solely from a gender perspective, McClure (2015: 129) analyses *ladies' styling* in salsa as part of wider cultural representations of femininity and does not refer to it as related to exoticising processes. My

Figure 4.2 Showing the arm moves in a *ladies' styling* workshop.
Source: © Valentin Behringer.

observations of *ladies' styling* classes and interviews with salsa dancers indicate the importance instructors place on the expression of a specific type of femininity, which in some cases draws on exoticising representations of the "hot Latina" but most often revolves around the importance of the apprenticeship of mastering one's body. While some dancers clearly ethnicise the practice of salsa dancing, for many others salsa's *ladies' styling* is related to something they "naturally" possess as women.

Paradoxically, the *ladies' styling* classes in salsa underline that femininity has to be learned, as the mastering of *ladies' styling* is not regarded as "natural" and instructors rather insist on the technical aspects of the gendered moves. One instructor reminded her students: "You can't let yourself go. All the magic happens when you can control your body!" The mastery of performances of salsa femininity requires hours of training and bodily control. In this way, female dancers learn to internalise body moves they can later include in their dancing and insert in the moments of the dance when the leader releases the partner hold – those instances Isabelle (quoted above) called her moments of free expression. For some dancers, the performance of a specific type of femininity is related to a space of expressive freedom and self-esteem, which for them comes with the cultivation of their body. This dovetails with Borland's (2009) analysis of salsa dancers in New Jersey and her argument:

> The structured and differential nature of the gendered exchange, which positions men as leaders and women as followers, paradoxically also offers a space of expressive freedom for women, since the recovery of partner dancing in this milieu allows women to engage in an admittedly exoticised but powerful expression of sexuality.
>
> (Borland 2009: 488)

This paradox of salsa *ladies' styling* has been analysed from a feminist perspective with reference to the imperative of self-cultivation in neoliberalism. Drawing on theories of post-feminism, McClure (2015) argues that *ladies' styling* serves as a mechanism to produce a specific "sexy" brand of femininity. In an understanding of individuals as responsible for their own self-cultivation, "ladies' styling can be read as a response to the neoliberal imperative for women in particular to work on and transform themselves according to ideals of femininity" (McClure 2015: 129). This process can be understood as a shift towards a post-feminist "resexualisation of women's bodies" (Gill 2003). Accordingly, as McClure (2015) concludes: "feelings of pleasure and empowerment associated with being sexually desirable are recruited to re-configure sexual objectification in terms of a freely choosing neoliberal feminine subject" (129). This analysis is helpful in understanding the paradox of female dancers experiencing the performances of a specific salsa femininity as empowering. At the same time, it leaves little room for an analysis of those voices that attempt to redo or undo gender in embodied ways, which is the main goal of this chapter.

In contrast to the numerous *ladies' styling* workshops offered during my research, *men's styling* workshops were rare. In those workshops, similar to the *ladies' styling* workshops, participants were taught dance technique (turning), and the highlighting of specific body parts, particularly the shoulders.[9] While *ladies' styling* classes and *men's styling* classes (re)produce a specific understanding of salsa femininity and salsa masculinity, other workshops were designed to improve the isolation of body parts, usually called body movement, and they addressed female and male dancers alike.

Some dancers are critical of the above definitions of salsa femininity and masculinity, especially some dancers of the younger generation of professionals. I already cited the case of Lavinia, who built up a considerable reputation with her powerful and unconventional salsa performances. Nara's case again illustrates well how gendered dance moves are currently negotiated in the salsa circuit:

> So that for example, for the longest time in salsa, anytime I would see women dancing, it's always like really delicate, always using their hands in this fashion [showing her two hands, fingers stretched out], or always moving with the hips and things like this that are feminine by this very narrow definition of femininity. Same thing goes for the men, their narrowly defined masculinity of being strong and brute almost. Whereas for me, my opinion of self-expression for the man and for the woman is going through a range of emotions, and we are not defined, like me being a strong person and me being angry or me being funny and joking around doesn't make me any less of a woman. For a man to be sensitive on the dance floor and to be delicate and elegant doesn't make him less of a man. And to define ourselves by oh, "men is macho, woman is like delicate", it is not contributing to the growth of an art form. Which should be about self-expression, it should not be about defining limitations to it, you know. So in that sense I'm also kind of going against the norm. Because I dance, I goof around, I do a lot of like, silly moves, people are like: oh, that's not very feminine. I don't shake my hips all the time, why, because I have no reason to do it, there's nothing in the music that makes me wanna go wam wam wam with my hips. So I'm not gonna create that movement. If the music is very strong then I'm equally strong in my movements and for most men [...] what I'm doing is so taboo, you know, it's just like [...] this is blasphemy, this is not what salsa is about.

In her account (as well as her dancing), Nara dissociates gender from salsa moves. She challenges "the essentialism of binary distinctions between people based on sex category" (Risman 2009: 83) and could be understood as undoing gender in Risman's terms. However, Nara's non-essentialist position in terms of gender has led to her being accused of lacking femininity by other (male) professionals. As she told me, she is sometimes asked: "Why don't you just move like a woman?" Nara is thus held accountable for not dancing in a way that is usually constructed as female.

If we do gender appropriately, we simultaneously sustain, reproduce, and render legitimate the institutional arrangements that are based on sex category. If we fail to do gender appropriately, we as individuals – not the institutional arrangements – may be called to account (for our character, motives, and predispositions).

(West and Zimmerman 1987: 146)

Following West and Zimmerman (2009), I therefore argue that in the above example Nara is redoing gender, as she is still held accountable for gender.

In a similar vein, the winner of an international salsa competition, a male dancer who performed a solo dance, prompted an online controversy: two of the established male dance professionals based in Europe quickly posted a video on YouTube and their Facebook account and explained how male dancers in salsa are supposed to move. Indirectly, the winner of the competition was thus accused of doing it wrong, because he did not hold his arms in a clear 90-degree angle but rather moved the arms while dancing, reminiscent of *ladies' styling*.

As these incidents demonstrate, dancers (of both sex categories) who challenge the gendered conventions of dance moves are held accountable for their doings. At the same time, dancers like Nara cater to the growing number of salsa practitioners interested in the communication between dance partners and musical understanding (rather than the performances of masculinity and femininity). Over the period of my research I observed an increase of festival workshops in "body movement", "spin technique" or "musicality", where aspects of body control and dance moves were learned without gendering them. In the situation of the workshops, in which they are accepted, these may be interpreted as gender-neglecting (Hirschauer 2001) dancing and thus a way of undoing gender in salsa.

Conclusion

This chapter has examined the gendered interactions of salsa dancers on the dance floor. Drawing on theoretical approaches of doing, redoing and undoing gender it has analysed the ongoing negotiations of gender conventions in the salsa circuit. Based on observations at workshops and interviews with salsa dancers and dance professionals, I have argued that salsa dancers constantly do gender when engaging in the salsa partnership.

Literature on partner dance has often analysed the gendered leader and follower structure as "reinforcing restrictive gender roles" (cf Borland 2009). While adding an important feminist critique, these analyses usually stay silent about the reasons for engaging in such activities. Furthermore, they do not necessarily discuss how the gender conventions are upheld. This chapter therefore offered an in-depth description and analysis of the ways in which salsa dancers are doing, redoing and undoing gender, thus adding to the extant literature on gender and social dance as well as the vast scholarship on doing and redoing gender (West and Zimmerman 1987, 2009) as well as undoing gender (Deutsch 2007; Hirschauer 1994, 2001; Risman 2009). The focus on gender conventions in salsa dancing here allowed for a particular attention to the ways in which (un/re)doing gender works "with and through" bodies (Messerschmidt 2009: 86), thus responding to calls to include the body more in analyses with the theoretical framework of doing gender.

As I have shown, dancers engage with the gender conventions and in particular the leader/follower structure in different ways. Those who perceive of it as a "nice role play" discursively embed it in other times (the past) and sometimes project it on "Latin culture", while constructing clear boundaries between the salsa space and other social situations of their lives, especially the workplace. Distancing themselves from their everyday practices, salsa dancers mark the gendered role play as a "game" (Villa 2003).

However, many dancers challenge the gender conventions in salsa, either through role switching or a redefinition of the partner structure of the dance. As shown in detail, role switching always needs some kind of legitimation or justification (see also McClure 2015; Schneider 2013). The potential of challenging the heteronormative structure of salsa is thus disrupted. Salsa dancers engage in a redoing and even undoing of gender in embodied ways when redefining the partner dance as "a conversation instead of a lecture". In some situations, dancers are able to create a connection between two dance partners, in which the connection with the music and the dance partner are the focus and gender is neglected (Hirschauer 2001).

At the same time, dancers who challenge the gendered dance moves are sometimes accused of lacking femininity or lacking masculinity. In this way, they are held accountable for gender. Furthermore, dancers who redefine the gendered leader/follower structure are also accused of not dancing salsa anymore. Not gender accountability but "salsa accountability" is here negotiated. A possible reason for the resistance to such redefinitions may be the following argument: as Becker (1982) observes, to challenge conventions is an attack not only on these conventions but also on the organisation or social structure of the world in question.

As Nara's case illustrates, salsa dance professionals (when endowed with a high amount of salsa capital) are able to initiate structural change: precisely through her insistence on redoing and undoing gender, Nara was able to build her career in the salsa circuit so that today she is one of the few female salsa dancers who has managed to build up a long-lasting successful transnational career as a solo artist. Hirschauer (2001: 228) argues that social change in the private relations between couples may bring a change in the organisation of the public labour market. In a similar vein, Nara's story may be interpreted as an example of how (re/un)doing gender on the dance floor actually changes not only the structure of salsa dance but also the gendered hierarchies at play in the construction of a transnational career in the salsa circuit, as further discussed in Chapter 7.

Notes

1 Here it is important to keep in mind that my research field did not include explicit same-sex or LGBT salsa spaces, due to my focus on the transnational salsa congresses. Same-sex or LGBT salsa spaces do exist in several cities worldwide (see Boulila 2015); at salsa competitions the category "same-gender" was introduced in 2010 (McMains 2015: 138).

2 McClure (2015) also problematises "the assumption that dancing salsa is about performing 'traditional' (Latino) gender roles" (8). While this chapter examines similar ethnographic situations at salsa events as McClure's study, I analyse them using different theoretical and methodological approaches.

3 Drawing on Butler (1990), the concept of heteronormativity (Warner 1991) points to the belief of two oppositional genders related by heterosexual desire, taken for granted as the norm. For a further discussion of heteronormativity in salsa spaces, see Boulila 2015; McClure 2015; McMains 2015.

4 I never observed a woman leading a man at a party, which might be due to the practical difficulties of identifying who leads whom in a dance couple, from the position of the observer.

5 See also McClure (2015: 103) for an elaborate discussion of these processes in terms of power relations between dance partners in social dancing.

6 In her article on tango dancers, Villa (2003) presents the practices of switching roles and of changing the partner structure of dance, arguing that the latter can be seen as a "subversive strategy" in Butler's sense, a strategy she as feminist sociologist wishes to implement. However, similar to the negative comments Nara is confronted with, Villa argues that the blurring of the leader/follower structure leads to other tango dancers not recognising the dance as tango anymore (Villa 2003: 153).

7 For a demonstration of ladies' styling after a festival workshop, see the following video: rebrand.ly/salsa-13.

8 See, for example Blanco Borelli (2016). In her book *She is Cuba: A genealogy of the Mulata Body*, the critical dance scholar builds a theoretical framework based on the hips, which she calls hip(g)nosis, "a feminist response to the mere objectification of the dancing *mulata*" (Blanco Borelli 2016: 13).

9 For a demonstration of men's styling after a festival workshop, see the following video: rebrand.ly/salsa-14.

Part III

Transnational careers

Introduction – conceptual notes on transnational careers

Part III of this book offers an analysis of the careers of salsa dance professionals of different nationalities from a transnational perspective. As the extant literature on salsa suggests, salsa dance professionals often develop local careers, characterised by their specifically local outreach in terms of students, reputation-building processes and the dance professionals' teaching activities concentrated in one place, usually a dance studio in a city.[1] However, due to salsa's successful development in many cities of Europe, North America and Asia, a new type of salsa dance professional has come into being: so-called *travelling artists*. To shed light on this understudied type of professional career, which often involves a large amount of cross-border mobility and reputation-building processes in different places, this book addresses the transnational careers of salsa dance professionals. Salsa dance professionals include the self-identified *travelling artists* who perform and teach salsa on a weekly basis at different festivals as well as dance studio owners who travel to salsa festivals to teach, both of whom make a living from salsa dance, mainly through teaching salsa in different places. I opted for the term "salsa dance professional" instead of "professional dancer" to underline the importance of other salsa-related activities and income-earning strategies in salsa dance professionals' careers, mainly teaching. Through this approach, I also revise prevalent framings of salsa dance instructors as *stars*, to allow for a sociological look at the work necessary to achieve fame.

My theoretical framework builds on the classical sociological concept of careers (Becker 1963; Hughes 1958) as well as more recent adaptations in studies of the sociology of art (Menger 1999; Wagner 2016) and migration (Martiniello and Rea 2014). Chicago sociologists such as Hughes (1958) developed a broad and flexible concept of career, used in the analysis of social organisation in general. In this line, Becker (1963) analyses the careers of dance musicians as a series of statuses and positions, while analysing individuals' adjustments in terms of self-conception. A career is thus not understood as a movement from one hierarchical level to the next; instead, the concept entails an objective and a subjective dimension. A career can be understood as a sequence of status passages, including the objective change in position and the subjective dimension of actors' own interpretation of it.

Drawing on this conceptualisation of careers, I will discuss the dilemmas salsa dance professionals face and the ways they adjust in order to pursue a transnational career in the salsa circuit. In this study, I identify three status passages: becoming a salsa dance professional, accessing the (European) salsa circuit and building up reputation (discussed in Chapters 5, 6 and 7 respectively). These passages are not always as clearly separable as presented and may sometimes overlap temporarily, but for analytical purposes they are here distinguished. It is important to keep in mind that the careers of salsa dance professionals happen outside enclosed organisations (see also Kirschbaum 2007) and therefore differ from the careers analysed in recent sociological and anthropological literature on professional dancers such as Laillier (2011) on ballet dancers at the Opéra de Paris, Marion (2012) on ballroom dancers in the "worldwide competition circuit" and Wulff (1998) on ballet dancers at ballet companies in London, New York, Stockholm and Frankfurt. Nevertheless, the cited literature is taken into account to discuss similarities and differences in the careers of salsa dance professionals as compared to other professional careers in dance.

To analyse salsa dancing and teaching in the salsa circuit in terms of a profession, I reconceptualise careers as transnational. "Transnational careers" are characterised by the transnational networks salsa dance professionals build up, the importance of geographical mobility and the importance of non-local forms of reputation building.[2] Through their mobile practices, salsa dance professionals link different hubs and actors of the salsa circuit to each other. Including a transnational perspective in the analysis of careers makes it possible to combine a focus on individual action with a focus on social structural dynamics (see also Martiniello and Rea 2014).

Becker (1963) analysed the careers of dance musicians as a deviant occupational group, "a group of 'outsiders' that considers itself and is considered by others as 'different'" (101). By using the concept of career to analyse transnationally active salsa dance professionals, I do not intend to categorise their activities as deviant. Instead, the analysis of (transnational salsa) careers, in Becker's sense, may be useful to better understand how particular forms of bodily practices are considered as belonging to a certain national territory as well as to specific (gendered) bodies. As a result, dancers often struggle with the non-recognition of salsa in European public spaces and cultural funding policies, as discussed in Chapter 5. In the discussion of the first status passage, I will look closely at how actors become salsa dancers and adjust to such perspectives.

Visible cross-border mobility is central in salsa dance professionals' transnational careers. Nevertheless, not everyone has the ability to actually be mobile and travel across national borders. I therefore deploy the already introduced "regimes-of-mobility framework" (Glick Schiller and Salazar 2013), which addresses the relationships between mobility and immobility, affirming the importance of social fields of differential power. This perspective makes it possible to take into account different forms of salsa dancers' mobility in one theoretical framework while addressing multiple forms of power such as legal status, which enable or hinder an individual's travels (Glick Schiller and Salazar 2013). In Chapter 6, I demonstrate how salsa dancers navigate the different possibilities of becoming mobile and the strategies they deploy in order to access the (European) salsa circuit; these are closely linked to an individual's mobility capital (in terms of networks, financial means and the legal right to travel).

Although the salsa circuit is not regarded as "different" in the ways Becker (1963: 101) describes the dance musicians' circuit, salsa dance professionals perceive the salsa circuit as "a small world" separate from other domains of society. In terms of economic capital and reputation, it can best be grasped as a form of alternative economy, what I term the "affective economy" of the salsa circuit, similar to that of the jazz musicians Becker studied in the 1950s. In Chapter 7, I discuss the ways dance professionals build up and maintain "salsa capital" inside the salsa circuit, including networking strategies and mobilising other forms of symbolic capital.

Before analysing the three status passages identified as crucial for the construction of transnational careers, I present portraits of three salsa dance professionals and their transnational careers diachronically. These career descriptions highlight the three main status passages – becoming a salsa dance professional, accessing the salsa circuit and building up reputation – and strategies used to construct a transnational career, all of which will be discussed in detail in the following chapters. The diachronic presentation here allows the construction of a clearer image of transnational careers, before they are disentangled and transversally discussed in the following chapters.

Marcos: "Salsa is making me travel all over the world"

Becoming a dancer

Marcos, 31 years old at the time of the interview, is a *travelling artist*, dancing at salsa events every weekend during the spring and twice a month during the rest of the year. He enthusiastically told me about his motivation to travel to salsa events:

> When I teach, I like to teach things that are functional for social dancing. That's what it is, I don't speak so many languages but because I know how to dance, I can connect with everybody, it's a huge tool of communication. Regardless of who you are, or where you're from. This connects people, and yeah it's a great tool, it's making me travel all over the world somehow, and I enjoy it a lot.

Like all the other interviewed dancers, Marcos uses the metaphor of language to describe what salsa means for him. Being a salsa dance professional not only allows him to meet and connect to other people. It also made it possible for him to become mobile, something that was not taken for granted when he was a child. Marcos grew up in Nicaragua and for a long time travelling was only a dream; as he stated: "It's not so common for a Nicaraguan guy to be out traveling. We are not so many out there".

Marcos started dancing salsa at the age of 12, helping his mother who ran dance classes for tourists. In the mid-1990s, a wave of couple dances like merengue spread throughout the Americas and formed part of Western tourists' expectations of their travel experience. Although Nicaragua is seldomly placed on the imaginary salsa map, his mother's dance studio catering for tourists was successful. Marcos thus went to school during the day and worked as a dance teacher in the evenings.

Through his teaching activities, Marcos had privileged access to foreigners who wanted to learn Latin dances. At the age of 17, he befriended a Japanese traveller who took lessons with him. When this friend had to go back to work in his job in a cultural centre in Japan, he asked Marcos for help in becoming a salsa teacher in Japan. Judging his friend's knowledge as insufficient, Marcos told him that he needed more time to teach him. His friend proposed that Marcos go to Japan and stay there for three months. He invited Marcos to live in his apartment and asked him to help him build up salsa classes.

> I was like, "why not?" After high school I didn't have any plan, I was fed up of studying and working at the same time, so I said, "OK, I'll do it". And I went, without knowing that I would really like it. [...] After two months, I said to him: "listen man, I don't want to go back. There are so many opportunities here that I don't have in my country, I want to stay. So what can I do?" He said, "Well, you have two options: either you get married here, or you have to fix your papers with a contract". And marriage was not an option, and I was not interested, I was 17 years old, so I said, "I want to try applications".

Once Marcos was in Japan, he realised that there was a market for salsa teachers like him and so he decided to try to stay. But in order to settle there, he needed to get a residence permit, which was impossible without a certification of his status as a professional dancer. He went back to Nicaragua, where he was able to obtain a diploma certifying his musical and dancing skills, through the help of his mother and his aunt (a music teacher) and finally obtained a working visa in Japan for one year. He worked for a company; after four years, he received a permanent visa. He then changed cities, formed a band and opened his own salsa school. Through his dancing at various salsa events in Japan, he started to build up his reputation.

Accessing the salsa circuit

In Japan, salsa dance events and academies had existed for several years, but as Iwanaga (2014: 214) states, in 1999, just one year before Marco's arrival, "salsa's popularity intensified". Around this time, information on salsa events in Japan became widely available, and salsa festivals were organised for the first time featuring New York-based salsa dancers in their workshops. As Iwanaga writes, "the Japanese Salsa Congress has played a significant role in uniting Japanese salsa lovers with the global salsa industry" (214). This congress was an important event for Marcos personally, as it led to another meeting that changed his career. Marcos was asked to translate Japanese to Spanish for an influential American salsa event organiser. On this occasion, the organiser saw him dancing what was – at that time – an unusual salsa performance: instead of dancing with a woman, he danced with another man, and they included samurai swords in the performance. Marcos was convinced that this innovative performance led to his being invited to perform at events in the US.

In the US, Marcos met up with his brother seven years after he had left Nicaragua for Japan. In the meantime, his brother had followed their father to Sweden, where he had studied dance and opened a salsa studio as well. After their reunion, his brother asked him to come to Sweden and teach in his studio. Marcos remembers:

> But I was feeling lonely in Japan, after 8 years already, I was tired. And I had never been in Europe, so [...] I said: "I close the school, and I will move to [city in Sweden] with you". So he opened a contract and I, no I didn't close the school, I just gave it to my students, who were good, and I moved my stuff and I just moved to Sweden. I started to work with him in the same company.

For the second time in his life, Marcos moved to a new country, this time through the help of his brother who was already established in Sweden and was able to help him with an initial working contract in his dance school. Marcos later worked in several other dance schools; at the time of the interview he had regularised his status and obtained a Swedish residence permit.

Building up reputation

Once in Europe, Marcos started to build up a reputation as a dance professional in the European salsa circuit. He used a strategy he had already applied in Japan: networking. In his own words:

> After a while, if you finally manage to establish a kind of reputation let's say, you actually have the possibility to choose where you wanna go. And that's a good thing because everything is based on networking. [...] You need a network. So networking, many times you can actually invest. You pay for your own ticket, you go and you present yourself. That's how everybody does it at the very beginning. If you wanna sell yourself, you have to start somewhere. And the best way to do it is just dance with people and, you know, try to start promoting yourself that way. But that's the thing. Sometimes I know organisers but I have probably not been there yet but I know them. So sometimes I say, "listen, I haven't been there yet, let's make

something together. I bring you this, this is what I offer, what do you offer?" You make a deal.

For Marcos, the importance of networks is obvious and he strategically uses his dancing and communication skills to promote himself. In this way, he was able to create a network of salsa contacts and people who booked him for other events. This was only possible once he had danced at salsa events in Europe: his physical presence in the European salsa circuit was thus a condition for starting his transnational career in Europe.

Yaimara: "Everybody here has got this energy"

Becoming a dancer

Yaimara, who at the time of the first interview was 26 years old, was born in an outer neighbourhood of Havana. She grew up in a family of musicians and dancers, seeing people dance and listening to music from a young age. In the first interview, Yaimara told me about her grandfather, a dancer and musician who is still today often cited as an important figure in the institutionalisation and implementation of the rumba as a national Cuban dance form by the revolutionary government. After the Cuban revolution in 1959, the government was keen to establish a National University of Dance, including so-called folkloric dances. They chose dancers mainly living in underprivileged and black neighbourhoods to help establish the school's programme, which was supposed to represent the Cuban people, including dance and rhythm traditions recognised as *Afro-Cuban*. Yaimara's grandfather was one of these dancers, and she still capitalises on his name. Her grandfather had many Cuban students, young dancers who wanted to learn from him. He was also asked to teach foreign students on salsa holidays organised by Cubans living in Italy in the 2000s. Yaimara helped her grandfather teach the classes, thus realising what she wanted to do later.

> You know, when I was a child, there were always many schools coming to take lessons with my grandfather. And they always told me about it, I was so interested and asked many questions: what is it like there? Can you go somewhere to dance? And they told me, "there and there", and where you can go dancing and that there are festivals. And I was like, "hey, I absolutely want to go to a festival" [laughs].

She decided to become a musician and dancer and joined a performance group of folkloric dancers. With this group, Yaimara performed in Havana and other places in Cuba. At the age of 21, she had the opportunity to go to Singapore with a group of musicians and work there for a year. During this time, she learned English, a skill she later used once travelling and teaching in the salsa circuit. She didn't like living in Singapore, so she returned to Cuba and continued with the first group until she met her future husband Felix, a man from Germany. After their marriage, she moved to Germany where she soon started teaching in an established salsa school.

Accessing the salsa circuit

As Yaimara started teaching locally, she also started to travel to festivals.[3] A friend of her family, who had already taught at European salsa events for many years, helped her. He partnered with her and asked a festival organiser to invite Yaimara to his event.

> And this person [event organiser] had invited him [her friend] and he told them they absolutely had to invite me as well. I had been in Germany only for a few months and he told them to invite me, so this was my first festival in Europe.

In this way, Yaimara was introduced to the organiser of a festival in Finland. She performed with her long-time friend and thus gained visibility and new contacts in the salsa circuit.

Building up reputation

Once she had performed at a salsa event with international outreach, Yaimara started to build up her reputation in the salsa circuit.

> People started watching the video on the internet, and I also wrote to some organisers that I had come from Cuba, that I am a dancer and that I'm interested in festivals, having heard good feedback about their festival, and that I'd like to work with them. So some of them said they already have the artists for this year, but next year they wish to work with me, others said, "yes, we would like to book you", etc.

Yaimara was thus able to perform at several events in different European countries and build up her name as a specialist in Cuban dances in the salsa circuit. She drew on a specific version of "Cubanness", constructing her dancing as a particularly "authentic" form of salsa. Furthermore, once in Europe, Yaimara quickly realised that there was a growing interest in the *Afro-Cuban* and folkloric dances she knew from her childhood. Parallel to her teaching and performance activities in Europe, she started to organise teaching opportunities at European festivals for her family members and friends still living in Cuba.

The process proved difficult and too expensive, as Yaimara told me in the interview I conducted with her in Havana:

> I had organised a tour in Europe with my family and of course everything cost us a lot. So I said, now we're gonna make an exchange, now

we're gonna bring European people to Cuba. Because we can't bring all the artists to Germany, it's too expensive, we don't have sponsors. So I'm gonna bring the people to Cuba!

Practically, Yaimara includes many family members and friends in the organisation of her dance holidays: her cousin organises the Cuban side while she is in Europe, her mother and her aunt cook, her sister leads the warm-ups before the classes and her father and grandfather teach lessons. Befriended dancers also teach the lessons, and a large number of "Cuban partners" are hired for every group to accompany the foreign dance students during the lessons.

> German people like learning, they can get to know my city: I as a Cuban can show them my home country, and that is important to me. Especially the people I teach, for example at [name of dance school in Germany], so they can understand where I've got all this energy I have while teaching. That's not only me, everybody here has got this energy! You just don't see it because you're in Germany. So I wanted you to understand why, where it comes from, this having fun while we dance, it's joy, you don't always have to concentrate so much, and uh, no laughing, no fun, no relaxing. It's different for us!

Yaimara's mobility allows her to stay connected to what she views as the roots of her art (the older generation of teachers in Cuba), which she then uses in her teaching in the European context. The "energy" and "fun" Cuban dancers are said to express form part of Yaimara's self-presentation as being well placed to guide foreign salsa students.

Maria: "I caught the salsa virus"

Becoming a dancer

Maria, a 33-year-old salsa dancer, has her own company as a "freelancer", working in different dance schools and at festivals as a teacher and performer, often with her dance partner. Born in Poland, Maria had musical and dance training during her childhood in different dance forms and sports. Besides regular school, she did a few years of ballet classes, then took piano lessons and later tried acrobatics. At the age of 19, she moved to a Polish city to study and discovered disco dancing, which she describes as "something closer to a video clip dance or something like that. So it was fun". She joined a group and started competing on a national level with the dance company, while doing a Master's degree in marketing and management. When she was 25, a friend invited Maria to a salsa party and she got into salsa dancing. Drawing on her skills in dancing, she learned quickly; she was soon asked to dance with a salsa company, as well as to perform and teach in a salsa studio in the evenings.

I was so hooked up to the salsa and so, you know, I caught the virus, so I wanted to learn as much as possible. And after experiencing my first festival in Warsaw [...] I liked it so much! And I was working, so I had my finances [sorted], so I could spend money on travelling on the weekends, so I started to travel pretty much.

In 2005, when Maria first experienced salsa, it was not very common in Eastern European countries; the first big salsa event took place in 2004. After realising that salsa events took place in other European cities, Maria started participating at salsa festivals all over Europe. She was "hooked" and realised how much she liked dancing and teaching salsa, a motivation that is still important to her, as she mentioned during the interview.

My motivation, the part of this whole job that feels most comfortable for me, is teaching. Definitely. Sharing the knowledge and teaching is the best part for me. I like it very much. And also sharing this culture, since I was caught up by salsa as a social experience, I liked this part very much as well, that you can just go out and dance, simply.

Maria thus started performing and teaching salsa at various events in Europe and slowly building a professional identification with her work as a salsa dance professional, which includes a large amount of teaching.

Accessing the salsa circuit

Unlike Marcos and Yaimara, to access the salsa circuit, Maria relied on her economic and legal capital, which allowed her to travel to an event as a participant. In terms of access to the European salsa circuit, geographical distance and restricted mobility are the main differences between Latin American and European salsa dance professionals. As Poland became a member state of the European Union in 2004, the subsequent free movement of EU nationals to and working in other EU member states became an option for European dancers like Maria. In the first years, she just travelled on the weekends to participate at salsa events in other European countries:

It was pretty a lot, like once a month. [...] So I was taking classes as much as I could and I was dancing, dancing, dancing. And meeting people. So during these three years because of my travelling and also because of working with the group [name of dance company], I met a lot of people. Many of my friends from now, I just know them from that time. [...] a lot of these artists, I met them at that time.

For Maria, the contacts she made during the years of travelling to events by herself were an investment not only in her dancing skills but also in the network, and thus important for her work as a freelance dancer later on.

Novice dancers need to invest in their careers and build up relationships with other actors in the salsa circuit. These ties often prove fruitful for collaborations and the exchange of information.

Building up reputation

At one salsa event, Maria met her future dance partner. As part of a dance company, Maria had performance and teaching experience, skills that were in demand. Her new dance partner was based in Norway and offered her a job in the dance studio as well as a partnership to travel to events. She accepted the offer and moved to Norway, which raised no difficulties in residency or working rights, thanks to Norway's association to the EU. After teaching for a while in Norway, Maria was able to build up a small network of local students, with the help of established salsa studios. She did not learn the local language, and she teaches in English. At the same time, she travels to salsa events in Europe and elsewhere several times a month.

When we discussed the different skills she needed, Maria told me that office work forms an important part of her daily schedule:

> This is the time I'm spending usually in the daytime, before the classes or before rehearsal, or in the evening sometimes, but mostly in the daytime. Answering emails, contacting people if something's needed. I also on top of … I also do some graphic design, I also do my own flyers, the website I did by myself and all that stuff. But I'm doing it because I like it, not everybody is doing it but I like it so I spend time on that as well. That's how it goes, on top of dancing, sometimes you also have to do other things [laughs].

To build up reputation and construct a transnational career, dance professionals need to do many more "other things", as Chapters 5, 6 and 7 will discuss.

The focus on these three careers has opened up the main themes of the next chapters, each of which deals with one aspect of the transnational careers of salsa dance professionals.

Notes

1 Though this ideal-typical definition of a local career focuses on the local outreach of salsa dance professionals' activities, their practices often also include participation in online networks as well as the construction and maintenance of transnational networks in the salsa circuit.
2 Such a clear-cut separation of career types is only helpful on a conceptual level, and what I refer to as local and transnational careers may overlap.
3 In the next chapter, the strategies and networks Yaimara mobilised to gain access to the salsa circuit will be discussed in detail. To avoid repetition, I keep this part short.

5   Becoming a salsa dance professional

In this chapter, I discuss some elements involved in the process of becoming a salsa dance professional. Other studies of artists' careers largely focus on the apprenticeship of a particular music or dance technique (e.g. Wagner 2015 on violinists) in enclosed organisations. To account for the variety of salsa dance professionals' backgrounds, their non-linear career paths as well and the specificities of the salsa circuit, this chapter concentrates on the process of professional identification, the "affective labour" (Ditmore 2007) it necessitates and negotiations involved in embarking on a professional career. Furthermore, it discusses the income-generating activities that salsa dance professionals build up. Drawing on literature in the sociology of art, namely work focusing on artists' careers, this chapter looks at the beginnings of salsa dance professionals' careers in terms of entering a profession. I discuss economic aspects of dancers' career paths, including the effects of salsa's low status in European countries' hierarchy of performance arts.

Professional identifications

In contrast to other artistic and professional careers, a career as a salsa dance professional is not regulated through one professional educational institution. While there exist several qualifying studies in related dance forms, there is no formal diploma in salsa dancing. The entry into and development of a career in the salsa circuit is a non-linear process, during which individuals develop an understanding of themselves as salsa artists. As this chapter argues, aspiring salsa dance professionals develop professional identifications based on a specific idea of "vocation" and construct a commodified persona (Bunten 2008) while adjusting to the affective economy of the salsa circuit.

"Then it truly became my life": salsa dancing as vocation

For Becker (1963), careers consist of a simultaneous learning process of the practice (as an individual moves from one step of the career to the next) and of a change in social identification. Status passages include a "fundamental change in an individual's identity, an alteration in the person's conception of self" (Barley 1989: 50). The interviewed salsa dance professionals often recalled their first encounters with salsa dancing as a life-changing event, a phenomenon Quayson (2014) found in his study of Accra's salsa scene. He uses the term "conversion narrative" in order to characterise salsa dancers' stories about their first encounters with salsa, due to the "sharp before-and-after quality of the stories" (Quayson 2014: 169). As biographical research has shown, individuals reconstruct their life history and constantly reinterpret experiences and events.

> The present perspective determines what the subject considers biographically relevant, how he or she develops thematic and temporal links between his or her various experiences and how past, present or anticipated future realities influence his or her personal interpretation of the meaning of his or her life.
>
> (Rosenthal 1993: 61)

Salsa dance professionals reinterpret their biographies in a similar manner with a strong before-and-after distinction.

ALICIA: So I was dancing since I was 6 years old, and I loved dance, but I did ballet for ten years. So when I changed country to study, I met salsa and all the other dances, and of course I went crazy, I really loved it. And then, one day, [...] at the university, Iannis came with his dance partner at that time, and I was like, wow! [...] And then a whole new world opened for me. And I went like, I think the next day, I went to his class, to his dance studio. And after that I was ready to change my whole life.

JOANNA: What kind of changes or implications did it have for your life?

ALICIA: Oh, everything! My whole orientation changed, OK I already knew that I loved salsa and it wouldn't be just a hobby. But then it truly became my life. Like, it's what I do in the morning, afternoon, nights, on the weekends, every every every day of the year. And it's truly amazing! I've been doing this now for five years and I want to keep doing it, like, for I don't know, forever.

Alicia's narrative includes this first encounter with salsa, in her case following the move from Cyprus to a Greek city for university studies. Once Alicia had met her future dance partner Iannis, she started to enter this "whole new world" and decided to take classes. Looking back on this during the interview, she describes this decision as a dramatic change in her life. The initial contact is thus followed by an intense period of acquiring the skills needed to dance. At this stage, dancers with experience in other dance forms are often advantaged. Eventually Alicia became Iannis' dance partner; at the time of the interview they taught classes in a Greek city during the week and performed at events at weekends. Like Maria in the portrait above, Alicia stresses the gradual shift from salsa dancing as a hobby to its becoming a serious and time-consuming professional activity, including a large social network. In this way, the mobile salsa trajectories of serious salsa students gradually develop into professional careers, with the partial or entire abandonment of other professional careers and jobs.

However, the choice of this career is likely to call for justification in relation to non-dancers, as salsa professionals often experience a lack of public recognition. In the interviews with dancers who had made salsa their full-time profession, two elements were particularly stressed in the process of adapting to their new professional identity: individuals who had given up jobs criticised their previous income-generating activities, and all dancers I interviewed insisted on the importance of following their "passion". This is exemplified in Clara's statement below, which demonstrates her distaste for her previous tasks as an office worker in a construction company.

> Of course there are some negative things, but, out of all the things that can go wrong, nothing is as bad as sitting in an office for 40 years without a clue what you are doing there. Where you do something just because you have done it for the last ten years and you will be able to do the same for the next ten years for sure. But nothing is as bad as that.

Clara is a dance studio owner and professional dancer based in Germany. Her partner, Gary, grew up on a Caribbean island and got into salsa during his studies in the Netherlands. He was also very clear about his career choices. He began dancing salsa in the Netherlands, spent some months in New York to improve his dancing and, once he met Clara, moved to Germany to live with her:

> I was a banker, quit my studies as accountant [...]. But I never had any regrets, I mean I threw away four years [of studies] but I don't regret it. Then I started from zero in Germany, with classes, also started my solo career, it wasn't easy, that wasn't easy at all.

Although Gary admitted that the construction of his career as a salsa dance professional entailed hardship and many difficulties, he presented his choice as the only right one, as he would not have liked to continue working "in an office" for the rest of his professional life. Although not all my interview participants gave up their jobs or studies (some of them kept a secondary job), the salsa dance professionals I spoke to generally described the decision to become a salsa dancer as a step towards a more interesting and rewarding life in terms of self-actualisation. Thus, the element of passion for salsa dancing recurs. As already seen, this element is particularly important in the conversion narratives of salsa dance students. As the interviews with salsa dance professionals revealed, it serves as an important argument to legitimate their career choice. As Nara explained: "There's a risk of things going wrong and you take that risk because the reward is much greater. [...] it's very fulfilling. [...] You find the things so that you can continue to do what you love". In dancers' explanations, "to do what you love" was often assessed as more important than the difficulties arising from a transnational career. In this sense, salsa dance professionals resemble other actors in the creative industries (encompassing activities and work strongly related to art, cf Mathieu 2011), as well as in other highly mobile careers (Wagner 2016). In his study of contemporary dancers in France, Sorignet (2014) also points out the importance of understanding dancers' careers in terms of a vocation. The dancers were less preoccupied with regard to financial difficulties than to self-fulfilment. In a similar vein, Laillier (2011) demonstrates the dynamic process of vocation of ballet dancers at the Opéra de Paris. He introduces the term "vocational rationalisation" to point to the importance of vocation that justifies dancers' commitment, as it is precisely through this commitment that dancers hope to realise their "calling" (Laillier 2011: 494). Although, based on my data, I cannot offer generalisations for all salsa dance professionals, the idea of a dance career as a possibility for self-actualisation was prominent. This point is illustrated by Andy, a *travelling salsa artist* based in London:

> You know, why would I wanna stay in London and dance, when I can go to another country and dance, everything paid for, you know. I'm not driven by money and stuff like that, I'm just driven by my passion. I guess one day it will go, but right now it's still on the high [smiling], very high.

The "passion" for salsa to which dance professionals refer can be understood as a prime motivator to pursue this type of career. At the same time, running across the transcripts as a common theme, the passion narrative could be read as a particular strategy of presenting themselves as legitimate salsa professionals. As I have shown in Chapter 2, part of salsa's affective economy is based on the importance of the expression of emotions of its practitioners. Being passionate about salsa as a profession is one more element of stressing one's professional status in salsa.

"Salsa is not recognised yet": struggling for legitimacy

The status passage from student dancer to salsa dance professional requires not only a reconfiguration of one's own professional identity inside the affective economy of the salsa circuit; dancers also need to position themselves in relation to non-dancers and their perceptions of salsa. Accordingly, nascent salsa dance professionals need to navigate historic representations that distinguish between art and popular culture, a distinction related to power relationships in a given society (see Bourdieu 1993).

Taking up the common complaint that salsa is not recognised as an art form in the US (see also McMains 2015: 98), this section asks how salsa dance professionals based in Europe deal with the perceived lack of recognition. Several salsa dance professionals told me about their negative experiences with non-dancers because they had to explain their profession as well as the fact that they can make a living out of salsa. Clara described salsa's lower status compared to other, more institutionalised dance forms:

> And it is because salsa will probably always stay underground, at least what we actually see. [...] Unfortunately, whenever someone asks you, "what do you do" – "well, I'm a dancer". The very moment I have to tell them that I'm a salsa dancer, they are like: [in a doubtful voice] "OK?" If I'd said that I'm a ballet dancer or jazz dancer or modern or whatever, they'd respect me more. It would be another impression than when I say I'm a salsa dancer.

In Clara's view, salsa should have the status of ballet, jazz and modern dance, which are all dance practices that have been formalised to a certain degree as well as institutionalised at universities or dance schools (see e.g. Wulff 1998 on ballet) and are recognised as performing arts. Clara's position mirrors many dancers' wish to be respected and for salsa to be perceived not only as entertainment but also as an art form that is performed on the stages of prestigious venues. Indeed "the stages on which salsa dancers perform tend to be those constructed in hotel ballrooms for the duration of a salsa congress, not established theaters" (McMains 2015: 317) (see Figure 5.1). Dancers' quest for legitimacy indicates a hierarchy of performance practices in the US as well as European countries.

Figure 5.1 Salsa show on the stage of a hotel at the Paris International Salsa Congress.
Source: © Valentin Behringer.

In his analysis of the artistic field, Bourdieu (1993) distinguishes three competing forms of legitimacy: "specific legitimacy", "bourgeois legitimacy" and "popular legitimacy". In Chapter 7, I analyse the recognition granted to salsa dancers inside the salsa circuit, which Bourdieu calls specific legitimacy. Here, I focus on the legitimacy related to the non-recognition of salsa dancers: the lack of bourgeois legitimacy. Bourdieu describes this as the:

> principle of legitimacy corresponding to "bourgeois" taste and to the consecration bestowed by the dominant fractions of the dominant class and by private tribunals, such as *salons*, or public, state-guaranteed ones, such as academies, which sanction the inseparably ethical and aesthetic (and therefore political) taste of the dominant.
>
> (Bourdieu 1993: 51)

Although Bourdieu's model was developed to analyse the field of cultural production in a specific national frame at a specific historical moment, it is helpful in situating contemporary salsa dancers' dilemma in terms of public recognition. The designation of salsa dance professionals as *artists* indicates their self-identification as producers of art, which they perceive as qualitatively different from "mere entertainment". In many interviews, the idea of salsa being an art form emerged vis a vis making sense of one's life as a dancer and artist. Dancers who develop professional careers in the salsa circuit therefore have to position themselves in relation to salsa's poor public recognition, which translates into lack of support from powerful institutions and the economic capital they provide. All the organisers of salsa events I talked to told me that it was difficult to obtain sponsorship money for salsa events.

Salsa events in European countries are based on private sponsorship, thus depending on "popular legitimacy", which Bourdieu (1993: 51) defines as "the consecration bestowed by the choice of ordinary consumers, the 'mass audience'". Hence, in terms of public recognition, salsa's relatively recent arrival as compared to longstanding local cultural practices may play a crucial role. Furthermore, from a nation state's perspective, "cultural funding" programmes are designed to support national artists (see e.g. Lipphardt 2012 on the establishment of EU funding schemes and the importance of national citizenship in acquiring them). As Becker (1982) argues:

> Governments may regard the arts, some or all of them, as integral parts of the nation's identity, things it is known for as Italy is known for opera, and subsidize them as they would any important feature of the national culture that could not support itself.
>
> (181)

During this research, I have never heard of salsa dancers being part of a funding scheme in Europe. Salsa dance professionals work as freelancers or entrepreneurs, a point that Yaimara, who had experienced state subsidisation in Cuba, criticised: "It would be great if there were an institution or something for dancers. [...] this would be great if Germany could do this. But I know there are other priorities". For Yaimara, compared to her experience of support in Cuba, there was non-recognition of salsa artists in Germany. Although similar criticism may be widespread among professionals in other artistic domains, such as performance or music, the described challenge of becoming salsa dance professionals points to the ongoing negotiations of what constitutes legitimate art in a (nationally defined) society. In many socialist countries, creating national dance academies and funding their artists was declared as a goal of the government to enhance "national culture". This phenomenon is known from Eastern European countries (Buckland 2006). The revolutionary government in Cuba established institutions to educate dancers in specific dance forms and, once they graduated, subsidised them in their activities, while regulating their travels. In this way, Becker's (1982) observation of the importance of political and administrative leaders for the functioning of art worlds still holds true: "The merging of politics and aesthetics thus affects what can be counted as art at all, the reputations of whole genres and media as well as those of individual artists" (166).

"You need to know how to sell yourself": salsa dancing as affective labour

The moment salsa dancers decide to make a living from their dancing they enter a market logic, which includes offering services to paying clients. Drawing on the concept of "self-commodification" (Bunten 2008) in tourism, this section argues that in the process of becoming salsa dance professionals, individuals need to engage in a specific form of "affective labour" (Ditmore 2007). Building on Hochschild's (1983) work on the "emotional labour"[1] of airline attendants, Bunten analyses "self-commodification" among Native American professionals in the cultural-tourism business. For Bunten (2008), self-commodification "involves any type of product performance that requires the individual to adjust his or her values, emotions, or both, to achieve an economic goal" (381). I show that salsa dancers' construction of a "commodified persona" (Bunten 2008) not only includes the marketing of specific services but also contains a specific form of "affective labour".

The notion of affective labour is employed in different ways in various fields of study, (see Gregg 2009 for an overview of the different definitions). While feminist studies have highlighted the significance of "emotion work" and "emotional labour" (Hochschild 1983) in care and service jobs since the 1970s, more recent theorisation dealing with the "immaterial labour" of the contemporary workplace (Hardt 1999; Lazzarato 1996) builds on principles of post-Marxism. In line with the "affective turn", studies on sex work combine these approaches and draw on an understanding of affective labour "as work that aims to evoke specific behaviors or sentiments in others as well as oneself, rather than it being merely about the production of a consumable product" (Ditmore 2007: 171). I build on these authors to demonstrate the significance of salsa dance professionals' affective labour.

In the field of affect studies, the debate about a clear distinction between emotions and affects is on-going (see Baier et al. 2014). In general, while "emotion is treated as a social or cultural expression of feeling and refers to the ways these feelings are managed in public spheres", affect "is generally considered to be the physical response to feeling, linked to the biological body" (Davis 2015b: 18). Contrary to the notion of emotions, the notion of affects thus locates feelings as experiences in the body and includes the possibility of affecting others, which is central in the processes discussed in this book.

In discussing the salsa dance profession, Maria mentioned the most common services salsa dance professionals offer to festival organisers:

> It depends whatever it's gonna be, [...] because you might be invited to the event for many different reasons. Because the event has different parts, they wanna fill up the different parts, some are invited because they are known for great shows, some because they are great teachers [...]. Social dancing and socialising with people, this is another story, you can see a lot of people having these skills, to pull up the party and just make it a great atmosphere [...]. So this is also a huge quality that the organisers need as well. So there are many ways to make your own mark and deliver the service that might be needed.

What Maria here calls services (show dancing, teaching and dancing socially) are the three basic tasks salsa dance professionals perform to sustain their livelihood.

Furthermore, salsa dance professionals need to develop a set of entrepreneurial skills such as the design of websites, flyers or a Facebook profile to market their product. Besides such classical marketing strategies necessary in every economic activity, salsa dance professionals often talked about the need to "sell themselves". Ajay framed this idea of adjusting the self according to the logics of the affective economy as follows:

> If you've done ten shows and done ten events and no one is inviting you, you need to do better. You need to evolve, change something about yourself as an artist. It's not just your dancing, it's your personality, it's who you are as a person, it's how you deal with people, how you communicate, it's language, it's all about stuff. You need to understand, "what can I do to make myself more likeable to the community".

As Ajay here explains, in developing a "commodified persona", salsa dance professionals develop entrepreneurial and social skills such as communication. Furthermore, they adjust their own persona and shape their self-presentation according to the demands of the dance students and congress organisers. Dancers thus need to work on their persona; they need to manage the expression of their own emotions according to the conventions of the affective economy of the salsa circuit. Furthermore, they are held responsible for the affective responses of the spectators (during a show) and salsa students (during social dancing).

In the interview with Valentina, co-organiser of a large salsa congress, I asked about her understanding of a "good" salsa artist. In the following extract she explains which types of salsa dance professionals she invites to her events.

> For me, a top artist is someone who really lives [all of] this, who lives this music. Not someone who just does a show with great technique with the latest steps he just made up or learned somewhere, but someone who interprets a story. Not the one who impresses you as a spectator with the splits [...] but [rather] with the emotions you have. There are people giving you so much with so little! And that is what I look for, as the guest is highly sensitive to this. And if the person is also a great teacher, then you are good for me. In this world you also need to be an entertainer, you cannot be a wallflower, you have a function, you are a personality, you need to know how to sell yourself. When you have all of this, then for me you are an artist.

As this salsa event organiser makes clear, to be invited to an event, salsa dance professionals are not only expected to have dancing and teaching skills, but also a whole set of embodied personal characteristics. To be accepted as salsa artists, dancers have to "live this"; they must embody being artists. In Valentina's reasoning, when on stage during a show, artists need to affirm their passion for and vocation of salsa, as it is not the technical mastery (such as the splits) but the ways the dancer "interprets a story" that will emotionally move or affect spectators (see Figure 5.2). In this way, Valentina relegates the responsibility for the emotions felt by the spectators of the show to the dancers on stage who, through their dancing, have the power to affect them. Furthermore, salsa dance professionals are supposed to be skilled entertainers, a related task that consists of affective labour, as entertainers in the salsa circuit are usually defined as the ones who "get the party started".

There is a second way salsa dance professionals engage in affective labour: what Maria calls "social dancing and socialising with people". Social dancing, which implies dancing with festival attendees during the night's parties, is a specificity of the salsa circuit. While the first two skills mentioned in Maria's quotation (show dancing and teaching) are remunerated and rendered explicit in signed or oral contracts between dance professionals and festival organisers, the third one – dancing socially – is only implicit.

The importance actors in the salsa circuit put on dance professionals' participation in social dancing – the "convention of tangible salsa *stars*" – often creates tensions. In an organised discussion round I observed at a festival, one of the topics was announced as "the problem of non-dancing salsa superstars". The moderator introduced the topic by telling the attendees that it was a pity that *salsa superstars* would no longer dance with festival participants. In the following discussion, one of the organisers clearly stated that he invited an artist only if he knew that the dancer in question would

Figure 5.2 Standing ovations at the end of a show.
Source: © Valentin Behringer.

also dance with the paying guests. Then the discussion centred on the question of whether dance professionals should be forced by contract and be paid to dance with amateurs. The majority of attending amateur dancers and organisers were against regulating the question on a contractual basis. The moderator closed the discussion round as follows: "you like to dance with *salsa stars* but you want them to do it because they like it – and not because they are paid for it".

As this short summary of the discussion makes clear, salsa dance professionals are not only expected to perform and/or teach at salsa events, they are also supposed to engage in an interpersonal relationship with amateur dancers who are eager to dance with a *salsa star*. In the context of salsa dancing, this relationship is necessarily highly gendered. As studies of affective labour argue, the relationship with clients is particularly significant: "Affective labor especially makes use of the interpersonal skills often as part of entrepreneurialism, where the relationship with clients and potential clients is paramount" (Ditmore 2007: 171, building on Lazzarato 1996). If dancers fail to adhere to this "convention of tangible *salsa stars*", their reputations may be in danger, and they run the risk of not being invited to subsequent salsa events.

It is precisely in this area of tension between dancing as a paid service and dancing as an interpersonal encounter that affective labour has to be performed. Although salsa dance professionals have many reasons not to dance with members of the public during festival nights,[2] the expectations of this profession do include dancing with paying salsa students, which can be analysed as a form of affective labour. Following the logics of the salsa circuit's affective economy, the gendered dance partnership between two salsa dancers is framed as the result of dancers' wish for the dance interaction. When the economic transaction is emphasised instead of the affective relationship, this convention is disrupted. From the perspective of the students, the exchange on the dance floor should not be framed in economic terms, as this reduces the dancing experience to a "product" bought in a market transaction.

In the literature, a similar phenomenon has been discussed in regard to so-called *taxi-dancers*, who work as temporary dance partners for visitors of the opposite sex (see Cressey 1932 on female taxi-dancers in the taxi-dance halls of Chicago, or, more recently, Törnqvist 2012 on male taxi-dancers catering to foreign women in the tango dance-halls of Buenos Aires). Although there is no direct economic exchange for a dance between a salsa dance professional and a salsa student in the context of a festival (as the transaction of money occurs through the intermediary of the event organiser), the above discussion demonstrates the similarities with the institution of taxi-dancers, as the boundaries between professional (and sometimes even contractually regulated) obligation and leisure, or between economic and affective relationships are blurred. Dance professionals are not only expected to dance with festival participants, they are also expected to "like it" and thus need to engage in affective labour. Salsa dance professionals at European festivals thus experience a similar dilemma as the professional dancers in Havana's salsa tourism space.

As this section has shown, to access paid jobs in the salsa circuit, dancers develop entrepreneurial skills and promote themselves, by developing their personality and focusing on one of their skills: performing salsa shows (sometimes competitions), teaching workshops or dancing socially. Furthermore, becoming a salsa dance professional includes an entrepreneurial approach to the self, as dance professionals not only change their social roles from dance student into dance professional, but they also need to adapt their self-images, entering an entrepreneurial logic to construct commodified personas, relying on the execution of gendered affective labour.

Income-generating activities

The construction of transnational careers enables actors to accumulate reputation or salsa capital, which is transferable into economic capital up to a certain extent, since famous dancers are in constant demand. Although salsa dance professionals claim status as artists, most of them do not make a living performing (in contrast, for example, to ballet dancers) but rather by teaching salsa to paying students. To become a salsa dance professional, dancers need to have income-generating activities.

As studies of artistic labour markets have shown, artists often face considerable risk due to the uncertainty of the fields they work in; therefore, they often follow a strategy of holding multiple jobs (Menger 1999: 562).

Here, teaching the specific skills of the practice is a frequent strategy (Menger 1999: 564). As argued in Chapter 3 in regards to the importance of the "teaching convention", becoming a salsa dance professional therefore includes developing skills not only in dancing, but importantly also in teaching. Teaching salsa dance is often learned on the spot, through imitation of one's own teachers and other salsa dance professionals active in the salsa circuit. Salsa dance professionals follow several strategies to make ends meet through teaching. These income-generating activities are sometimes combined; sometimes they follow one another in the course of a dancer's career. Basically, salsa dance professionals travel as salsa artists, often combined with teaching locally as freelancers, or they own (and teach in) dance studios. In this section, I discuss the rationale for taking up each of these activities and the ways they are related to different degrees of geographical mobility and different social networks, as each one requires and results in different degrees of local rootedness and transnational connections.

"You don't have a regular contract": travelling as *salsa artist*

Travelling artists are highly prestigious dancers, whose photographs figure on festival advertisements, thus attracting salsa students to a particular event. Most of them are based in one country, moving to other places several times a month for the duration of a weekend in order to work. Once they have obtained residency rights in a country in Europe, they work mostly at salsa events in Europe, with occasional events in other countries.

Lavinia told me about the places she had performed and taught salsa with her dance partner:

> We can go all around Europe, we also went to Japan, we went to Turkey, we went to Australia, to Dubai, to Russia, ehm … Lebanon, Israel, Africa – I mean that's a continent but we went to Morocco. Yeah, like I think to each continent we have gone at least once, in one country.

Some salsa dance professionals also tour for longer periods, for example if they are invited to teach in a school for several weeks, or if organisers of different events jointly pay for the travel and accommodation of an artist living on another continent. In this way, dancers based in the USA (in this study Nara), Singapore (in this study Ajay) or Australia are also present on European festival stages and dance floors, as European dancers are at Asian festivals.[3]

Although becoming a *travelling artist* and developing a transnational career is often cited as a dream for many salsa dancers, the material conditions are rather precarious even for those who have gained considerable reputation inside the circuit. Salsa events are not stable sources of income, and personal networks with event organisers and other actors play a crucial role in organising jobs. Job opportunities for salsa dance professionals thus often depend on the organisers and their interests and calendars. Sometimes events are cancelled at short notice due to financial difficulties. In these cases, the invited artists are not paid. Several of my interviewees told me about such difficulties, such as Clara who mentioned several occasions she and her partner Gary received no payment for their work:

> Two years ago, we worked five weekends for nothing because they couldn't pay us. Later we saw the money, for two [of the weekends], some of them couldn't pay for us or only half of it, or whatever. But there's nothing where you can say, "OK, we can count on this".

Several of the interviewed dancers told me about such experiences with cancelled events or work they had done unpaid. Other dancers mentioned the unstable working conditions, such as Yaimara: "The thing I find most difficult with dancing is that you don't have a regular contract, it is hard. Because one month you can have a lot and the other month nothing, you have to be careful".

To diversify their income-generating strategies, many salsa dance professionals teach not only at salsa events but also locally on weekdays, for example in the salsa studios of others. This is the case for Maria, who set up her own small company in order to formally freelance with different schools. Thus, she teaches regularly alone as well as with her dance partner in the city where the two are living. Based in Norway, Maria and her dance partner often travel to other dance schools in Scandinavia and other European countries and to bigger events where they teach and perform. Although she works half the weekends in a year, she does not like the idea of making a living only out of these jobs. Instead, she insists on keeping her regular students and teaching locally: "I don't think I would feel comfortable relying only on the events, it would be too stressful. So having a more steady base like classes or another job is definitely needed". As a freelancer without her own studio, Maria is able to combine the need for a regular income with the wish for a transnational career.

Dancers who start building up professional careers often concentrate on the organisation of their travelling and establishment of transnational networks and have to find ways to teach classes in someone else's dance school or in a rented room during the week.

"Either you are on the move or you manage a school": owning a dance studio

Since the salsa wave in European countries of the late 1990s, salsa dance studios (also called dance schools) have flourished in many European cities. They range from a one-room studio up to several rooms where more than one class can be taught at a time. In order to open up their own studio, dancers require not only economic capital, but also the necessary legal status, organisational skills, local networks and teaching experience. Therefore, dancers at the beginning of their careers rarely choose to open up their own studios, as they first need to acquire these resources. Nevertheless, several of my research participants mentioned being owners of dance studios, planning to become owners or having already closed their studios and moved on.

Several of my research participants considered dance schools as stable sources of income, where they depend on themselves instead of waiting for others to invite them to teach. When I discussed this point with Iannis and Alicia, a Greek salsa couple performing and teaching together, Iannis said: "That's why we have the studio. I mean it's like, it gives a little bit of security, although it's hard in Greece to have a small business, with the taxes". Although it brings a lot of work under difficult conditions, Iannis considers running a dance studio worth it because it provides some security, even though the economic crisis in Greece has affected his business. He plans to continue teaching salsa and considers his studio a good place to do this on a regular basis.

After several years of teaching salsa in different German cities and at festivals, Gary and his partner Clara decided to open a studio. Although they continue travelling to festivals, they manage their studio in a German city. For them, the studio has advantages in economic terms, as Clara explains:

> The dance school is "stable", in quotation mark, it's between 150 and 170 people [students], sometimes more, sometimes less, the money arrives most of the time, with few problems, but at the beginning or in the middle of the month it should be there, that's what you can count on.

In order to make a living out of dancing, Clara and Gary follow a two-fold strategy similar to Alicia and Iannis: on one hand they rely on the regular income of their dance studio, on the other hand they travel to events to teach and perform. For them, running a studio has the advantage of a more or less regular income, especially compared to jobs at salsa events.

The decision to concentrate on a local business is often taken after a transnational career as *travelling artist*, and the decision to run a studio and settle down is also linked to age and gender. The case of Anna is illustrative of this. Anna runs the studio on her own and employs several teachers, managing "a little enterprise", as she says. Her decision to settle down and stop travelling was linked to her wish to have a family and become a mother, something she did not want to combine with a transnational career. She thus decided to open a school and stop working at festivals: "Either you are on the move internationally or you manage a school, you can't do both". The difficulties lie in the necessitated personal presence in order to keep students and get oneself known locally. In this context, the reputation gained in the (transnationally oriented) salsa circuit is not directly transferable, as local students don't necessarily know about their dance teachers' transnational activities.[4] Furthermore, once a studio is running, owners have to attract new students constantly while keeping old ones in order to gain a regular income. Asked if she ever thought about opening her own school in Germany, Yaimara replied:

I've really thought about this but at the moment I don't have the time. Because during the week I am at [name of a big dance studio in a German city], I could do this as well in my own dance school. But on the weekends I am away, at festivals. That would really stress me, because it means that I need employees to do the administration, for example if someone is sick in a couple class and I have to organise a temporary partner. So I would need someone for the whole organisation, it needs a lot of force, a lot of energy, a lot of time for everything. And at this moment I have so many other things going on.

Yaimara refers to a practice I experienced several times, with schools organising an equal number of students for the couples classes. As she explains, being the owner of a studio demands not only a lot of administrative work but also a lot of work in terms of building up local relationships with students in order to keep them coming to classes as well as attracting new ones. Teachers of local schools usually organise monthly or weekly parties in their locations and go to parties with their students regularly. Similarly, in a study on Argentinean tango performers in New York, Viladrich (2013) notes that the dancers' work involves "a steady investment of time, energy, and even money, as they must attend tango parlors regularly for the sake of displaying their tango skills with peers, as well as dancing with current and potential students" (80). This work in terms of presenting oneself and networking is crucial to running a local dance school.

This strategy of salsa dancers' economic activities – owning a dance school – is place-bound and based on local networks with organisers of local salsa nights, as well as a network of local students. (The most prestigious salsa dancers teaching in New York or Milan do have visiting students coming from outside, but most dance schools rely on the local salsa scene.) Opening a dance school is an economic investment and an option only for dancers with at least a residence permit in the country in question, as seen in the case of Marcos who had to wait to become a resident of Japan before he opened his own studio. Furthermore, opening a dance studio needs business and other skills such as knowledge of the local language.

As this brief discussion of the different income-generating activities of salsa dance professionals shows, the establishment of a transnational career relies on the acquisition of various resources that can be deployed differently in different places. In order to travel, salsa dance professionals need to build up reputation in the salsa circuit and transnational networks of peers and event organisers to secure job opportunities. Nevertheless, relying solely on such irregular jobs at salsa events is often regarded as too uncertain. Salsa dance professionals therefore often hold secondary jobs. Owning a salsa studio is one possibility to secure a more regular income, relying on local resources, networks and relationships to local salsa students and events. All in all, salsa dance professionals often perform independent, self-managed work building on various skills.

Conclusion

This chapter has provided an analysis of the first status passage of becoming a salsa dance professional. As argued, becoming a salsa dance professional in Europe involves negotiations of a new professional identity, which is related to salsa's lack of "bourgeois legitimacy" (Bourdieu 1993). I have demonstrated in which ways nascent salsa dance professionals negotiate their professional identities outside the salsa circuit. Some salsa dancers are able to gain considerable reputation inside the salsa circuit, including economic rewards. However, as salsa has no institutional anchor in any European country, this achieved symbolic status is not recognised in other social fields (the national or local context in which these dancers live).

Transnational salsa careers can be understood as a particular form of vocational careers. They are legitimised by a strong narrative of passion. The motivations of salsa dance professionals thus resemble those of professionals in other performance arts such as ballet or music (Laillier 2011; Sorignet 2014; Wagner 2015). On the other hand, as I have shown, salsa dance professionals become entrepreneurs of themselves, as they develop a "commodified persona" (Bunten 2008) and engage in "affective labour" (Ditmore 2007) to sustain their livelihood with salsa. They have to negotiate the gendered "convention of tangible salsa *stars*" in order to build their careers. In this respect, professional careers in the salsa circuit differ from other professional careers in dance, music or performance as studied in the above-mentioned literature. Indeed, the independent, self-managed work shares similarities with the careers of capoeira instructors in North America, explored by Robitaille (2013).

In her study, Robitaille (2013) frames capoeira as a "cultural resource", and analyses Brazilian *mestres* (teachers) and the ways they engage in capoeira in North America as a context of "transnational neoliberalism". She describes the network facilitating the transnational "exportation" of capoeira at large, arguing that within this network, it is the labour of each *mestre* that transforms capoeira into a resource that ensures individuals' livelihoods (Robitaille 2013: 161). The Brazilian capoeira *mestres* locally organise their schools as small enterprises within a neoliberal economy. While the work of salsa dance professionals resembles the one of the described Capoeira *mestres*, this book demonstrates the importance of the construction of a specific salsa imaginary of an *Esperanto of the body* instead of a "cultural resource", due to this study's different framing of salsa as a bodily social practice.

To start building up the activities described in this chapter, salsa dance professionals need to access the salsa circuit, a status passage that often includes many obstacles, as explored in the next chapter.

Notes

1 Hochschild's (1983) widely cited concept of emotional labour describes the process by which workers are expected to manage their feelings and expressions in accordance with employer-defined rules.

2 Many salsa dancers who consider themselves artists are reluctant to dance with paying festival participants, a task they consider not part of their art. They prefer to stay behind the scene with other dance professionals, thus demonstrating their status as salsa artists. Furthermore, in informal discussions, female dancers mentioned the risk of injuries through dancing with inexperienced leaders as well as tiredness after a long day of teaching, rehearsing and performing as reasons for their absence during festival night parties. Some artists compromise to some degree by dancing in public but choosing their dance partners from the circle of more experienced dancers they already know.

3 For a video of two *salsa stars* based in Europe, filmed after their workshop at the China Latin Dance Festival, see rebrand.ly/salsa-15.

4 This is different in the case of salsa schools in Havana, which rely on the influx of salsa students from abroad and therefore deploy strategies to attract them.

6   Accessing the European salsa circuit

Access to the salsa circuit, in particular the prestigious European salsa circuit, is regulated through diverse elements whereby relationships with strategic actors (dance students, more experienced dancers, event organisers) as well as the possibility of travel play a crucial role. The ways dance professionals build up ties to these specific actors will be discussed in Chapter 7. However, before being able to establish ties with relevant actors of the European salsa circuit, aspiring salsa dance professionals need to be able to create opportunities to meet them. Dancers living in Europe and possessing sufficient economic means and time to travel to salsa events maximise their exposure in the salsa circuit as much as possible and thus their chances to be seen and invited by more experienced dance professionals or event organisers. However, aspiring salsa dancers living outside Europe have to overcome several barriers in order to access the European salsa circuit.

I will now turn to the salsa careers of non-European dancers and the social networks and other resources they mobilise to access the European salsa circuit. In this chapter, I combine perspectives and findings from the field of mobility studies with the already developed theoretical framework of transnational careers. Drawing on the concept of "mobility capital", this chapter sheds light on an important aspect of salsa dance professionals' working conditions and careers that is completely absent from public tales of salsa as an inclusive moment where "everybody can participate" and from literature on salsa, which usually presumes the participation of *Latinos/Latinas* and *non-Latinos/Latinas* in the transnational circuit. In this literature, salsa dancers' mobility across national borders is implicitly taken for granted and their strategies usually remain unacknowledged. The same holds for much of the literature on other "mobile professionals" (be it so-called highly skilled or others). Focusing on actors that actually are mobile, studies tend to neglect the fact that this mobility is not automatically granted but has to be obtained by many, thus glossing over an important aspect of unequal access to resources.

As Shamir (2005: 200) claims, "the differential ability to move in space – and even more so to have access to opportunities for movements – has become a major stratifying force in the global social hierarchy". In a similar vein, Mau et al. (2015) speak of a global "mobility divide". They demonstrate that while citizens of OECD countries can largely travel visa-free to many parts of the world, nationals from non-OECD countries face high levels of travel restrictions (Mau et al. 2015). Passports and visas structure individual salsa dancers' short-term travels as well as their long-term mobility to a considerable degree. To travel to European countries, passport holders of many Latin American countries have to obtain a tourist visa (Neumayer 2010), which generally allows for a stay of 90 days. Once this period is over, dancers can leave the country or overstay their visa and find other ways to consolidate their legal status.

In recent approaches to the study of mobilities, mobility has been conceptualised as a capital in Bourdieu's sense (Kaufmann et al. 2004; Moret 2016; Sheller 2011; for an overview see Jayaram 2016). Kaufmann et al. (2004) define this ability to move, "motility", as "the capacity of entities (e.g. goods, information or persons) to be mobile in social and geographic space or as the way in which entities access and appropriate the capacity for socio-spatial mobility according to their circumstances" (Kaufmann et al. 2004: 750). In this framework, the potential to be mobile is as important as the actual act of moving. As Sheller (2011) writes, mobility capital can be conceptualised "as the uneven distribution of these capacities and competences, in relation to the surrounding physical, social and political affordances for movement (with the legal structures regulating who or what can and cannot move being crucial)" (5).

Furthermore, the concept of motility links spatial mobility to social mobility, "as the ability to be mobile is related to the ability to deploy strategies to improve one's situation" (Moret 2018: 103). Drawing on what Cresswell (2010) terms "the politics of mobility", Moret (2016) theorises mobility "as an element of social differentiation involved in the production of power relations and inequalities" (1458). In this perspective, mobility is seen as an unequally distributed resource "that can, under certain conditions, be mobilised and transformed into social and economic advantages" (Moret 2016: 1458), and thus becomes mobility capital.

As this chapter demonstrates, salsa dancers of non-European origin are endowed with different volumes of mobility capital. Many of my research participants first had to acquire the necessary skills, contacts and legal documents before they were able to access the European salsa circuit and build a successful transnational career, thereby drawing on other resources. In this study, mobility is understood as capital that can be acquired (through the deployment of other forms of capital, such as social capital) as well as mobilised and converted into other forms of capital (such as reputation in the salsa circuit, and/or economic advantages).

This chapter includes a second argument put forward by scholarship of "mobility studies": it brings together forms of mobility that are usually conceived of separately, such as tourism, migration or circular mobility, in one theoretical framework (see also Dahinden 2010; Schapendonk et al. 2015). In my research, this was particularly striking in the encounters and relationships built between tourists from European countries and their Cuban salsa teachers. The tourist's mobility is normalised whereas the teacher's wish to partake in mobility as part of a "cosmopolitan lifestyle" was often hindered by diverse exclusionary mechanisms of "migration regimes" (Amelina 2017). In bringing together this theoretical argument with a focus on the transnational careers of salsa dance professionals, I am able to add a better understanding of the construction of such careers. Drawing on Martiniello and Rea's (2014: 1089) insights in their discussion of "migratory careers", I acknowledge not only individual characteristics such as nationality, marital status, level of education, age and gender, but I also take into account the role of the state "as a key actor that structures the context of reception or departure of migrants" in one analytical framework. To account for the interdependency of the various forms of mobility I suggest the notion of "entangled mobilities", which will be further theorised in the conclusion of this chapter.

In the following, I look at three consecutive phases of the process of accessing the salsa circuit. The first phase is of "imaginative travels" to account for the importance of imaginaries in salsa dance professionals' careers. The second phase I explore is the ways Cuban dancers first gained access to the European salsa circuit and the strategies they mobilised (more or less successfully) during the process. To illustrate this second phase, I draw on the individual cases of selected dancers, chosen for their relevance (Flick 2014) and variation (Becker 1998). The third phase is the way in which Latin American dancers consolidated "legal capital" once in Europe in order to be able to continue their transnational careers in the salsa circuit.

Imaginaries of a "cosmopolitan lifestyle"

Most of the salsa dance professionals I interviewed who had been born in a Latin American country had already danced salsa or similar dances where they grew up. Before they started their transnational careers as salsa professionals, usually initiated by migration to a European country, they imagined being mobile and had ideas of other possible places to live. Salazar (2011) defines such historically laden imaginaries as "socially shared and transmitted (both within and between cultures) representational assemblages that interact with people's personal imaginings and are used as meaning-making and world-shaping devices" (576). In his discussion of different "scapes", Appadurai (1990: 296) proposes to explore the links between imagination and social life, as actors navigate scapes and build "imagined worlds". There are various motivations to cross borders and live elsewhere, and imaginaries of other places and lives play an important role in this process, as scholarship on migration and mobility has demonstrated (Riaño and Baghdadi 2007; Salazar 2011). In their analysis of transnational spaces, geographers have argued for an inclusion not only of "the *material geographies* of labour migration" but also "the *symbolic and imaginary geographies*" (Jackson et al. 2004: 3). Contrary to a simplistic understanding of people migrating solely due to economic hardship, imaginaries that inform the choices of individual migrants should be taken into account when analysing dancers' careers.

The research participants mentioned how they had imagined salsa in "Europe" (imagined as a geographic unit) and their own careers as salsa dancers while living in their countries of origin. The "cosmopolitan lifestyle" the interviewed salsa dancers imagined entails two dimensions: ideas of professional opportunities in the (European) salsa circuit and the dream of travelling. Furthermore, part of such imaginaries was also openness to meeting new people and newly arising opportunities (which shaped later mobility). While the notion of cosmopolitanism is used in many different ways in the literature,[1] a thorough discussion is not the goal of this section. Rather, understanding cosmopolitanism as a "practice which is apparent in things that people do and say to positively engage with 'the otherness of the other' and the oneness of the world" (Nowicka and Rovisco 2009: 2), the idea of a "cosmopolitan lifestyle" is here used as a descriptive notion to account for my interviewees' claims to ideas of being mobile and meeting "others".

Salsa dancers living in Latin American countries often knew about the European salsa circuit through the internet (via YouTube and Facebook) or the stories of others. Alejandro, a salsa dance professional who was born in Costa Rica, worked as a dance teacher in a dance school for tourists in Costa Rica, where he befriended some Swiss students who suggested he come to Switzerland. I asked him about his plans before leaving Costa Rica and he told me that he thought that he would be able to teach and compete in other European countries:

> I knew that in Europe more salsa was going on than in Costa Rica, 'cause everything is open, you can do competitions and congresses everywhere. This didn't exist in Costa Rica or in Latin America. When I left, there were two congresses: one in Puerto Rico and the other one somewhere in America, not many. [...] Nowadays you have congresses in Brazil, Argentina, Chile, Peru, everywhere. At that time, they didn't exist yet. But in Europe they existed already, in Italy, in Germany, even in Switzerland. Before I came here they already existed and I knew that. And most important was that I had good friends from Switzerland. So that's why I'm here now.

As salsa congresses proliferated during the early 2000s in many European countries, Alejandro perceived Europe as more interesting in terms of salsa activity than Latin America. As he told me later on, though he knew about salsa congresses going on in the US, he had no chance to enter the country, as he was not acquainted with dancers who would invite him to a salsa event. On the other hand, once in Switzerland with a tourist visa, he knew he would be able to travel to salsa events. In this sense, "everything is open". He had knowledge of salsa competitions and planned to participate in them to build up his reputation. Furthermore, Alejandro's explanation also identifies the importance of social ties – his good friends from Switzerland – in the construction of his imaginaries. Though not all dancers had such a clear idea of how they would proceed once in

Europe, imaginaries of professional opportunities linked to salsa in Europe played an important role in their decision to try their luck in the European salsa circuit.

Moreover, several of my interviewees dreamed of mobility from an early age. Yaimara started imagining her own travels early: "When I was a child, I always knew that one day ... I always wanted to travel, get to know cultures and people". This underlines the importance of imaginaries of a mobile lifestyle including travelling and the chance to "get to know others".

As the discussed cases illustrate, imaginary forms of participation in the salsa circuit are possible even for individuals who do not physically cross national borders. Urry (2007) also discusses the possibility of "imaginative travel" and states: "Such travel can sometimes substitute for physical travel [...] but more often seems to generate the desire for travel and for being bodily in other places" (169). In terms of salsa dancers' identifications and constructions of belonging, imaginary forms of mobility and participation in the salsa circuit may be of high significance.[2] However, this "imaginary mobility" is not the same as physical, geographical mobility, which in some cases leads to the construction of successful transnational careers. In this way, imaginaries precede travels, but they cannot replace them in terms of the accumulation of mobility capital.

The imagined mobility is further characterised by an idea of openness to self-transformation through mobility. Lavinia, born in Mexico, met her Italian dance partner at a salsa event in Mexico when she was 21 years old. He asked her to move to Milan to work with him and his dance company. Although in this case, the mobility had not been imagined as part of her career, in Lavinia's narration it became a decisive element of self-transformation.

JOANNA: Can you tell me some more about the decision to move to Milano?
LAVINIA: Yes? Because of my personality, I always love challenges, like, when someone tells me, "let's try to do this", I will try it. Maybe after, I won't like it, maybe after I will, maybe not very much, but I always love to try things. And when this proposal came out of nothing, when you didn't expect, that someone could say, "move to the other part of the world", I said, "why not". [...] it was, you know, such a big opportunity, maybe to open my mind or my world. [...] And now, it's five years that I'm here.

In this case, although she had not imagined it as part of her career from an early age, Lavinia embraced the idea of moving to Europe and participating in the salsa circuit as an opportunity and experience for personal development, to "open her mind".

A part of Lavinia's imaginary was her openness to newly arising opportunities. The above quotation illustrates how salsa dancers' career plans and goals change with new experiences and unforeseen opportunities, for instance arising out of encounters with new dance partners. Becker (1963) did not conceive of careers as linear processes; the same holds for transnational careers of salsa dance professionals: they develop over time and allow for adjustments.

A Cuban case study

In Chapter 2, I discussed the importance of salsa hubs outside Europe, and in particular Havana, in salsa dancers' imaginary salsa map. Many salsa dance professionals in the European salsa circuit are of Cuban origin. I now turn to the conditions dancers had to meet and the strategies they mobilised to access the salsa circuit, with a focus on Cuba for the reasons outlined above. This section discusses the manifold ways in which four emerging dance professionals in Havana mobilised specific resources, which in turn allowed them to access the European salsa circuit.

Before they could build up the necessary networks, dancers generally had to move from a village to Havana, where salsa tourism is established. As scholars of mobility studies have pointed out, internal movements such as going to live in a city can sometimes imply bigger changes than the crossing of a border (see Kalir 2013). For these dancers, their move to Havana and their activities in the informal spaces of dance tourism implied a decisive change in their career paths. Gaudette (2013) shares a similar analysis in regards to Guinean jembe musicians who wish to achieve global mobility through playing this drum, and for whom being "in the right place at the right time" is crucial (Gaudette 2013: 304). Similar to the musicians in Guinea who strived to be present at jembe workshops in Conakry, the Cuban salsa dancers in my study had endeavoured to enter spaces of dance tourism in Havana where they could meet tourists. Once established as teachers of salsa dance in a tourist context in Havana, they had a privileged access to visitors.

By considering mobility as an unequally distributed resource that needs to be acquired, as well as an asset that may lead to the improvement of one's situation, this case study demonstrates that the interviewed Cuban dancers needed to actively strategise various ways to access the salsa circuit. In this respect, as I will demonstrate, the mobility of others, in particular European salsa dancers, often allowed for the mobility of Cuban dancers, through an invitation or a marriage. Established networks of salsa students in Europe and cultural capital were also door-openers to the salsa circuit. However, in many cases, the imagined move to Europe – and thus access to the European salsa circuit – does not work, and dancers remain "stuck" at the edge of the salsa circuit.

Juli: "They helped me a lot": mobilising friendship networks

Before my first research trip to Havana, I asked dancer friends and dance studio owners in Switzerland for their recommendations for dance teachers. All of them mentioned Juli's school in Havana as a place to take lessons, which demonstrates her efforts in building and sustaining networks in Switzerland. In Havana, I took several lessons with Juli and other teachers at her school. I met Juli for an interview at her house in central Havana, after a day of work in her school.

Juli started dancing at young age and later enrolled at the university to study dance at the National Arts School (ENA). During this time, in the early 1990s, she also started to teach foreign visitors and to build up contacts: "I studied in the ENA, but I had many family problems, I didn't have any money, I had to work. So I left the ENA, I went to Switzerland and worked, you understand". Due to economic difficulties, Juli had to interrupt her studies and followed an opportunity to go abroad and teach dancing:

> The first time I went was in '98, I went to Switzerland. I knew two Swiss guys, Harry and Frank they are students of mine. They are very good people [...]. I went to Switzerland, gave classes with Barbara, a dance teacher in [Swiss city], she had a dance school. Barbara organised some work for me in Switzerland, in 1998, and I worked in Barbara's school and slept at the house of my friend Harry and it was a great time. Because I worked a lot and I was very happy to be able to go to Switzerland, to get to meet good friends and to earn some money. I don't know, I made 1000 or 2000 francs [at the time 1500 or 3000 Euro], it was a lot of money 'cause here I had nothing. I will always be very grateful to Harry and Frank who helped me with this. I was there for three months, I worked with Barbara for one month and then I worked in other places as well, in [a smaller Swiss city]. There was a project of intercultural exchange, with an official contract with the state. They helped me always for the official part, the legal part, the school [name of Swiss dance school run by Cuban-born dancers]. Therefore I am very grateful to [name of dance school] because they helped me a lot. She's a very good friend of mine, she helped me a lot, until this day.

Like many other dancers, Juli managed to meet enthusiastic students who invited her to travel to Switzerland and helped her with the administrative and practical questions. The money was not a lot in the Swiss context but it was a significant sum in Cuba, which allowed Juli to contemplate opening her own dance studio in a central house. She also relied on the help of others in her network to deal with the paperwork to get an artist's visa that allowed her to travel out of Cuba to Switzerland. She had an artist's contract with the Cuban government, declaring her travel as "intercultural exchange", one of the rare possibilities to leave the country legally during this time. In Switzerland, she obtained a tourist visa of three months. During this first trip, with the help of her former students, Juli taught successfully in different places in Switzerland and made new connections. Building on these, she was able to leave Havana again for a three-month visit to Switzerland one year later and then continued her teaching visits to Switzerland and soon France, Germany, Spain and Denmark, extending her network of interested schools and students every time she was there. Soon, dance students who saw her in Europe started travelling to Havana in order to take classes in her school, attracted by her personality, dancing and teaching skills. After several years of travelling back and forth between Cuba and Europe, Juli was able to buy a house in Havana and subsequently enlarge the dance school by several floors. She relied on the help of family members and friends to look after the school while she was abroad, as well as on a befriended lawyer who helped her deal with the Cuban bureaucracy.

Juli met her future husband during one of her teaching tours in Switzerland. Ten years after her first trip to Switzerland, they married and later had a child. Her husband supports her teaching activities with his own network and knowledge of the language; he helps her organise teaching opportunities. Since her marriage, Juli spends half of the year in Havana and the rest of the year in Switzerland and Europe. This to-and-fro movement between two places allows Juli to keep her dance studio in Havana, where she manages a group of around 15 teachers and 10 assistants. During the interview, she stressed the importance of living near other family members and the emotional costs of being away from Cuba.

Juli's physical presence in Europe for several months of the year allows her to make more money than she can in Cuba and to attract new students to Havana. As she told me, her Swiss residence permit enables her to travel to other countries more easily and with fewer visa restrictions and difficulties than with the Cuban passport alone. When I met Juli, this model had worked for six years, but as their daughter grew older, she and her husband started to discuss where the child would attend school and the place the family should mainly live.

These snapshots of Juli's transnational career demonstrate the ways in which dance professionals are able to mobilise networks they built up in Havana to access the European salsa circuit. Only the initial invitation from someone established in Europe provided Juli with the opportunity to demonstrate her skills in dancing and teaching in dance studios and at small festivals in Europe and to subsequently enlarge her network of inviting dance studios and festivals. Juli's story reveals the ways in which dance professionals can mobilise resources located in two places: not only did she develop her own career as a salsa teacher in Europe, but she also attracted European students to Havana, where she built up a successful school with many Cuban teachers. In the literature, this form of regular movements between two places has been called "circulation" (Duany 2002), "commuting" (Nowicka 2013) or "pendular migration" (Morokvasic-Muller 1999). It allows actors to build up "mobile livelihoods" through a strategy that extends the means of subsistence across borders in situations where economic opportunities are not distributed equally between places (Duany 2002).

After a while, Juli's dance studio became a salsa hub, bringing together Cuban dance teachers and European students. She proudly told me the names of all the Cuban dancers who had left Havana due to invitations from or marriages with European students they had met in her school. Despite this apparently successful transnational career, Juli experiences the incessant travel as extremely exhausting and is always under pressure to keep up her contacts.

The mobilisation of her large network of people in Cuba and Switzerland enables her to continue with this business.

Yaimara: "I found my media naranja": mobilising transnational marriage

Alongside cultivating friendships with foreigners, marriage was a strategy that often stood at the beginning of a transnational salsa career. Especially in the Cuban context, since the economic crisis in the 1990s and the increase in foreign tourism, marriage has become for many people a way of leaving the island. As Fernandez (2013) writes: "Both kin-making and cultivating friendships with foreigners have become key strategies for Cubans to ensure their own and their family's well-being" (281). For Cuban dancers, marriage is not only a way to leave the country, it is a way to enter (and remain in) Europe legally. In fact, for people of non-EU origin countries, marriage is often a way to extend their legal stay in Europe and benefit from the family reunification rights conferred to spouses of EU citizens (Andrikopoulos 2019). Due to Europe's selective migration policies, "family migration is one of the few remaining channels for those who do not fit into the privileged categories of mobility" (Moret et al. 2019: 2). The significance of a marriage with a European citizen will be demonstrated with the case of Yaimara.

Yaimara met her German husband, Felix, who was interested in Cuban music and dance, when he was in Havana to interview Yaimara's grandfather. They became friends, and whenever Felix was in Havana Yaimara helped him with his research projects. After a while they realised that they wanted to live together, and Felix invited Yaimara to Germany. "He wanted to invite me so that I could find out if I actually liked Germany or not, so he invited me", but the couple could not obtain a visa for Yaimara. They tried a second time, but "the embassy said no. Then he [Felix] said: 'OK, so I will come to Cuba, we will marry, so they can't say no anymore'". The couple thus married in Cuba, but it took another six months before Yaimara could leave the country. As scholars of cross-border marriages have pointed out, "bringing spouses from elsewhere into a European country is increasingly difficult, as many EU Member States have been tightening regulations governing spousal immigration" (Charsley 2012: 8). Thus, going through the family reunification process is often an expensive and time-consuming enterprise, as Fernandez (2013) demonstrates for Cuban marriage migration to Denmark. This was the case for Yaimara. As a further complication, she had applied for a Cuban foreign residency permit (*permiso de residencia en el exterior*), which (until 2013) was necessary to leave Cuba legally and at the same time retain one's residency, inheritance and property rights (cf Fernandez 2013: 277).

Once Yaimara had obtained all the necessary documents, she settled in Germany where she soon got a job at a big dance school and after a while started teaching regularly. She was introduced to the festival circuit through an old family friend, and thus she started her career as a *travelling artist* at European festivals. She also taught almost every day of the week in the dance school.

After some years she also started to organise dance holidays in Cuba, mobilising her networks in both places, bringing European salsa students to Havana.

Looking at Yaimara's transnational career, the marriage with a German, the mobility capital she thus acquired and the subsequent relocation to Europe proved to be turning points that opened the door to her successful transnational career. In this way, Yaimara's story reveals the importance of "kin-making" (Fernandez 2013) as a strategy to access Europe and its salsa circuit – not exclusively, but importantly for Cuban dancers.

Although I asked dancers a general question about how they had come to Europe and, due to time restraints, did not ask for an in-depth story of how they met their partners, Yaimara felt the need to label her marriage as a "love marriage". During our stay in Havana, and without my asking, she told me:

> I am married because I love my husband! You can see how many people one can get to know here, there are many tourists, but this was never important for me. When I found my half-orange,[3] I went with him.

Yaimara distanced herself from a supposed instrumental vision of marriage, a practice I also encountered in discussions with other salsa dancers. Marrying a European is a common practice for both male and female dancers. However, many interviewees were somewhat hesitant to tell me that they were married, that they had come to Europe through the legal route of family reunification and that they had obtained residency rights through marriage. This reservation can be understood because of public discourses about so-called fraudulent marriages and the politicisation of transnational marriage in many European countries (Beck-Gernsheim 2011). As Bonjour and de Hart (2013) demonstrate, increasingly restrictive family migration policies have been implemented in many European countries over recent years. This migration policy-making is shaped by (and informs) constructions of collective identities, through gendered and ethnicised practices of "othering" (Bonjour and de Hart 2013). Marriage migration is often normatively evaluated because of its "affinity to instrumental motives that represent a violation of the Western ideal of love, the breaching of a cultural taboo" (Beck-Gernsheim 2011: 61). The salsa dance professionals I interviewed know about the politicisation of transnational marriage and distance themselves from practices that could harm their images.

This distancing also points to the entanglement of emotions and instrumental or strategically motivated practices (see Charsley 2012). As scholarship on marriage demonstrates, the categorisation of "sham" versus "genuine" marriages draws on a distinction between interest and emotions (Andrikopoulos 2019). However, as Andrikopoulos (2019) argues, "material and emotive resources" may circulate between spouses (14). Though a marriage may provide Latin American dancers with considerable advantages in terms of travel opportunities, residency rights or economic gains, the emotions involved should not be overlooked, and Yaimara's insistence illustrates the significance of emotions in her marriage in her understanding and self-presentation.

Juan: "I started touring in Italy with the Tropicana": mobilising cultural capital

For dancers with a professional background in dance or music, including a diploma from one of the national universities or art schools in Cuba, there are other possibilities to leave the country and travel: the state grants selected artists and musicians foreign residency permits to live abroad (Fernandez 2013: 277). Numerous Cuban dancers in the European salsa circuit do have formal training in so-called folkloric dances in the Cuban National Folkloric Company or the National Art School or have graduated from the Cabaret Tropicana School in Havana. Many of these dancers first travelled to Europe through official "cultural exchange" arranged by the Cuban state. Several of the interviewees left Cuba for the first time on an organised tour with their dance or music ensembles. Juan's story reveals that this touring stood at the beginning of his transnational career in the European salsa circuit.

Juan, at the time of the interview in his late 40s and often cited as being among the most influential professional dancers of *Cuban salsa* in Europe, grew up in Havana. He started dancing in a *casa de cultura* and became part of a group exhibiting performances for tourists in Varadero, the main tourist hotspot in Cuba at the end of the 1990s. He started to make a living from dancing and soon became a member of the dance group at a well-known cabaret. Through his visibility as a dancer of this group, Juan eventually became a dancer at the renowned Cabaret Tropicana in Havana, a theatre offering dance spectacles since the 1940s. In the beginning of the 1990s, dancers from this company were touring in Europe (Juan mentioned Italy, Spain, Switzerland and France). On one of these occasions, the director of the company was asked to recommend two Cuban dancers who wished to teach dance in Italy. Juan seized the opportunity and started teaching dance in Italy, travelling back and forth between Cuba and Italy for several years.

JUAN: He suggested a couple to teach in Italy: salsa, Cuban dances. My teacher [name] proposed me and another girl [...] and so my career in Italy and in Europe started, let's say from a professional perspective, solo. [...] Then I got to know many people, because I worked across Italy, I started working in discos, did animations, taught. I started working in various schools. [...]

JOANNA: So, the Tropicana was finished?

JUAN: I did six months in Italy, then I went back to Cuba to dance in the Tropicana, to see my family. And sometimes I did three months in Italy, then three months there, three months here ... And from this moment my story here in Europe started.

After several years, Juan decided to stay in Italy full time. He married an Italian citizen, and he slowly started to enlarge the circle of his own students and founded his own school in Milano. He started with 200 students, and at its best times the school had about 1000 enrolled students. He also founded a dance company with Cuban dancers; now he performs on festival stages worldwide. Juan himself became an important figure, and his studio became a hub for other dancers who followed him to Italy, especially Milan, which subsequently became a spatial hub for salsa dancers of *Cuban salsa*.

Gaining access to the circuit through tours with a dance company is not uncommon for Cuban dancers. Similar to the two women discussed earlier, Juan had to build networks and legal capital in Italy before he was able to start his own dance business and the subsequent transnational career. The strategy of leaving Cuba with an officially state-sponsored company is possible for dancers with formal dance training and a diploma, whereas dancers like Yaimara (and to a certain degree Juli) had to rely on informal networks and the reputations built up in Havana itself.

As Juan's case demonstrates, the cultural capital institutionalised in the form of a diploma is convertible into mobility capital. Another dance professional Vilson, whom I met in Havana, also rendered this explicit during the interview. Vilson, a member of Cuba's national dance ensemble *Conjunto Folklórico* in Havana, had already toured and taught *Cuban dance* in several European countries (mainly in established dance academies), always returning to Cuba after some weeks. When I asked him about his travels, he told me that for him leaving and returning to Cuba did not entail difficulties, at least not in terms of the necessary legal documents.

> I never had any problems, as I am a personality of the culture of this country I never had any problems, I left, came back, left again. This happens a lot more with the *bailadores*, they don't have a title, they are not graduated, you know? They have more problems to leave than the professional *bailarínes*.

The distinction between professional dancers with institutionalised cultural capital (*bailarínes*) and the ones who have learned to dance "on the street" (*bailadores*) here becomes an important criterion in the ways mobility and thus the European salsa circuit is accessed, as it influences the possibility of leaving Cuba through official routes.

Wilfredo: "Up to now I haven't had the opportunity to travel": teaching at the edge of the salsa circuit

The previous cases demonstrate different strategies for leaving Cuba and accessing Europe, all of which were important turning points in terms of dance careers in the salsa circuit. In this last part of the Cuban case study, I turn to those dancers whose strategies to leave the country and start a dance career outside Cuba do not work. They are "stuck" at the edge of the salsa circuit, taking part through teaching tourists but unable to move outward – as exemplified by the case of Wilfredo.

I met Wilfredo during an organised salsa holiday where he assisted as a dance partner for the female participants during the lessons. In his 40s, Wilfredo has been dancing and teaching *casino* for over 20 years, after he learned to dance "on the street". He never received formal training but danced in several show groups that performed in Varadero and Havana, both tourist hotspots in Cuba. Unlike Juan, he never danced in the Tropicana or another official dance company and had no diploma. Wilfredo, a *bailador*, was keen to present himself as a serious dancer throughout the interview with me, insisting on his professionalism with visitors, despite having no diploma to prove his skills. He referred to his Cubanness and positioned himself as an authentic dancer: "because *casino* is mine, it's Cuban. No one can take this from me, it comes from my soil".

To distance himself from the numerous young men who, in his view, only dance to get to know tourists, he positioned himself as a good teacher who knew a lot about the dance and wanted to share it with interested people. During the interview, he criticised other Cuban teachers who, without having his knowledge of dance, did the same job in order to "be with tourists to have a better life" and ultimately "get a visa and get a passport". In his view, some young men in Havana are hired as dance teachers even though they do not dance very well just because they are needed as teachers for a tourist group. Talking about these men, he said:

> But the person doesn't come with this idea. You know why? Because you are giving them the passport and you are giving them the visa and everything you are giving them directly into their hands.

Wilfredo, who has been dancing and teaching in Havana for many years, saw the informal encounters made possible during dance classes in Havana as a clear opportunity for some to leave the country. He has witnessed numerous times how young men who taught dance in Havana left the country because they had married one of their female students and, less often, young women who had married their male students. Wilfredo, instead, has rarely had the opportunity to travel and has only left Cuba twice. The first time was when he was working as a tourist entertainer on a cruise ship and the second time when he travelled with a performance group Juli had organised to Europe. Wilfredo came back to Cuba and continued teaching salsa to tourists in a dance school in Havana as well as working as a dancer for organised salsa holidays. His second attempt to teach at a small salsa event in Switzerland, organised by Juli, failed due to the denial of the necessary visa: "It's not that I wouldn't like to travel, it's that up to now I haven't had the opportunity to do it. One day it will come, I don't despair. I know that someday I will be able to do it". Although Wilfredo would like to partake in the European salsa circuit, he has no possibility of doing so. Conscious of the economic differences between himself and his European salsa students, he was very clear that he would like to travel or live abroad only if he could also work there:

I'd like to [travel], but for work. I don't like to go on holidays. You know why? The moment I go on holidays, I depend on another person. You understand what I mean? The bills go on you. For example, you invite me and the bills are for you. […] I like to have my own. I'd like to buy a bottle of water and I buy it. If I'd like to buy a pair of flip-flops, I buy them. I don't need to wait for you to come from work and I sit around, chatting or watching the computer or the TV, or sleeping or eating, [wait for] you to buy something for me. No! I have two hands and two feet.

Wilfredo was well aware of the difficulties he could have finding a job elsewhere and he wants to stay independent. In his statement, he pointed to the economic disparities between the European researcher or an eventual European girlfriend and himself. He also told me about his dream of having his own dance school in Havana, but for the time being worked in Juli's school as well as joining groups like the one organised by Yaimara.

Wilfredo was able to access these job opportunities through his contacts made at a young age in a dance company. However, for other *bailadores* even finding these teaching opportunities may be impossible. The dance schools in Havana, whose rise I have described above, tend to work with formally trained dancers with a diploma in so-called folkloric dances, contemporary dance or ballet at one of Cuba's state universities. In 2014, I overheard a discussion between dance school owner Juli and one of her teachers, who suggested she hire a dancer friend. Although he insisted on the dancer's abilities, Juli did not want to hire the dancer in question because he lacked the necessary licence to engage in private-sector activities. In a study on rumba dancers in Cuba, Ana (2017) also indicates the professionalisation of Havana's dance-school scene and the potential exclusion this leads to: "This often excluded practitioners without formal training, as well as those who came from families of self-taught *rumberos* or acknowledged performers, who did not have the same opportunities to interact with tourists" (Ana 2017: 172).

Wilfredo's story demonstrates the ways in which dancers in Havana may find themselves stuck in a position at the edge of the salsa circuit: themselves hindered from partaking in transnational mobility, they are dependent on the mobility of others. They can only dream of the mobility their international students take for granted. To fly to Cuba, holders of a European passport just have to purchase a ticket and fill out a visa application, a "very small administrative detail" as Gaudette (2013: 302) calls it, pointing to the asymmetric power at work between Western students of jembe in Guinea and their teachers. Facing the same asymmetric power relations, Cuban salsa teachers in Havana depend on *Cuban salsa*'s dissemination abroad, which attracts foreign students to Cuba.

These dancers' situations are related to their positions in a transnational field where class, age, unequal travel opportunities and gender intersect. In particular, I met male dance teachers of a certain age (such as Wilfredo) as well as younger female dance teachers with family obligations, who were "stuck" in this condition. They do not perceive their localised careers as dance professionals in Havana as satisfying, because they feel completely dependent on the flow of incoming tourists. Their stuck position is furthermore amplified through tourists' imaginaries of an "authentic" Cuba, "frozen" in time (Ana 2017, see Chapter 3). In these unequal relations, dancers like Wilfredo redefine their position as legitimate dance teachers through reference to their Cubanness, embracing an essentialist position to legitimise his status as instructor.

Consolidating legal status

As became clear through the stories, dancers with Latin American passports were unable to mobilise their dancing skills and personal networks in Europe without the necessary legal documents. To access the salsa circuit for longer than the duration of one tourist visa, dancers eventually need to consolidate their legal status in Europe.

Scholars working on various economic activities related to mobility have emphasised the existence of circulatory migration patterns as an alternative to (sedentary) migration (Tarrius 1993, 2002). These authors have shown that individuals cross borders regularly to engage in economic activities such as "suitcase trading" around the Mediterranean (Peraldi 2007; Schmoll 2005). As discussed, many of the salsa dance professionals in this study developed similar forms of mobile activities, in the case of Latin American dancers initiated by a first migration to Europe. In a second step, these dancers may develop circulatory practices within and beyond Europe. However, in order to do this, they first need to establish themselves in a specific place. This is Dahinden's (2010) argument in her study on cabaret dancers who circulate between different countries to work in different cabarets. As she argues in her article, entitled "Settle down in order to stay mobile?" the women need to develop familiarity with the local context in order to keep up their circulatory movement between different places. As she states, "circular transnational mobility is only possible when the women develop some 'sedentarizing' elements in their transnational way of being" (Dahinden 2010: 330). Similarly, Qacha (2013), in a study on migration trajectories, illustrates how stages of sedentariness allow migrant women to acquire local knowledge, social networks and residency rights, which they later use to develop circulatory practices within Europe.

In her study on the mobility practices of migrants of Somali origin based in Europe, Moret (2018) demonstrates that legal status can be considered a form of capital: "legal capital". For her research participants who engage in transnational mobility, international travel was difficult with the Somali passport. For them, it was crucial to acquire legal documents that grant the possibility of crossing borders. "Legal capital ensues from migrants' social and structural position within a given context, that of their country of residence. In parallel, it is linked to the position of this state in geopolitical hierarchies of power" (Moret 2018: 115). The acquisition of a residence permit or passport of a country that scores highly in terms of legal capital is essential for dance professionals who wish to travel to salsa festivals in the USA or Europe. Furthermore, they require legal documents in order to return to their place of residence. Riccio (2001) observes similar mechanisms in the case of Senegalese transmigrants in Italy, and he concludes: "It is only when the permit is obtained and the re-entry to Italy guaranteed that Senegalese can start going backwards and forwards and manifest transnational mobility" (Riccio 2001: 590). In other words, being undocumented does not allow for cross-border mobility in the ways discussed above.

In this section, I look more closely at the phase in which some dancers are stuck; they have neither the right to stay nor the right to travel. In this way, I shed light on the legal dimensions of mobility after an initial migration and the importance of access to visa documents and residence permits in terms of working opportunities for salsa dance professionals.

Lavinia, at the time of the interview 26 years old, found herself in such difficulties: born in Mexico, she moved to Italy at the age of 21 in order to join a dance company, and started to work in Italy but had troubles regularising her status:

> The first years I was there, I didn't have the regular permit, now I have it, but the first years it was a little bit difficult to find a solution because the schools which I was working with, they were supposed to help me get my permit, but then after two years of working in the first school, we had some economic discussion, or difference, and we stopped working together. So then I lost two years of a possible, you know, because we didn't work anymore together. So it was tough, but now, it's slow the process, we have to wait and wait and pay, and pay, and wait. So yeah, bureaucracy is not easy, you have to be patient. […] I had to do it all by myself, you know, I didn't have […] a person that said, oh maybe you can do this. It was me that was always asking, what can I do, without, you know, the easiest thing that everyone does, is getting married. I didn't wanna do this. I don't know, it didn't seem correct to me, or the best thing if I could try another thing. So then I asked for their work permit. And now it's processing, it's slow, but at least I hope that I'll have it soon.

In the above quote, it is not clear whether Lavinia gained an Italian residence permit, which includes the right to work. Some months after the interview, she moved to another European country where she enrolled in a university to study dance and resided with a student visa, an alternative to marriage-based legalisation in Europe, which she refused for moral reasons.

Lavinia's story reveals again the difficulties for non-EU nationals to regularise their status in Europe in order to participate in the salsa circuit. Although she was lucky and finally found a way to stay, others are not. Many dance professionals experience periods of irregular and precarious situations.

Marcos, introduced earlier, also recalled a difficult period when he was stuck in terms of his legal rights to stay in a European country:

> I once had a problem with my visa in Sweden. And I didn't know where to go because one of the companies I was working with messed up with my taxes and I had to leave the country for a period of time. And I was pretty shocked because I didn't know what to do. And … go back to my country … come on … I cannot do that. So I said "okay, where can I go that is not in Schengen area, where I can actually stay for a while?" I called a friend from Slovenia, he said "listen, I might know the right person. Do you remember the festival in Sarajevo? You remember Eric?" I said "yes … ". "I think he can help you out". So I called him, he said, "yes man, come over here, you have an apartment". And I stayed six months [laughs].

Marcos was thus able to mobilise his network of salsa connections to get out of a difficult situation. During his stay in Sarajevo, he taught salsa and helped to organise an event locally. After the six months, he went back to Sweden, and at the time of the interview he had obtained a residence permit.

For dancers who wish to make a living by teaching salsa, residency rights and the legal right to work are essential. Acquiring these is often difficult, as the dancers depend on employers to sponsor their quest for a work permit, and the stories of dancers who had to leave Europe due to visa issues are numerous. Only those who acquired legal capital are able to build a successful career in the European salsa circuit. Legal capital is also a resource that can be transformed into mobility capital, as many dancers can only travel to limited places.

Such visa restrictions for the USA hindered Yaimara from performing at a festival she was invited to.

> Yaimara: For us Cubans it is unbelievably difficult. There are not many countries where I don't need a visa, for example Serbia, Russia and some others […]. But when I want to fly to the United States, I need a visa. Or to Turkey or other countries […] For example I wanted to go to the USA but they said no, just no.

Yaimara refers to often-cited difficulties for dancers of Cuban nationality to travel to salsa festivals in other countries; the USA is particularly difficult to enter due to the political relations between the two countries. To address these difficulties, the dancers and the inviting organisers usually try to request the necessary travel visa early, although this strategy does not always work, as Yaimara's account demonstrates.

Conclusion

This chapter has dealt with the second status passage in salsa dance professionals' transnational careers, particularly dancers with Latin American nationality. It discussed the ways Cuban dancers accessed the European salsa circuit, taking into account the opportunity structures and constraints related to diverse regimes of mobility.

As I have shown, in order to access the European salsa circuit, Latin American dance professionals need more than dancing skills. They need to physically be in a salsa hub to mobilise manifold resources and build up social networks, mobility capital and legal capital to leave their country as well as consolidate their legal status to be mobile later on. To account for the related cross-border mobility of differently positioned salsa dancers, I suggest applying the notion of "entangled mobilities". In this respect, the circulation of imaginaries and the mobility of salsa tourists play a crucial role.

In addition, the strategies of the discussed dancers often included the mobilisation of resources in social networks and thus demonstrate the importance of social capital in accessing the European salsa circuit. As literature on migration has demonstrated, social networks are often vital, as they provide information and facilitate migration (Massey et al. 1987). A large body of literature in migration research builds on the idea of "chain migration", explaining international migration systems with "the presence of social relations channelling migrants and developing an ever denser network of connections between places" (Pathirage and Collyer 2011: 318). This literature usually focuses on social relations between aspiring migrants and established migrants from the same country of origin, thus focusing on social capital present in family or ethnic ties, people of a supposed "group". In the case of the salsa dancers I spoke to, relations to other Cuban dancers already established in Europe were occasionally mentioned and proved helpful in some cases. However, in many cases the dancers I interviewed relied on social ties they had created with European salsa students, who had come to Cuba to improve their dancing. Therefore, as I have shown, for salsa dance professionals engaged in practices of circulation in or migration to Europe, social capital often derives from friendship instead of family or ethnic networks, as is often assumed in migration studies (Dahinden 2013; Ryan 2015).

In a study on the dissemination of the Senegalese dance sabar in Europe, Aterianus-Owanga (2019) notes the importance of European women for the organisation of Senegalese dancers' careers in Europe. As she writes about European women:

> Some of them are married with Senegalese musicians or dancers and organise workshops for them in their home city in Europe, contributing largely to the promotion of sabar and Senegal in European contexts, by making their economic and cultural capitals available for their husbands' or friends' activities.
>
> (Aterianus-Owanga 2019: 354)

Similarly, this chapter has shown that for Cuban salsa dancers, contacts with salsa students were established and nurtured; in some cases they proved highly effective in gaining access to the European salsa circuit.

"Entangled mobilities" encompass more than social capital; they also encompass mobility capital. However, I would argue that the cited model of motility omits an important element: the imaginaries of other places and different lives. As this chapter's analysis of the strategies of Latin American salsa dance professionals to access the European salsa circuit has made clear, in many cases, imaginaries of a certain "cosmopolitan lifestyle" lie at the base of a first move into the direction of a transnational career. I would thus argue to enlarge the concept of "mobility capital" (Kaufmann et al. 2004) with the dimension of imaginaries, in line with Appadurai's (1990) and Salazar's (2011) arguments of the importance of the imagination in structuring human mobility.

However, access to the European salsa circuit is but one passage in the transnational career: once invited to a festival or another salsa event, dance professionals need to build their reputations in the festival circuit, a process entailing social capital and salsa capital, as the next chapter will explore.

Notes

1 Beck and Sznaider (2006), for example, argue for a "methodological cosmopolitanism" in social sciences, while Nowicka and Rovisco (2009) distinguish between cosmopolitanism as a practice and as a moral ideal.
2 As has been argued, "virtual travel" (Urry 2007) is also a form of mobility interconnected with the here-described "imaginative travel". As McMains (2015: 268) shows, online connections between dancers based in the USA and in Europe indeed played an important role in the development of the European salsa circuit in the early 2000s. However, when it comes to access to the circuit, "virtual travel" does not appear to be of particular importance in my data. In this, the limited cases and the overrepresentation of Cuban dance professionals in my data may also play a role, as these dancers often had no access to the internet in their own country, unlike the dancers based in the USA studied by McMains.
3 Yaimara said "meine orange Hälfte" in German, which is a direct translation from *mi media naranja*, used in Spanish to describe "one's soulmate".

7   Building up reputation

This chapter addresses the third status passage of salsa dance professionals' transnational careers: the building and maintenance of reputation in the affective economy of the salsa circuit. According to Bourdieu's (1993, 1986) framework, artistic fields are characterised by struggles over reputation inside the field in question. In these struggles, a specific set of resources is particularly valuable, once recognised by other actors of the salsa circuit: social capital, but also mobility, "authenticity" and bodily attributes. Following Bourdieu's capital theory, the distribution of these resources influences a dancer's position and structures the social order of dancers in the salsa circuit. This chapter draws on a Bourdieusian perspective on the question of power relations and enlarges it to account for dancers' embodied doings. Reputation is here understood as being linked to a dance professional's social capital with what I coined "salsa capital".

Chapters 5 and 6 have both addressed the importance of social networks and the social capital therein. However, the notion of social capital has thus far remained under-theorised. Drawing on parts of the already cited material, the first section of this chapter suggests an analysis of salsa dancers' social capital through the perspective of (qualitative) social network literature (Dahinden 2010, 2013; Ryan and Mulholland 2014; Schapendonk 2015). It asks how dancers access social capital embedded in their networks.

The second part of this chapter discusses the resources mobilised in the construction of "salsa capital". Salsa capital varies in volume and structure, and it must be contextualised. Salsa capital is valid inside the salsa circuit but difficult to transfer to other contexts. It has to be enhanced through a dancer's presence at events in the salsa circuit, and dancers face a constant struggle to maintain their capital. Individuals' "position-taking" further mediates their capital; hence, actors strategise to mobilise resources and build capital (Bourdieu 1986). Salsa dance professionals endowed with a large volume of salsa capital are able to pursue successful transnational careers, including teaching and performance opportunities, thus converting salsa capital into economic capital, a process further discussed in this chapter's conclusion.

Social capital in the salsa circuit

To construct successful careers, dance professionals need to create and maintain social relationships with a variety of other actors in and outside of the salsa circuit. To theorise social capital in the process of reputation building, I draw on literature of qualitative social network analysis in migration studies (Dahinden 2010, 2013; Ryan and Mulholland 2014; Schapendonk 2015) and in studies of professions (Burt 1998; Granovetter 1983; Wagner 2006, 2015). The main goal of studies of social network analysis is to describe the embeddedness of actors in a web of specific social relations (Dahinden 2010). Social relations introduce possibilities and constraints that affect actors' scopes of action (Schweizer 1988).

Drawing on Bourdieu's conceptualisation of social capital, Lin (1999) develops a "network theory of social capital" and defines social capital as "resources embedded in a social structure which are accessed and/or mobilized in purposive actions" (35). In other words, "The core idea of network social capital is that people better equipped with social resources – in the sense of their social relations and the resources of others that they can draw upon – will succeed better in attaining their goals" (Dahinden 2013: 44). However, social networks are not a "natural given"; rather they have to be created and sustained, and they are products of maintenance work (Bourdieu 1980a: 2). Following the argument for a "practice approach" to social networks by Schapendonk (2015), I consider networks not as static structures but rather as dynamic. This approach is particularly well suited to analyse the ways salsa dance professionals build up reputation because it demonstrates in detail how "networking practices" (Schapendonk 2015) lead to the evolution of transnational careers.

The first two parts of this section consider social relationships inside the salsa circuit, which provide salsa dance professionals with salsa-related resources. First, I look at the importance of co-presence and networking practices in accessing and building up relations with various actors. Next, I explore the ties to four categories of social actors that are crucial, as they may play the role of gatekeeper in the process of accessing performance and teaching opportunities, thus gaining more visibility and recognition: salsa event organisers, promoters and dance students, as well as fellow dance professionals. In the last section, the focus is broadened to include relationships with actors outside the salsa circuit and a discussion of how such ties may actually hinder the development of transnational careers.

"It doesn't matter how great you are, if you don't have the network": organisers, promoters and dance students

To access the salsa circuit, dancers sometimes rely on the travels of others, as I discussed in Chapter 6. However, once they aspire to work at salsa festivals and construct successful transnational careers, dancers need to travel themselves, in order to access new networks and open up new working opportunities. Hence, social capital is accessed through the mobilisation of mobility capital.

Salsa festivals represent the most important hub: actors of the salsa circuit meet and exchange in co-present encounters. Building on Goffman (1963), Urry (2003) writes, "These co-present encounters are located within time and space, there is a 'gathering' in which people must sense that they are close enough to be seen and to see others" (165). In such face-to-face interactions, dance professionals exchange information, establish trust and build up their reputations. However, this relies on active networking strategies. The salsa dance professionals I interviewed all mentioned the importance of active networking in building reputations. In Maria's words: "If you choose to be present at the international events, then of course it's all about kind of making contacts". Dancers were "conscious of, and reflexive about, the ways they networked" (Ryan and Mulholland 2014: 154), similar to the highly skilled migrants in London in Ryan and Mulholland's study.

Networking strategies rely on specific skills such as sociability and communication skills. The way Marcos put it is telling: "It doesn't matter how great you are, if you don't have the network". Becker (1963) describes a similar process in his study on (male-only) jazz musicians:

> In short, to get these job positions requires both ability and the formation of informal relationships of mutual obligation with men who can sponsor one for the jobs. Without the necessary minimum of ability one cannot perform successfully at the new level, but this ability will command the appropriate kind of work only if a man has made the proper connection.
>
> (Becker 1963: 107)

Male and female salsa dance professionals thus strive to make the "proper connection" in the salsa circuit.

As scholars of network social capital have demonstrated, social capital varies with network composition (Burt 1983; Dahinden 2013). Building social ties with a diverse range of people is likely to create "entrepreneurial opportunity" (Burt 1998: 9). To construct a successful career, salsa dance professionals not only need large and expansive networks; their networks also need to be diversified in terms of positions in the salsa circuit, as this guarantees access to different resources. The following sections focus on the different actors with whom salsa dance professionals form ties.

Menger (1999) describes creative artists as freelancing workers who "may themselves be seen as small firms building subcontractual relations with artistic organizations" (546). In the case of salsa dance professionals, these "artistic organizations" mainly consist of event organisers and event promoters. Event organisers are often dancers themselves who have been active in the salsa circuit for a long time and thus possess a large network of fellow organisers and dance professionals. They take charge of or delegate all tasks behind the organisation of the salsa event: financial aspects and organisational tasks regarding the room location, publicity and programme of an event, including the invitation of dance instructors and performers. Organisers work closely with so-called promoters, whose task consists of attracting paying guests to an event through advertising strategies in local dance studios or at other dance events. Promoters are usually remunerated with free entry tickets or spots on a prestigious stage.

For dance professionals, building direct ties to organisers may prove particularly beneficial as these actors, once convinced to collaborate, are in the position to help advance dancers' careers by inviting them to their event, as seen in the case of Marcos who was invited to the US through a contact he made while in Japan. When dancers wish to participate at an event but have no direct contact to the organisers, other actors may become important. Here, promoters are crucial, as they may "broker the flow of information" (Burt 1998: 8) between event organisers and salsa dance professionals. As scholars of social networks have argued, bridges in networks are essential in facilitating information and influence (Burt 1992; Granovetter 1983). For locating and obtaining resources, such as looking for a job or a better job, actors need to access and extend bridges in the network (Lin 1999: 34).

His relationship to an event promoter enabled Alejandro to perform and teach at a prestigious festival. Karl, in his role of event promoter, told me in the interview that he can "bring on stage" a dancer every year. He had mobilised about 40 paying attendees and could thus recommend a chosen salsa dance professional to the organiser of the event. As a dance student, Karl had known Alejandro for several years and had taken private lessons with him. As he told me, he particularly likes Alejandro's school: "it's one of the coolest schools, thanks to its family-character". Karl thus approached Alejandro, who was more than willing to participate in the festival. In this way, Alejandro and his dance partner had a chance to perform at a festival, which they would not have had without ties to Karl. In the salsa circuit, promoters like Karl create links between different actors, thus spanning "structural holes" (Burt 1992).

A third category of people is indirectly important in salsa dance professionals' networking strategies: students. After gaining their first access to the salsa circuit, dancers invest in their own careers and concentrate on jobs that contribute to their reputation building even if they have to work unpaid (for a similar observation see Freakley and Neelands 2003: 55). In this way, dancers in the early stage of their career actively contact festival organisers and promoters and offer performance and teaching – for free. They also invest in their own travel, accommodation and entry fees, thus drawing on economic capital. Moreover, their ties to salsa students may be a crucial element, as the following explanation from an interview with a salsa promoter illustrates:

> Very often you don't get anything. In general, without having a name, you have to assume that you don't get anything. Additionally you even have to bring something to be allowed to perform. [...] If you bring enough people [paying attendees], and you have to be a good dancer [...] And if you bring really a lot of people, they may pay for your hotel. And if you really really bring a lot of people, like 50 people or maybe 35, 40 people, then you get the hotel and the flight. And if you really

want money, like [names some of the *salsa stars*], [...] they really get money, but there, you know, they are the headliners, they bring people [through their reputation].

Congress organisers always invite some of the well-known *salsa stars* to attract paying participants to their events. Salsa dance professionals of lesser reputation in the salsa circuit may nevertheless have a large group of local students at their disposal. As congress organisers wish to attract these students to travel to their event, some of them do promotional deals like the example described above. For dance professionals with teaching activities in a local school, this means that the ties they have built with their own students become a resource to mobilise in the process of the construction of a transnational career. Students become a resource only under the condition that they have the necessary means and are willing to travel. As already discussed, dance professionals who teach in local salsa studios develop several strategies to keep their students interested and loyal: besides an evolving curriculum with ever new content, they organise monthly or weekly parties in their studios, go out together at weekends or organise dance trips to other countries. As Ryan and Mulholland (2014) argue, based on Bourdieu's classical argument, "social ties are not spontaneous but require effort and nurturing" (148). Salsa dance professionals thus nurture relationships with their students who then follow them to events.

"We performed together in a show": dance partners

Besides ties to event organisers, promoters and dance students, building up relationships with a fourth category of actors in the salsa circuit is of high interest: other salsa dance professionals or peers. Dancers exchange information about job opportunities or they may introduce a new dancer to an event organiser they already know. Gary, who struggled to build up a salsa career after his arrival in Germany in the late 1990s, told me about his meeting with a more experienced dancer:

> And then I met [name of a salsa dancer], he's a legend from New York. And he toured in Europe and I was by chance in [city in Germany] and there I got to know him and he helped me, he opened up the door for me, to be solo at a congress for the first time, in Germany in 2000. And I'm so grateful to him, we performed together in a show, then I had my solo, I taught workshops and then it started rolling.

Although the collaboration between Gary and the more experienced dancer lasted for only the duration of this one event, it takes an important place in Gary's description of his career. Through his performance on the stage of a salsa event with international outreach, being seen together with a well-known dancer, Gary was able to enhance his prestige in the salsa circuit. As sociologists of art have noticed, "being seen" is of high interest in any artistic field.

> To be seen, discovered and recognized, to be attributed to the field or to
> be given the opportunity to take part of certain assets of the field, that is,
> to have symbolic capital, is of decisive importance in the field of art in
> particular.
>
> (Svensson 2015: 4)

Furthermore, Gary made contacts with fellow dancers; in this way his
transnational career started unfolding. As this example illustrates, fellow dance
professionals may "open up the door" for dancers and become gatekeepers to
the salsa circuit.

A specific form of the professional relationship salsa dance professionals engage
in are dance partners, who are often decisive for reputation building and the
construction of a dancer's transnational career. Although there are different forms
of work constellations, from travelling and performing solo to being part of
a dance company, most salsa dance professionals perform and teach with another
dance professional (most commonly of the opposite sex) for periods of time. To
analyse these relationships, I loosely draw on Wagner's model of "career
coupling", adding a focus on gender and romance, whose importance in the salsa
couple is specific to the salsa profession. Career coupling is defined as a "social
process, which concerns the parallel professional routes of two or more actors
who cooperate, each in their own specialty, during the time necessary for them
to change their rank in their respective professional worlds" (Wagner 2006: 78).
Wagner develops the idea of career coupling in her analysis of the interaction
between the careers of virtuoso musicians and elite scientists. The actors in her
study collaborate closely and jointly build their careers, with the goal of moving
up in the professional hierarchy of their respective fields. Career coupling
happens between people at different stages in their careers: newcomers and
initiators, whereby both categories depend on the work of the other (Wagner
2006: 85). In the salsa circuit as well, newcomers strive to become dance partners
of established dancers whose reputations and networks may help to construct
their own careers. Established dancers may need to find a new dance partner
after a break-up with a former partner or a change of location.

Obviously, the process of career coupling in salsa dancing is gendered, as
the roles during salsa performances and teaching are often highly gendered
(see Figure 7.1). Romance plays an important role in dance partnerships: salsa
couples often not only form professional dance couples but also publicly share
that they are involved romantically, for example on Facebook.

In the first phase of the career coupling process, the "matching", two
dancers decide to become professional dance partners. Salsa dancers often
decide to perform together after becoming a couple in private life. In the
process of matching, different criteria have to be considered, such as a similar
dedication to construct a transnational career, including time and location
constraints as well as questions of aesthetic–artistic elements. If dancers live in
separate places and wish to work together in a local school or with a local
company, one of them may move to the other's location, as seen with the

Figure 7.1 A salsa couple performing at a show.
Source: © Valentin Behringer.

case of Lavinia, who left Mexico and moved to Italy to work and train on a daily basis with her new dance partner. The same holds for Maria, who met her future dance partner at one of the festivals, whereupon she was offered a teaching job in his dance studio in Norway.

During the phase of matching, dancers need to clarify and match their career goals and the ways they wish to work together, including the decision for a place to meet for joint trainings. Additionally, aesthetic elements are often mentioned as important criteria. Ajay told me how he met his current dance partner, with whom he has been working for eight years.

> [I found my partner] at a salsa festival. She attended my workshop, I saw what she was doing and she picked up very fast, and her style and movement is very similar to mine. She was almost a carbon copy of what I was doing. So that really fascinated me, and she also liked my style in dancing a show. I asked her if she would like to work together, and she agreed. And the rest is history.

Once two dancers match and decide to become dance partners, they enter the phase of "active collaboration" (Wagner 2006: 79). In this phase, the other actors in the salsa circuit learn about the collaboration and "the names of the collaborators are joined" (Wagner 2006: 79). They now construct their careers together and reputation is attached to their joint names. In the salsa circuit, salsa couples are announced in festival programmes and on stages with their names, for example "Iannis and Alicia".[1] In this process, private and professional life often becomes intertwined, as famous salsa couples celebrate their love story on social media and romance becomes part of the marketing strategy of the couple. In this phase, dance partners travel together to salsa events, and they are able to build on the networks of both dancers, thus enlarging their job opportunities. The lesser-known actor becomes recognised in the salsa circuit through the well-known partner while established actors are able to maintain their reputations as *travelling artists* through collaboration with a matching partner. Whenever a relationship ends, the dancers need to renegotiate their dance partnership, and often the search for a new dance partner begins.

"It's too much all over the place": mobility's implications

So far, I have discussed social networks inside the salsa circuit as enabling dance professionals to access new resources and construct their transnational careers. However, as research on social networks has highlighted, social ties may also hinder actors from developing mobile careers. Faist (2000) argues that social ties keep people in one place. Furthermore, "life courses cannot be fully understood as individual trajectories only" (Leemann 2010: 613), often they also affect other family members or partners, as studies on the mobility of academics have argued (e.g. Leemann 2010; Schaer et al. 2017).

In this vein, dancers mentioned challenges in terms of relationships related to their *travelling* to different salsa events. These difficulties are especially common in social relationships outside of salsa. Several of the interviewed dancers mentioned the inverse working rhythm they follow, which render meetings with non-salsa friends and family difficult as the dancers often work during the evenings (teach) and are away at weekends. Clara told me that she really missed her dog during their weekends away, which was for her a reason to stay at home at least one weekend a month and travel less to salsa events. The constant travelling also influences the couple relationships. As mentioned above, some of the research participants travelled with their partner, forming a dance couple as well. Others preferred to stay single in order to be independent. Andy, who pursues a solo career as dance teacher in the festival circuit, stated:

> You know, I'm gonna say it, I'm very selfish about what I do because I love it so much. And selfish because I don't wanna give up my passion for, you know, if you find a woman or wife or children, you need to compromise, you know, I don't think I'm ready for that yet. So and I'm happy with what I am.

Several of the interviewed dancers felt that their transnational careers were more important to them than a stable relationship. Others wished to be in a stable relationship but accepted that it was not compatible with their travelling.

> I'm actually single. And being all the time that kind of on the way … It's hard to be with someone when you have a lifestyle this way. You know, you travel all the time, you're devoted to your job. Yeah, for now I think it's OK. Until I kind of finally settle down, maybe it will be much easier.

Like Marcos in this statement, several of the interviewed dancers affirmed that they see their mobile lifestyle as temporary due to the sacrifices it entails in terms of romantic relationships or starting a family. Studies of highly mobile professionals have indicated the difficulties related to such a mobile lifestyle. Lipphardt, in her research with EU-funded artists, argues against a too narrow celebration of artists' mobility:

> What gets lost in these official narratives is an understanding of the highly ambivalent character of this lifestyle and work-mode: artists nowadays may indeed enjoy the most privileged form of mobility, but for many this also means to live permanently on the edge, financially, socially and emotionally.
>
> (Lipphardt 2012: 121)

While my data does not allow me to draw such a precarious image of salsa dance professionals' careers or the opposite, the mobile lifestyle clearly has its limitations, and they are often articulated at the intersections of family life/ partnership, gender and mobility.

While male dancers mentioned the need to compromise between partners and their transnational careers, several female interviewees told me that they could not imagine travelling to salsa events once they had children. Gendered representations of childcare work as a female activity were particularly strong in female salsa dancers' discourse (see also McMains 2015: 307). Anna's case demonstrates this. A dancer in her late 40s, Anna consciously changed her career from a transnational to a local one, due to her age and the birth of a child. As she explained to me: "And now it is calmer, now I have a child. Many have a child first and then a career, but I had first a dance career and now a child, in the last moment [laughs]". For Anna, the transnational career could not be combined with having a child, so she decided to travel less and concentrate on her own studio. In a similar vein, the young salsa dance professional Irena clearly sees her transnational career as temporary:

> I love dancing, this is my passion, I can't imagine my live without this, but I know this is not really forever, you know. Especially for women. You know, you wanna have a family, you need to look after kids, all that and I definitely would love to have kids in the future. So the life- style we have, I don't see this working for starting a family. Because it's too much all over the place, you know.

Irena's account of her imagined future is gendered, as she sees the high mobility necessary for her work as incompatible with her wish to start a family and relates this to her being a woman. Her partner, who was present during this interview, on the contrary, did not express the same concern for a more stable lifestyle in the future. Such gendered representations, which assign women responsibility over childcare and men the role of breadwinner may therefore produce gendered practices of mobility, whereby female dancers choose to stop travelling and male dancers continue.

Academic literature about gender and mobility/migration amply demonstrates the effects that gendered representations of care work in general have on the professional life and mobility trajectories of women (Kofman and Raghuram 2015). In a study about work careers among academics in Europe and North America, Scheibelhofer (2008) found gendered patterns of mobility over the life course, explaining that physical presence to provide care for the elderly and the children was often expected from women. Similarly, Jöns (2011) states:

> Although men are also increasingly affected by mobility constraints result- ing from dual-career relationships, gendered patterns of partnering and household labour are the main reasons for why most female researchers still face greater barriers for participating in transnational academic mobil- ity than their male colleagues.
>
> (205)

Schaer et al. (2017) also observe that becoming parents "stands out as a key turning point in a couple's configuration" (1304), as it may lead early-career academics to embrace less equal gender roles in the family organisation. While these studies underline the importance of gendered representations of care work as well as structural issues such as access to the provision of childcare, they also hint to individuals' possibility to contest such gendered roles (Schaer et al. 2017; Shinozaki 2014). Similarly, my findings indicate that some salsa dance professionals find new arrangements, for example, with other family members and continue being mobile (such as Juli), while others renounce their transnational careers. Social ties to family members and gendered patterns of care work may therefore also lead to the abandonment of a transnational career.

Although being mobile (or *travelling* in salsa dancers' emic term) is often represented as an achievement and linked to a dancer's position in the salsa circuit, for many dancers it is also a necessity that affects other domains of their lives. In sum, to build a reputation in the salsa circuit, dancers need to travel and make new connections, but this travelling depends not only on themselves but also on other actors such as friends, partners or family members, and the transnational careers are thus gendered.

Salsa capital in the salsa circuit

Drawing on Bourdieu's work on economies of symbolic goods (1980b) and inspired by Törnqvist's (2013) analysis of the "intimate dance economy" of

Argentinean tango in Buenos Aires, this section explores the construction of "salsa capital" in the affective economy of the salsa circuit. Salsa capital is a form of capital dancers construct by mobilising different resources and forms of social and symbolic capital (as well as, less discussed here, economic and cultural capital). Bourdieu defines symbolic capital as follows:

> Symbolic capital is an ordinary property (physical strength, wealth, warlike valor, etc.) which, perceived by social agents endowed with the categories of perception and appreciation permitting them to perceive, know and recognize it, becomes symbolically efficient, like a veritable *magical power*: a property which, because it responds to socially constituted "collective expectations" and beliefs, exercised a sort of action from a distance, without physical contact.
>
> (Bourdieu 1998: 102)

This section looks at some of those "ordinary properties" that are loaded with special significance. It explores different ordinary properties that are recognised as values in the salsa circuit and thus figure as resources that dance professionals may use in the process of reputation building.[2]

Salsa capital builds on the negotiations between differently positioned actors, whereby dance professionals mobilise various resources to distinguish themselves from other dancers. To be acknowledged as a legitimate salsa dance performer and teacher, dancing skills are crucial, but they are far from the only skills their salsa capital is built on; salsa dance professionals also have to develop teaching skills, a certain degree of entertainment skills and comfort with being a public persona (Bunten 2008) at congresses, as the discussion of affective labour in Chapter 5 has demonstrated. This section discusses other resources dance professionals build on to construct salsa capital in the affective economy of the salsa circuit: visible geographical mobility, as well as embodied, gendered and ethnicised resources.

"Off to ... ?? I don't know, lol": mobility and salsa capital

As argued throughout this book, mobility is an important resource dance professionals need to acquire, first, to access the salsa circuit and, second, to access new networks related to job opportunities (social capital). Visible geographical mobility can enhance a dancer's salsa capital in two ways: as a form of credential of symbolic capital and as a form of investment in "authenticity".

In interviews with dance professionals, being on the move was often represented as a sign of a successful career. I term this symbolic dimension of mobility as a resource the "tale of mobility". As Iannis put it, "you have a dream, to achieve a goal and travel. When somebody says 'I will bring you [to an event]', I feel really really nice". In the salsa circuit, the practice of regular cross-border mobility is not only part of the dream of a "cosmopolitan lifestyle"; it also enhances dance professionals with salsa capital.

JOANNA: And what are your actual projects right now?

ANDY: There is no project, it's just, I'm booked up till next October, every weekend.

JOANNA: Every weekend?

ANDY: Yeah, we all travel every weekend, so everybody you see here this weekend, we are booked up in other events for the whole year. I've been like this from 2001, I wouldn't have a weekend off for about 14 years now.

In this quote from an interview during the month of October, Andy boasts of his *travelling* to salsa events for the next 12 months. The importance of the "tale of mobility" is also demonstrated by numerous descriptions in artist biographies on websites, on Facebook and in festival programmes and clearly illustrated by the following marketing sentence: "Taught in more than 70 countries".

To be recognised as a form of symbolic resource, mobility has to be rendered visible. Similarly, speaking of professional ballroom dancers, Marion (2012) writes: "Just as the dancing costumes of ballroom dance competitors are designed to help them be seen on the competition floor, their wide-ranging travel raises their visibility and status as competitors and performers" (8). The above quotations exemplify the performative dimension of mobility. To add to their physical presence at an event, salsa dance professionals use Facebook as the main tool for self-promotion. Dancers here state where they will travel, sometimes putting a whole list of confirmed workshops, sometimes just letting their followers know where they will go next, such as this Germany-based dancer: "only 12 hours at home then off to Singapore". Through such status news, the dancers not only demonstrate their importance as invited artists in such faraway places but also render their mobility visible for others.

In this process, with the exception of Cuba and New York, the actual destination becomes secondary, as the following Facebook status of a travelling salsa artist exemplifies: "Off to … ?? I don't know, lol".[3] In terms of reputation building, the fact that a dancer *travels* to perform at salsa events is more important than the actual place or country of the festival. In the case of the salsa circuit, practices of cross-border mobility are often reduced to a short period of time, such as teaching and performance opportunities at salsa events for three days or, in rare cases, up to a week. This short-term travelling must be visible through constant performance and repetition in virtual space for reputation to grow.

The phenomenon of mobility as a career-enhancing element and a form of symbolic capital is known from studies of other professional fields. Bauder, Hannan and Lujan (2016: 3) adapt the notion of "mobility fetishism" in the academic field to indicate the importance of mobility in the careers of academic researchers. As they write, "researchers strategically pursue mobility to enhance their value as researchers" (Bauder et al. 2016: 3). In a similar vein, Schaer et al. (2017) critically indicate the "imperative of mobility" in academia. However, in academia, the specific place or university a researcher goes to is important as well: a "post-doctoral experience at a prestigious foreign university can generate 'reputational capital' that is appreciated by hiring committees" (Bauder et al. 2016: 3). The same holds true for the processes of reputation building in the salsa circuit, where the travel to specific teachers or places ranked highly in the salsa circuit is significant, due to salsa's supposed historical "roots" imagined in specific geographic places.

Hence, secondly, mobility is used as an investment in authenticity: as seen, salsa dancers at an early stage of their transnational careers often choose to take dance lessons at specific places that are historically associated with salsa. Greece-based Iannis told me why it was important for him to go to New York.

> Actually that summer I went to New York, again to take some work-shops and to learn new things, I was at the congress there as well. And I was thinking of coming back and opening it [dance studio], because I wanted to do New York-style salsa. I wanted to bring something new to Greece […] I had some classes already, in other studios, and I had a degree in Latin International ballroom, you know. But I wanted to teach salsa so I went to New York and I said I'm gonna bring this to [Greek city]. That happened in 2008.

Taking lessons with teachers based in New York or Cuba not only enhances a dancer's technique but also creates value for use back home. As Iannis puts it, in order to "bring this to Greece", he needed to be in physical contact with salsa instructors in a specific place – New York. Once they have been "there", dancers are able to transfer the acquired "danced knowledge" (Farnell 2012: 2) through their own mobility and validate their teaching practices. The acquired dance skills as well as the fact that they have "acquired context" (Bizas 2014) through "being there" legitimises and authorises these dancers as knowledgeable. As the discussion demonstrated, mobility can be transformed into social advantages in reputation and thus becomes mobility capital.

"She looks exotic": bodies and salsa capital

In her analysis of the intimate economy of tango in Buenos Aires, Törnqvist (2013) describes tango as an "economy of the flesh". She states, "The fact that dancers enter into the tango with and through their bodies, implying that the practice is primarily an economy of the flesh, stresses the significance of appearance" (Törnqvist 2013: 69). Keeping in mind this chapter's focus on salsa capital of dance professionals (as opposed to the mixed tango salons of Törnqvist's study design), a similar claim can be made for salsa: bodily appearance matters. As in other parts of social life, popular physiognomic features may be an asset, as Hakim (2010) argues in terms of the importance of "erotic capital" and "erotic power" in late-modern societies. In the affective economy of the salsa circuit, salsa capital can be enhanced through the values attached to bodies considered beautiful and sexually attractive, defined along a salsa-related aesthetic sometimes including authenticity markers such as dark hair or dark skin (see Törnqvist 2013: 69 for a similar discussion in tango tourism).

Salsa dance professionals engage in various forms of what has been termed "body work" (Gimlin 2007) to shape their bodies in particular ways. They engage in techniques such as dieting, working out, hairstyling and hair removal, the application of cosmetics and cosmetic surgery (cf McClure 2015: 39). Dark sunglasses, fancy shoes and tight clothes are popular accessories among male and female salsa dancers alike. In addition, salsa artists need special costumes for performances as well as social dancing, as the parties at salsa events often propose a themed party with a dress code. McClure even writes of "the image era of salsa" (see also Marion 2014 for a discussion of glamour and style in dancesport). The "body work" is used to attain a certain appearance particularly valued in the affective economy of the salsa circuit, which also changes with general trends in pop cultural and the fashion industry.

Furthermore, bodies are used to construct specific looks with attached ethnicised and racialised meanings. Iannis and Alicia, a young Greek salsa couple, discussed the importance of "looks" during the interview:

IANNIS: Another thing that I like [about salsa], on the dance floor: it doesn't matter, I mean if you are a doctor or a lawyer or you are a painter or whatever. It doesn't, no one asks you. If you are black or white, it doesn't matter … Maybe it matters, if you are black.

ALICIA: It's better!

IANNIS: It's better [laughs] You know, you look more like a Latino, and it feels nice. […]

ALICIA: I've heard this, because in summer I'm even […] darker [laughs]. Yeah, I get this sometimes. Because you know, dancing, and the hair and …

IANNIS: She looks exotic, that's why, that's the truth.

ALICIA: In summer maybe.

JOANNA: So is it a plus for a salsa dancer?

ALICIA: Yes, I think so, as a salsa dancer yes.

As this discussion suggests, to "look like a Latino" may enhance a dancer's salsa capital. Here, "Latino" is stereotypically equated with black or dark skin, a state Alicia reaches through tanning during the summer. The other signifier of Latinness for female dancers is long, wavy hair, exactly the way Alicia wears it – like many other female salsa performers. She is thus able to obtain an "exotic" look, as Iannis puts it, a resource that is regarded as valuable in performing on salsa stages.

The interview extract exemplifies the ways that female bodies in particular are exoticised in the salsa circuit. Studies of the exoticisation of black male and female bodies in performance spaces have pointed to the sexualisation of these bodies (García 2013). In salsa, not only female bodies are exoticised and racialised, as already seen in Ernesto's description of "young black Cubans with open shirts" (who threaten his career) in Chapter 3. Following Ernesto's logic, *Cuban salsa* in the festival context is racialised, and blackness may enhance a male dancer's embodied salsa capital as a marker of "authenticity". The cited examples point to the importance of the intersections of gender and race in the construction of salsa capital related to a dancer's body (a point I will further discuss in the conclusion of this book). Hence, bodily appearance and "body work" (Gimlin 2007) are mobilised to construct salsa capital.

"Girls are just 'the dancer of'": gender and salsa capital

Chapter 4 has analysed in detail how gender is (re)produced through the doings of salsa dancers. To analyse the specific ways in which differently positioned dancers negotiate and do gender, it was necessary to explore the gender conventions in depth. However, gender is also a key resource, which salsa dance professionals mobilise in the construction of reputation. I will now focus on gendered representations of dance professionals' roles in order to shed light on gendered strategies to access salsa capital.

Scholars of salsa dance have noted "gender inequalities" regarding dance professionals' careers in the salsa industry (McMains 2015; Pietrobruno 2006). McMains (2015) notes that female salsa teachers and performers often earn less money than their male counterparts. She furthermore argues that the inequalities stem "from broader sexual inequalities in society: the expectation that women will have primary caretaking responsibilities for children and a culture of courtship that makes women more vulnerable to harassment and exploitation when working in nightlife industries" (McMains 2015: 286). These findings were echoed during my interviews with female salsa dance professionals, several of whom raised the topic of sexism. Recalling her first steps in the salsa circuit, Lavinia told me that in her perspective, the salsa industry is "a men's world":

> I remember in the beginning, when no one knew me, no one talked to me. And no one said hi, and no one said, "oh who are you", [they rather said:] "ah you are the dancer of ...." You know, because they were used to seeing things like that, the girls are just "the dancer of". And for me it was not respectful because it's not that I am not taking credit from my dance partner, I know he has more experience, but it's also like: I have done my school, I have paid for my lessons, I have done a lot of things for my career, so I'm also a professional.

Female salsa dancers often experience being treated as just "the dancer of" their male dance partner, and feel they have to struggle to gain respect in salsa. Lavinia links the non-recognition with the fact of being a female dancer and predominant ideas of salsa femininities. In a similar vein, scholarship on popular music has demonstrated that music critics often privilege male performers (Schmutz and Faupel 2010). As Whiteley (2000) argues, in discussions of "authorship", male performers and male-dominated musical styles are often more advantaged than their female counterparts. Similarly, in the salsa music industry cultural production is found to be primarily in the hands of male musicians (Aparicio 1998; Washburne 2008). The common expression "the dancer of", which is reserved for female salsa dancers, indicates underlying gendered representations of autonomous male dancers and dependent female dancers. Feminist scholars have analysed such representations as being informed by longstanding notions of autonomy and agency as related to masculinity, whereas femininity has been portrayed as dependent (see Butler 1990). In the salsa circuit, gender thus influences how salsa capital can be accumulated – in different ways for male and female dance professionals.

Teresa, former owner of a dance studio who then moved to join her well-known dance partner (and later husband) in Italy, told me that she often has to clarify her status as not just "playing the teacher":

> Sometimes people see you as "just the wife", she's trying to play the teacher. But it was never like that. I could just come with him without working. But why, if I can do it, it's my job as well.

Teresa is often looked at as "just the wife" who helps her partner teach, without being acknowledged for her own efforts and experiences as a salsa dancer who even built her own school. In her case, the fact that her partner achieved considerable status in the salsa circuit before she met him may contribute to the misrepresentation of her own work. Similar to Lavinia, Teresa recalls how she had "to fight" her way in order to be acknowledged and visible in the salsa circuit.

The cited experiences are not singular cases; they indicate gendered hierarchies in the salsa circuit, which attribute some activities to male dancers and others to female dancers. They suggest that activities such as teaching are often gendered as male activities. At the same time, these activities are related to higher salsa capital and directly transferable into economic capital. In some contexts, aspects of "hegemonic masculinity" (Connell 1995) inform salsa capital, which can be termed a "hegemonic male salsa capital".

The couple classes taught at salsa congresses are most often led and verbally explained by male dancers, while female dancers demonstrate the steps without talking. This leader-centred way of presenting salsa dancing endows male dancers with more symbolic capital than female dancers.

In a short interview, salsa professional Andy told me that he travels every weekend of the year to a different salsa event, as a solo artist. As he only teaches and never performs, he has no fixed dance partner:

> Me I just get on a plane on Friday, I go to sleep, I wake up, I party. Saturday I pick a girl from a class I've never met in my life, teach a routine. You know, my life is very easy compared to my other colleagues.

Interested only in the leading, this dancer can just "pick a girl" before a workshop he has to teach, even though he has never danced with her before, and ask her to assist him during the workshop. Andy, a professional male leader, is endowed with high salsa capital. At congress parties I observed several times how groups of women actually queued in order to dance with this particular dancer, something reserved for the *salsa superstars*. He never has problems finding a willing dance partner for the class. This example sheds light on the status relations at work in the salsa couple. Although the two partners are mutually dependent, the leader/male dancer is often considered more important than the follower/female dancer. Through the weight given to the leader function in salsa dance and the gendering of this role as male, female salsa professionals have fewer opportunities to gain reputation in the teaching business.

Confronted with this hegemonic male salsa capital, female dancers use strategies to accumulate salsa capital based on other gendered properties. Female salsa professionals have developed ways to compete with male overrepresentation in the teaching business through the innovation of *styling*. With the establishment of *ladies' styling* classes, female dancers have been able to create a specific "female salsa capital" (see Figure 7.2).

As Bourdieu argues, struggle over symbolic capital constitutes all artistic fields. As I demonstrate, these struggles lead to processes of change and innovation. In the salsa circuit, one strategy for female dancers consisted of

Figure 7.2 Students film the learned sequence at the end of a *ladies' styling* workshop.
Source: © Valentin Behringer.

promoting a new definition of salsa dancing and thus opening up new performance and teaching opportunities. I suggest that this is exactly what happened with the *ladies' styling* classes, which developed at the end of the 1990s and still today form a branch of salsa dancing that is mainly in women's hands.

Anna, the before-cited German dance professional, used this strategy. She told me how she was able to continue her dance career after separating from her dance partner (after ten years of performing together). She first danced with other partners but then identified a new way of being a *travelling artist*:

> And I had a great *ladies' styling* formation with flamenco, I was "famous" in quotation marks, in salsa, and went to many congresses and taught my *ladies' styling* 'cause I had a particular touch in *ladies' styling* through flamenco and my Argentinean tango, because I had an interest in these dances as well. So I had a special styling, people really liked it. And I think I was one of the first with *ladies' styling*, this didn't exist at that time.

Through the creative integration of other dance techniques into her styling, Anna was able to continue her international travelling even after the breakup with her former partner and succeed as a solo artist. Although Anna was supposedly not the first woman to teach *ladies' styling* at salsa events on an international level, since the time she mentions (around the early 2000s) *ladies' styling* has been developing and still forms one of the main teaching opportunities for female professionals. As the historical example of *ladies' styling* demonstrates, by taking "ownership of this aspect of the evolving dance style" (Borland 2009: 485), some female dance professionals thus created a new means of acquiring salsa capital.

However, as the detailed analysis of Lavinia's and Nara's strategies of redoing and even undoing gender in salsa dancing (see Chapter 4) also shows, some female dancers are able to do things differently and challenge gendered assumptions. I would argue that Nara was actually in a position to engage in redefinitions of salsa thanks to a certain volume of salsa capital and her status in the hierarchy of *travelling artists*. Even though some other professionals might exclude her, she is very successful and accepted among students at salsa festivals in North America, Europe and Asia. At the same time, her (and others') success with a rebranded form of salsa informs her salsa capital.

"He was looking for a Cuban": ethnicity and salsa capital

In Chapter 3, the importance of ethnicity in the construction of authenticity among salsa dance professionals has already been addressed. This section further clarifies the ethnicised strategies to access salsa capital. As I argue, in cases where cultural authenticity is acknowledged as a resource, the mobilisation of ethnicity may invert the power dynamics between actors of European and non-European nationality (in terms of legal capital and mobility capital), which I demonstrated in the last chapter. At the same time, it comes with an objectifying essentialism. The underlying mechanisms can be understood as a form of "strategic essentialism" (Spivak 2012 (1988)), which, according to Eide (2010), "entails that members of groups, while being highly differentiated internally, may engage in an essentializing and to some extent a standardizing of their public image, thus advancing their group identity in a simplified, collectivised way to achieve certain objectives" (76). I illustrate the mobilisation of ethnicity with the example of so-called *Afro-Cuban* dance styles in the salsa circuit.

Similar to the innovation and spread of *ladies' styling* discussed above, the so-called *Afro-Cuban* dances have gained in importance in the salsa circuit. As argued before, I have observed a growing offer of *Afro-Cuban and rumba* dance workshops at salsa events in Europe. This particular style of dancing is often presented as an "ancestor" of salsa, and part of its steps and movements are integrated into the repertory of standardised salsa movements. Through this ethnicisation/racialisation of a style, (racialised) dancers of Cuban origin are most sought after to teach it, as they are perceived as experts in these dances. Male and female dance professionals of Cuban origin were thus able to draw on ethnicity to carve a niche in the salsa teaching business and build salsa capital.

The case of Yaimara helps to illustrate this point. When she arrived in Germany, she first had no job but was put in contact with the owner of the successful dance school where she started working soon after. Yaimara recalls:

> And in this time, the other Cuban was not in the school anymore, and Franz [German owner of dance school] was looking for another Cuban woman to teach the rumba lesson with Willy [...] and then I had an interview. And so I started with the rumba lesson. I remember very well, I had only one lesson in the beginning, and today I teach 14 hours [a week] [laughs].

As Yaimara told me, she and the other teacher, Willy, are the only Cuban teachers in the school. This explicit wish for two Cubans to teach the rumba classes demonstrates the way this dance style is ethnicised in a European context and constructed as directly linked to the Caribbean island.

Being identified as carrier of "authentic" salsa may enhance a dancer's salsa capital (and thus shape opportunities for transnational career development inside the salsa circuit). In this process, global power hierarchies that considerably shape dancers' ability to be mobile are temporary inverted. The ethnicisation and racialisation that exclude certain bodies from European territory (and exclusionary immigration and labour market politics are often based on) is valued inside salsa circuit and may enhance a dancer's salsa capital. However, this form of salsa capital often builds on ideas of cultural otherness, including assumptions of essential cultural differences. As literature on the exoticisation of Latin dances has demonstrated (McMains 2016), such representations may also perpetuate colonial categorisations and reinforce ethnicised and racialised hierarchies. Cuban salsa dance professionals therefore perform a balancing act when engaging in the mobilisation of ethnicity to construct salsa capital, which is valuable only inside the salsa circuit. This is also reflected in the fact that during my research I was unable to find a Cuban salsa dance professional who did not engage in "authenticity work" or who actively challenged ethnicised and racialised representations, for instance by "undoing Cubanness". The processes of authentication of *salsa Cubana* in the European salsa circuit can therefore best be understood as a part of the (rather successful) strategies of Cuban dance professionals to participate in the salsa circuit – though in a constrained field, as further discussed in the Conclusion of this study.

Conclusion

In this chapter, I have used a theoretical framework drawing on Bourdieu's capital theory and social network theory to analyse the process of reputation building, the third status passage in the construction of salsa dance professionals' transnational careers.

By applying some of the considerations of classic social network analysis to salsa dance professionals' careers, I demonstrated how dancers form networks to better understand how networking strategies inform the process of reputation building. I also highlighted the significance of differently positioned actors of the salsa circuit. Hence, all actors of the salsa circuit may play the important role of gatekeepers in the process of accessing more prestigious performance or teaching opportunities. Nevertheless, social relations are not always helpful in producing (mobile) transnational careers. In some cases, they keep dancers in a specific place. Also, contrary to the celebratory narrative of mobile careers, this privileged form of mobility often entails costs in regard to social relations, also demonstrated in other studies with highly mobile artists (Lipphardt 2012). Furthermore, as I have shown, the transnational careers of salsa dance professionals are gendered.

As the discussion has demonstrated, dance professionals draw on various resources to enhance their reputations in the salsa circuit and construct what I have termed salsa capital. Salsa capital is constructed differently, depending on dancers' position in and outside of the salsa circuit and their endowment with other forms of capital. I have especially demonstrated the significance of mobility, bodies, gender and ethnicity in this process.

An important point of Bourdieu's capital theory is the question of the convertibility of different forms of capital, which I now address. Salsa capital can be transformed into economic capital in various ways, as has been indicated throughout the last chapters. In this process, the most obvious exchange happens in the form of remuneration for teaching and performing at salsa events. Alongside such activities, many salsa dance professionals sell teaching material such as DVDs or online classes, which they promote during their travelling. Other dancers with a large volume of salsa capital sell choreographies of their routines to other dance instructors, who teach them to their own students, using the logo of the well-recognised *salsa stars* as a marketing tool to attract more paying students. Some of the experienced dancers also start organising larger events, drawing on their transnational networks of fellow *artists* and their reputations built during years of travelling to events. Established salsa dancers who dispose of social capital and salsa capital can thus become salsa event organisers, once they see business opportunities arising.

As argued in other studies, Bourdieu's theory of forms of capital can be adapted to a transnational perspective on mobility by analysing how the different forms of capital transfer across national borders (cf Moret 2018; Nowicka 2013). As Nowicka (2013) writes in her study on the positioning strategies of Polish entrepreneurs in Germany, migration

> disrupts accumulation and valorisation of capital but it also enables migrants to strategically employ these resources which are symbolically monopolised within a nation-state; this is in particular visible when migrants use the ethnic stereotypes to flexibly react to labour market demands abroad.
>
> (43)

This particularly holds true for the case of Cuban salsa dance professionals in this study: the construction of their salsa capital differs from that of their European counterparts. Although the latter may be endowed with more mobility capital, they do not dispose of the specific form of salsa capital, which is enhanced through the organisation of dance holidays in Cuba and the mobilisation of social networks in Cuba.

Cuban dance professionals active in the European salsa circuit are able to mobilise the resources of their networks in two different places and thus link them and convert different forms of capital thanks to their transnational mobility. These actors are able to not only convert social, cultural and symbolic capital from Cuba into salsa capital, which eventually translates into economic capital in the European salsa circuit; they are also able to convert their economic and social capital from Europe into social, economic or cultural capital in Cuba and thus improve their positions (and those of their family and friends) at their birthplaces.

Notes

1 For a video of a show of a professional salsa dance couple, see rebrand.ly/salsa-16.
2 Chapters 3 and 4 respectively have explored in depth the ways in which gender and "authenticity" (based on ethnicity as well as other criteria) are construed and negotiated between differently positioned actors in the salsa circuit. By focusing on how gendered, ethnicised and embodied properties may form "salsa capital", I now draw attention to the ways the outcome of such negotiations affects the construction of careers.
3 Lol is an often-used abbreviation in online communication, meaning "laughing out loud".

Part IV

Conclusion

This book set out to explore transnational processes at the intersections of salsa dance, circulating representations of gender and ethnicity and professional careers. It serves as a case study to illuminate how gender, ethnicity and race shape globalisation processes, demonstrating the complex interplay of different levels of analysis. Focusing on the connections between differently situated individuals in a world of "entangled modernities" (Randeria 1999), this study suggests current globalisation processes should be considered beyond global-local and North-South dichotomies. I argued that the salsa circuit might best be grasped as a rhizome-like, transnational formation produced through the circulation of people, imaginaries and affects, enabling professional careers at the crossroads of human movement in geographical space and on the dance floor. Including an (im)mobilities perspective, I tried to identify the conditions that allow those movements to happen and suggest the notion of "entangled mobilities" to analyse them.

As argued at the beginning of this book, most literature on salsa dance focuses on localised scenes and the ways salsa is "reterritorialised" in specific cities or national contexts. Due to this focus, the transnational careers of salsa dance professionals and the mobile practices of salsa dancers are rarely acknowledged. Furthermore, the studies that mention the participation of European and non-European dancers in salsa implicitly take the presence of Latin American dancers for granted. In this way, they neglect the importance of social capital and mobility capital, shaped by unequal power relations between countries and the historically grown migration regimes, to actually access and participate in the (European) salsa circuit.

To address this puzzle, this book builds on migration and mobility studies, transnational studies, gender studies and scholarship on art and dance. The starting point for this research was an epistemological stance based on a constructivist understanding of social "reality", notably in regard to gender and ethnicity. At the same time, it included the "embodied knowledge" (Crosby 1997). I adopted a transnational perspective (e.g. Dahinden 2016, 2017) and a "regimes-of-mobility" approach (Glick Schiller and Salazar 2013) to account for the importance of nation states in regulating the cross-border mobility of people. Drawing on scholarship interested in the construction of "transnational networks" (Kiwan and Meinhof 2011) or "large-scale systems" (Mueller 2016), I proposed a conceptualisation of salsa as a circuit with several hubs. Paired with concepts developed in the analysis of art (Becker 1982) and cultural production (Bourdieu 1993) as well as Bourdieu's capital approach, my theoretical framework allowed an exploration of salsa dancers' transnational practices on and off the dance floor. The combined interpretive framework focusing on a "logic of practices" (Villa 2010) as well as a perspective on structural power relations allowed me to gain different insights into dancers' opportunities and constraints.

I adopted a specific mobile methodology of diverse data-gathering methods designed to address the research questions relating to a research field in constant circulation. To grasp the importance of circulation in the salsa circuit, I developed an embodied, multi-sited (Hannerz 2003; Marcus 1995) research strategy, including several field "sites", notably salsa congresses, dance studios and an organised salsa holiday. The study is based on a triangulation of qualitative data-gathering methods, including semi-structured, problem-centred interviews (Witzel 2000) and participant observation/observant participation (Daniel 1995; Skinner 2010). Moreover, this study draws on a burgeoning field of embodied research methodologies, which stress the importance of "embodied knowledge" (Crosby 1997). Taking up calls for the reintroduction of the researcher's body into the research process, I also employed techniques of embodied research, common in dance ethnographies (Buckland 2010; Crosby 1997) and "carnal sociology" (Wacquant 2004). The acknowledgement of the researcher's own body in the research process is still often neglected in social science literature and its importance is often unrecognised. As I have demonstrated, combining embodied research techniques with more classical research strategies proves a valuable approach not only in studying dance but also for studying (other) transnational phenomena in general.

This book explored a transnational field developing between European countries, the Americas and in particular Cuba, demonstrating the importance of social relationships related to salsa. While this study examined some of salsa's transnational routes, several questions still remain to be answered, notably regarding the transnational networks between other places and people, and the ways the salsa circuit works in other parts of the world. Further research might explore more in depth the role of post-colonial ties and new migration routes in salsa dancers' careers.

This book explicitly seeks to go beyond the accounts of localised salsa scenes, sometimes described as having a "sedentary bias" (Sheller and Urry 2006). I therefore chose to explore the transnational circulation of people and imaginaries; this focus also bears the risk of a "mobility bias". I tried to counter this risk by addressing the immobilities and actors' difficulties in gaining access to mobility. Nevertheless, this book draws an image of highly mobile actors, who are actually the minority of salsa dancers.

Furthermore, the recent changes in the political and economic landscape between Cuba and the USA, and the subsequent changes in tourism and salsa entrepreneurship, offer a fruitful area for further work. These changes also brought shifts in the access to and use of the internet in Cuba: during the final stage of my research, I noticed an increase in commentaries on YouTube videos of dance. These commentaries demonstrate the negotiations around "authenticity", related to power relations between Cubans on the island, those living in Miami and Cubans based in Europe, who all criticise each other for teaching the dance moves in the wrong ways, particularly since "new" actors have access to online spaces. Though I was not able to include an analysis of these online negotiations in this book due to time restraints, they provide interesting research avenues for future netnographies.

Despite these limits, this book's findings add new insights to the literature, thus contributing to larger debates in the social sciences, notably in transnational studies, mobility studies, gender studies and the anthropology of dance.

Beyond the "migration container"

Based on an argument developed in transnational studies (Dahinden 2016), this book addresses current social transformations beyond the "migration container". It does so in the following three ways. First, adopting a transnational perspective (Dahinden 2017) in the analysis of the salsa circuit allowed me to go beyond statements of the "transnational" character of the dance world as mere metaphor. I not only analysed the construction of transnational careers, networks and subjectivities but also demonstrated the importance of the "national" in the notion of "transnational", notably nation states' borders and regimes of mobility. While dancers may feel part of a "global community", access to and participation in travelling is highly restricted by the nation state in question. Thus addressing global inequalities, I showed that the possibility to cross a border and to participate in circulation is unequally distributed.

Second, and related, while I focused on the circulation of salsa dancers, I also included the theoretical reflections of mobilities studies, urging scholars not to forget about the immobilities and moorings. Framing salsa dancers' circulation from a "regimes-of-mobility" perspective (Glick Schiller and Salazar 2013) allowed an understanding of the importance of salsa students' travels in the construction of salsa dance professionals' careers and a conceptualisation of some relations as "entangled mobilities". The notion of entangled mobilities points to the significance not only of social capital but also of imaginaries and mobility capital. Furthermore, as demonstrated throughout this book, entangled mobilities are gendered and ethnicised/racialised. As illustrated with the manifold cases in this study, the perspective of "entangled mobilities" makes it possible to consider the (im)mobilities of differently positioned individuals without naturalising either mobility or stasis.

Third, this study started with an interest in a "group" defined in terms of members' common activity, instead of focusing on a group defined in ethnic or national terms, as is still common in much of the research on migration and transnationalism as well as some studies on transnational careers in dance.

Salsa proved to be a particularly fruitful research context to establish a "de-ethnicized" (Wimmer 2009) and "de-migranticized" (Dahinden 2016) research design due to its attraction to differently positioned individuals. Entering the field through specific events in Europe and Cuba, and focusing on the present actors and their common activity (salsa dancing) allowed for a diverse sample in terms of origin countries. I thus included salsa dance professionals of various origin countries, as well as their students, in order to analyse how these individuals construct their careers and negotiate ethnicity and gender in specific situations. These situations were then analysed as one of several strategies to make claims of "authenticity" and legitimacy in the highly competitive field of the salsa circuit. In this way, strategies of claiming ownership through ethnicity were interpreted as responses to specific configurations of power relations (such as unequal distribution of economic and mobility capital between European salsa students and Cuban salsa teachers). Furthermore, focusing on salsa dancers with different nationalities has rendered visible the often-neglected importance of regimes of mobility and mobility capital – and thus the labour necessary in the construction of a transnational career.

Therefore, this study also differs from research on other cultural/dance practices such as Bizas' (2014) study analysing West African dance teachers and North American students or Robitaille's (2013) study interested in Brazilian capoeira masters and their North American students. As I argue, by choosing another approach to construct the research sample, this book is able to demonstrate commonalities and differences between dancers both as related to structural factors and as a result of actors' negotiations. In this way it minimises the risk of presenting individuals as cultural actors drawing on cultural resources alone.

The *Esperanto of the body* and the affective economy

To address the internal structure and logics of the salsa circuit, I used the notion of "affective economy", drawing on Bourdieu's approach to economies of symbolic goods (1980b, 1993, see also Törnqvist 2013) and on reflections from the field of "affect studies" (Ahmed 2004; Bakko and Merz 2015; Clough 2007; Davis 2015b). Salsa students as well as salsa dance professionals participate in the (re)production of a set of shared beliefs in specific values as part of the rules of the game (Bourdieu 1980b) or conventions (Becker 1982). At the same time, they stress circulating affects.

As I have shown, dancers draw on the interrelated arguments that salsa is accessible for anyone and that the shared bodily practice is a common "language": the *Esperanto of the body*. Salsa events are collectively imagined and generated as spaces of diversity and equality in terms of nationality, class, age, race and religion. As I have suggested, salsa dancers' arguments can be compared to public debates about political multiculturalism (Taylor 1992). Furthermore, actors of the salsa circuit share an understanding of the significance of affects, which they locate in bodily experiences. Against this backdrop, dance students' unease about the commercialised relationship to their dance teachers and *Cuban dance partners* (taxi-dancers) can be analysed. As I have shown, framing the dance partnership in economic terms instead of a voluntary "authentic" and gendered experience generates discussions at European salsa festivals as well as in the salsa tourism space in Havana. This finding is echoed in other studies looking at dance and tourism, such as Törnqvist (2013), who argues in her analysis of the interactions between tourists and tango dancers in Buenos Aires that "subjecting the tango to up-front economic deals through which a *price tag* is put on the experiences [...] conflicts with the *taboo of making things explicit*, the *mystification* and the *myth-making* central to the tango culture" (219). As demonstrated, part of such "myth-making" is also the gendered convention in regards to the partnering in salsa dancing. The issues at stake also resemble those described by Aterianus-Owanga's (forthcoming) account of sabar dancers circulating between Europe and Senegal. Building on Cole and Groes' (2016) notion of "affective circuits", she describes the entanglement of material and emotional dimensions and analyses the shifting borders between commerce and intimacy during dance workshops in Senegal. Similarly, salsa dancers' relations cannot be analysed as purely motivated by economic interests and need to be analysed as intimately enlaced with emotions and imaginaries.

I further provided a closer look at the processes through which salsa dance professionals develop a "commodified persona" (Bunten 2008) as they construct a marketable product beyond their dancing through engaging in "affective labour". Drawing on scholarship on "emotional labour" in service industries (Hochschild 1983) and, more specifically, "affective labour" in the sex industry (Ditmore 2007), I demonstrated the significance of interpersonal skills such as creating a relationship with potential clients/students. In these gendered relations, salsa dance professionals negotiate the convention of "tangible salsa *stars*".

Following calls to take emotions and affects more seriously (Clough 2007), this book draws attention to the affective economy on which the salsa circuit builds. It thus contributes to a better empirical understanding of the role of emotions and affects in transnational processes.

Ethnicity and gender as negotiable resources in unequal fields of power

Salsa dance has been described as a global dance form that has been "de-ethnicised" (see, for instance, Urquía 2005) in the process of its transnationalisation. While this is certainly true for some of the danced salsa styles, this book nuances the picture. As this study has demonstrated, salsa dancers of various countries of origin engage in symbolic struggles of boundary-work to legitimate their position. In this process, they negotiate salsa's "Latinness" in terms of a group-based authenticity versus an individualised skill, which can be acquired and learned through dance training. They further draw on arguments of cultural authenticity and a specific set of pedagogical techniques.

While the boundaries of ethnicity are challenged or even seemingly irrelevant for many of the female and male European and North American salsa dance professionals, this is not the case for Cuban dancers. I have demonstrated the ways in which dancers with a Cuban passport engage in "authenticity work" (Peterson 2005), a form of "strategic essentialism" (Spivak 2012 (1988)). A similar process has been described with regard to musicians and the "commodification of difference" in the so-called world music market (Connell and Gibson 2004; Kiwan and Meinhof 2011). Connell and Gibson (2004) cite musicians who felt constrained to play the "ethnic card" in a Western context demanding "authenticity". By demonstrating the processes of what could be termed a "re-ethnicisation" of salsa, this study has positioned salsa Cubanness as a result of the negotiations in the salsa circuit (see also Boulila 2018).

This book has underlined the importance of embodied doings in the construction of the social order (see Villa 2010). However, the micro-sociological analysis of how dancers are "doing being Cuban" alone does not allow for an interpretation of this phenomenon. Therefore, I added a perspective from Bourdieu's field approach to account for dancers' different positions in the salsa circuit. Furthermore, as argued in the debates on intersectionality, ethnicity, gender and other categories of difference always intersect (Villa 2010). This interpretative framework takes into account the Cuban interviewees' position at the intersections of ethnicised/racialised, class-based and gendered inequalities that leave little scope left to renegotiate ethnicity. It is against this backdrop that Cuban dancers' mobilisation of the "cultural authenticity" argument may best be understood.

Unlike ethnicity, gender is negotiated in manifold ways in the salsa circuit. Here, a micro-sociological interpretive framework was helpful in going beyond established literature on gender in salsa: Instead of presenting gender relations in salsa as stable and a simple result of dancers' wish to engage in "traditional" or "exotic" gender roles, I presented the ongoing negotiations of gender conventions (Schulze 2015). These negotiations happen primarily in embodied ways. Through a focus on gender conventions in the dancing, I demonstrated the ways in which (un/re)doing gender works "with and through" bodies (Messerschmidt 2009: 86). Hence, this study takes up calls for an inclusion of the body in analyses with the theoretical framework of doing gender.

Gender and ethnicity as identity categories are thus discussed very differently in the salsa circuit. These findings may partly be explained by the processes around an "unsettling of identities" that Brubaker (2016) analyses in a book entitled *trans*. Starting from the public debates around the pairing of transgender and transracial identities in the USA in 2015, he states: "In this landscape of unsettled identities, sex/gender and ethnoracial categories have ceased to be taken for granted and have become the focus of self-conscious choices and political claims" (Brubaker 2016: 5). However, as Brubaker (2016) argues, in public understanding these two forms of embodied identities are perceived as different: "even as gender identities have come to be reimagined in far-reaching and unprecedented ways, racial identities continue to be widely understood as unchanging and un-chosen" (Brubaker

2016: 132). While the context of the salsa circuit and the negotiations discussed herein turn around different questions from those discussed by Brubaker, his analysis parallels my findings. Brubaker (2016) claims:

> Paradoxically, while sex is a biological category in a way that race is not, sex and gender are understood to be more open to choice and change than are race and ethnicity. The distinction between sex and gender – and the irrelevance of ancestry to definitions of sex and gender – has made it possible to construe gender identity as a subjective individual property that is uncoupled from the body. Racial identity, however, is understood to be tightly coupled to the body and to be grounded in social relations, specifically in family and ancestry.
>
> (Brubaker 2016: 6)

The different understandings of these categories are also at work in the salsa circuit, where gender and ethnicity are construed in different ways. Although gender conventions are highly heteronormative and often reproduced, some male and female dancers are able to neglect gender (Hirschauer 2001) and thus challenge the current order. By contrast, when it comes to ethnicity, I have not observed a similar possibility of neglect for all dancers, and in particular for Cuban dancers. As argued above, dancers in the European salsa circuit are constrained to "play the ethnic card" as they lack the resources other salsa dance professionals are able to mobilise in the construction of "salsa capital".

Mobility capital and imaginaries

The current study highlighted the importance of mobility capital in the construction of transnational careers and the ways in which it has to be acquired. Scholars argued for a conceptualisation of mobility capital as including the capacities and competences to be mobile (Kaufmann et al. 2004; Moret 2016). As I have shown, additionally the imaginaries of dancers play an important role in the construction of mobility capital. Often imaginaries lie at the beginning of any spatial travels (Salazar 2011), of salsa students, teachers and performers alike. Imaginaries of salsa as the *Esperanto of the body*, allowing for new encounters on the dance floor, as well as the imaginaries of Cuba as salsa's "birthplace", bring salsa students to engage in travelling to salsa events in Europe and Cuba. At the same time, Latin American salsa dancers told me about the imaginaries of salsa as a way to engage in a "cosmopolitan lifestyle", to travel themselves, but also as possibility of self-transformation. Bizas (2014) similarly analyses the importance of imagination in the travels of students and artists of the Senegalese dance form sabar. As Bizas (2014) concludes, "imagination plays an important role in mobilizing U.S. students to West Africa, and West African artists to the United States" (127). Likewise Davis (2015a) describes the importance of tango dancers' fantasies about "the other" and frames their transnational connections as "a passionate encounter across many different borders between dancers with a shared desire for difference and a taste of 'elsewhere'" (181).

However, the actors in the salsa circuit are endowed with different volumes of mobility capital. In order to build mobility capital, many dance professionals first need to access the right contacts. The interviewed Cuban dancers relied on the mobility of others. Moreover, in the process of career construction, salsa dance professionals need to travel to salsa events, and it becomes a condition of this transnational career. Mobility capital is thus not only necessitated in the first stage of access to the salsa circuit but also in the construction of social networks in the subsequent stage of reputation-building.

Social capital and "entangled mobilities"

This book analysed the importance of several types of capital in salsa dance professionals' transnational careers. It proposed to analyse salsa dance professionals' transnational careers from a sociological and anthropological perspective, thus shedding light on a specific form of a professional career at the intersections of industries as diverse as art, entertainment/performance and teaching. It particularly addressed the importance of social capital in the construction of these careers, defined as "resources embedded in a social structure which are accessed and/or mobilized in purposive actions" (Lin 1999: 35). Going beyond the mere observation of the importance of social capital, I also analysed which types of actors are important, how social capital may relate to the social networks actors build up and the ways it is gendered. While resources present in social networks are mobilised at all three of the stages I identified in salsa dance professionals' careers, I particularly shed light on the roles and working of social capital in the passage of accessing the salsa circuit as well as in the passage of reputation building.

The literature on migrants' social capital often focuses on ties between family members or other people from the same origin country (e.g. Pathirage and Collyer 2011). Contrary to this literature, I have shown that the Latin American salsa dancers I interviewed mainly drew on resources from networks built with their European students. The networks in the salsa circuit can therefore be described as transnational and highly diversified in terms of gender, nationality and place of residence.

This is also the case for the social networks the dancers build on to construct their careers in the salsa circuit, including the organisation of teaching and performance opportunities to gain visibility and reputation. As demonstrated, dancers need to be present at salsa events in "co-present encounters" (Urry 2003) in order to network and meet event organisers, promoters, dance partners as well as their students — all of whom may play the role of gatekeepers to access new opportunities. Social capital is therefore mobilised to access mobility capital, which in turn allows actors in the salsa circuit to access new networks and deploy resources in different places, which leads to the accumulation of salsa capital.

To account for the specific relations between differently positioned actors in the salsa circuit I suggested the notion of "entangled mobilities". Analysing salsa dancers' careers through a perspective of entangled mobilities allows taking into account not only dancers' social capital and different volumes of mobility capital but also gendered, ethnicised and racialised representations. Literature on intimate relationships in tourist destinations in Latin America often frames these encounters as "sex tourism" or "romance tourism". While these studies deliver important insights, their focus necessarily means that they tend to present intimate relationships under the light of sex tourism. Based on my research, I would argue that the perspective of "entangled mobilities" allows for an analysis of the "tourist-local" relationship adding to existing approaches. As I have shown, the relationships built between salsa dance students and teachers cover a large spectrum of possible intimacy; starting from a student-teacher relationship, they may occasionally involve sexual encounters, romances or marriage. They are shaped by complex power relations between the European students and their Cuban teachers, based on unequal access to mobility capital, economic and legal capital and a shared understanding of "passion" for salsa.

Approaching dancers' mobility through the perspective of "entangled mobilities" also sheds light on the mobility practices of a group of people who are usually glossed over in studies on highly skilled mobile actors.

This book serves as a case study to illuminate processes of social organisation, transnational encounters and global inequalities through the entry point of salsa dance. It suggests that the prism of dance allows for alternative perspectives in research on spatial mobility and transnational networks. It combines theoretical and methodological perspectives from different fields of study in an approach that I hope may fruitfully be used in further research on transnational phenomena to foster our understanding of the interconnectedness of the world.

Bibliography

Ahmed, Sara. 2004. Affective economies. *Social Text* 22(3):117–139.

Amelina, Anna. 2017. *Transnationalizing inequalities in Europe. Sociocultural boundaries, assemblages and regimes of intersection.* New York: Routledge.

Amelina, Anna, and Thomas Faist. 2012. De-naturalizing the national in research methodologies: key concepts of transnational studies in migration. *Ethnic and Racial Studies* 35(10):1707–1724. DOI: 10.1080/01419870.2012.659273.

Ana, Ruxandra. 2017. Rumba: heritage, tourism and the "authentic" Afro-Cuban experience. In *Collaborative intimacies in music and dance: anthropologies of sound and movement.* Evangelos Chrysagis and Panas Karampampas, eds. New York: Berghahn, pp. 163-186.

Ana, Ruxandra, and Oskar Lubiński. 2018. Cuban private entrepreneurship – from periphery to key sector of the economy in tourism-oriented market socialism. *Regional Science Policy & Practice* 11(3):467–477. DOI: 10.1111/rsp3.12154.

Andrikopoulos, Apostolos. 2019. Love, money and papers in the affective circuits of cross-border marriages: beyond the "sham"/"genuine" dichotomy. *Journal of Ethnic and Migration Studies* 1–18. DOI: 10.1080/1369183X.2019.1625129.

Aparicio, Frances R. 1998. *Listening to salsa: gender, Latin popular music, and Puerto Rican cultures.* Middletown: Wesleyan University Press.

Appadurai, Arjun, ed. 1986. *The social life of things. Commodities in cultural perspective.* Cambridge: Cambridge University Press.

Appadurai, Arjun. 1990. Disjuncture and difference in the global cultural economy. *Theory, Culture & Society* 7(2–3):295–310. DOI: 10.1177/026327690007002017.

Appadurai, Arjun. 1996. *Modernity at large: cultural dimensions of globalization.* Minneapolis, MN: University of Minnesota Press.

Apprill, Christophe. 2005. *Sociologie des danses de couple. Une pratique entre résurgence et folklorisation.* Paris: L'Harmattan.

Aterianus-Owanga, Alice. 2019. Dancing an open Africanity: playing with "tradition" and identity in the spreading of sabar in Europe. *Open Cultural Studies* 3(1):347. DOI: 10.1515/culture-2019-0030.

Aterianus-Owanga, Alice. forthcoming. "Kaay fecc!" (Come dance!). Economic, cultural and emotional flows in the "dance tourism" of sabar (Senegal-Europe). In *Destination Africa. Contemporary Africa as a global meeting point.* Mayke Kaag, Guive Khan Mohammad, and Stefan Schmid, eds. Brill.

Babb, Florence E. 2011. Che, Chevys, and Hemingway's Daiquiris: Cuban tourism in a time of globalisation. *Bulletin of Latin American Research* 30(1):50–63. DOI: 10.1111/j.1470-9856.2010.00450.x.

Baier, Angelika, Christa Binswanger, Jana Häberlein, Yv Eveline Nay, and Andrea Zimmermann, eds. 2014. *Affekt und Geschlecht: eine einführende Anthologie.* Wien: Zaglossus.

Bakko, Matthew, and Sibille Merz. 2015. Towards an affective turn in social science research? Theorising affect, rethinking methods and (re)envisioning the social. *Graduate Journal of Social Science* 11(1):7–14.

Balbuena Gutiérrez, Barbara. 2014. Dancing salsa in Cuba: another look. In *Salsa world. A global dance in local contexts.* Sydney Hutchinson, ed. Philadelphia, PA: Temple University Press, pp. 98–116.

Barley, Stephen R. 1989. Careers, identities, and institutions: the legacy of the Chicago school of sociology. *Handbook of Career Theory* 41:65.

Barth, Fredrik, ed. 1969. *Ethnic groups and boundaries. The social organization of culture difference.* Oslo: Universitetsferlaget.

Basch, Linda, Nina Glick Schiller, and Christina Blanc-Szanton. 1994. *Nations unbound: transnational projects, postcolonial predicaments, and deterritorialized Nation-States.* New York: Gordon and Breach.

Bauder, Harald, Charity-Ann Hannan, and Omar Lujan. 2016. International experience in the academic field: knowledge production, symbolic capital, and mobility fetishism. *Population, Space and Place* 23(6):e2040. DOI: 10.1002/psp.2040.

Baumann, Gerd. 1996. *Contesting culture. Discourses of identity in multi-ethnic London.* Cambridge: Cambridge University Press.

Beck, Ulrich, and Natan Sznaider. 2006. Unpacking cosmopolitanism for the social sciences: a research agenda. *The British Journal of Sociology* 57(1):1–23.

Becker, Howard S. 1963. *Outsiders: studies in the sociology of deviance.* London: Free Press.

Becker, Howard S. 1982. *Art worlds.* Berkeley, CA: University of California Press.

Becker, Howard S. 1986. *Doing things together.* Evanston, IL: Northwestern University Press.

Becker, Howard S. 1998. *Tricks of the trade. How to think about your research while you're doing it.* Chicago, IL and London: University of Chicago Press.

Beck-Gernsheim, Elisabeth. 2011. The marriage route to migration: of border artists, transnational matchmaking and imported spouses. *Nordic Journal of Migration Research* 1 (2):60–68. DOI: 10.2478/v10202-011-0008-y.

Beljaars, Ine. 2016. Difference making in the Dutch kizomba scene. *LOVA, the Netherlands Association for Gender Studies and Feminist Anthropology* 36:26–37.

Bessin, Marc, Claire Bidart, and Michel Grossetti. 2010. *Bifurcations: les sciences sociales face aux ruptures et à l'événement.* Paris: La Découverte.

Bizas, Eleni. 2012. Navigating trans-Atlantic flows: New York's Senegalese Sabar teachers. *Journal for the Anthropological Study of Human Movement* (2), http://jashm.press.uillinois. edu/17.2/bizas.html.

Bizas, Eleni. 2014. *Learning Senegalese Sabar. Dancers and embodiment in New York and Dakar.* New York: Berghahn.

Blanco Borelli, Melissa. 2016. *She is Cuba. A genealogy of the mulata body.* New York: Oxford University Press.

Bock, Sheila, and Katherine Borland. 2011. Exotic identities: dance, difference, and self-fashioning. *Journal of Folklore Research* 48(1):1–36. DOI: 10.2979/jfolkrese.48.1.1.

Bodenheimer, Rebecca M. 2013. National symbol or "a black thing"?: rumba and racial politics in cuba in the era of cultural tourism. *Black Music Research Journal* 33(2):177–205.

Bonjour, Saskia, and Betty de Hart. 2013. A proper wife, a proper marriage: constructions of "us" and "them" in Dutch family migration policy. *European Journal of Women's Studies* 20 (1):61–76. DOI: 10.1177/1350506812456459.

Borland, Katherine. 2009. Embracing difference: salsa fever in New Jersey. *The Journal of American Folklore* 122(486):466–492. DOI: 10.2307/40390082.

Bosse, Joanna. 2008. Salsa dance and the transformation of style: an ethnographic study of movement and meaning in a cross-cultural context. *Dance Research Journal* 40(1):45–64.

Bosse, Joanna. 2013. Salsa dance as cosmopolitan formation: cooperation, conflict and commerce in the Midwest United States. *Ethnomusicology Forum* 22(2):210–231. DOI: 10.1080/17411912.2013.809256.

Bottero, Wendy, and Nick Crossley. 2011. Worlds, fields and networks: Becker, Bourdieu and the structures of social relations. *Cultural Sociology* 5(1):99–119.

Boulila, Stefanie Claudine. 2015. What makes a lesbian salsa space comfortable? Reconceptualising safety and homophobia. In *Lesbian geographies. Gender, place and power.* Kath Browne and Eduarda Ferreira, eds. Farnham: Ashgate, pp. 133–152.

Boulila, Stefanie Claudine. 2018. Salsa cosmopolitanism? Consuming racialised difference in the European social dance industry. *Leisure Studies* 37(3):243–255. DOI: 10.1080/02614367.2017.1405459.

Bourdieu, Pierre. 1980a. Le capital social. *Actes de la recherche en sciences sociales* 31:2–3.

Bourdieu, Pierre. 1980b. The production of belief: contribution to an economy of symbolic goods. *Media, Culture and Society* 2:261–293.

Bourdieu, Pierre. 1983. The field of cultural production, or: the economic world reversed. *Poetics* 12(4):311–356. DOI: 10.1016/0304-422X(83)90012-8.

Bourdieu, Pierre. 1986. The forms of capital. In *Handbook of theory and research for the sociology of education.* John G. Richardson, ed. Westport, CT: Greenwood, pp. 241–258.

Bourdieu, Pierre. 1993. *The field of cultural production. Essays on art and literature.* Randal Johnson, ed. Cambridge: Polity Press.

Bourdieu, Pierre. 1998. *Practical reason. On the theory of action.* London: Polity Press.

Bourdieu, Pierre, and Loïc Wacquant. 1992. *An invitation to reflexive sociology.* Cambridge: Polity Press.

Brubaker, Rogers. 2002. Ethnicity without groups. *European Journal of Sociology* 43(2):163–189. DOI: 10.1017/S0003975602001066.

Brubaker, Rogers. 2016. *Trans. Gender and race in an age of unsettled identities.* Princeton, NJ: Princeton University Press.

Buckland, Theresa Jill. 2006. Dance, history, and ethnography. Frameworks, sources, and identities of past and present. In *Dancing from past to present: nation, culture, identities.* Theresa Jill Buckland, ed. Madison, WI: University of Wisconsin Press, pp. 3–24.

Buckland, Theresa Jill. 2010. Shifting perspectives on dance ethnography. In *The dance studies reader.* Alexandra Carter and Janet O'Shea, eds. London: Routledge, pp. 335–343.

Bunten, Alexis Celeste. 2008. Sharing culture or selling out? Developing the commodified persona in the heritage industry. *American Ethnologist* 35(3):380–395. DOI: 10.1111/j.1548-1425.2008.00041.x.

Burt, Ronald S. 1983. Range. In *Applied network analysis: a methodological introductoin.* Ronald S. Burt and Michael J. Minor, eds. Beverly Hills, CA: Sage, pp. 176–194.

Burt, Ronald S. 1992. *Structural holes.* Cambridge, MA: Harvard University Press.

Burt, Ronald S. 1998. The gender of social capital. *Rationality and Society* 10(1):5–46. DOI: 10.1177/104346398010001001.

Butler, Judith. 1990. *Gender trouble: feminism and the subversion of identity.* New York: Routledge.

Butler, Judith. 1993. Critically queer. In *Identity: a reader.* Paul du Gay, Jessica Evans, and Peter Redman, eds. London: Sage, pp. 108–118.

Calhoun, Craig. 1993. Habitus, field and capital: the question of historical specificity. In *Bourdieu: critical perspectives*. Craig Calhoun, Edward LiPuma, and Moishe Postone, eds. Chicago, IL: University of Chicago Press, pp. 61–88.

Candea, Matei. 2007. Arbitrary locations: in defence of the bounded field-site. *Journal of the Royal Anthropological Institute* 13(1):167–184. DOI: 10.1111/j.1467-9655.2007.00419.x.

Carwile, Christey. 2017. "The clave comes home": salsa dance and Pan-African identity in Ghana. *African Studies Review* 60(2):183–207. DOI: 10.1017/asr.2017.6.

Charmaz, Kathy. 2006. *Constructing grounded theory: a practical guide through qualitative analysis*. London: Sage.

Charsley, Katharine, ed. 2012. *Transnational marriage. New perspectives from Europe and beyond*. New York: Routledge.

Chrysagis, Evangelos, and Panas Karampampas. 2017. Collaborative intimacies. In *Collaborative intimacies in music and dance: anthropology of sound and movement*. Evangelos Chrysagis and Panas Karampampas, eds. New York: Berghahn, pp. 1–26.

Clealand, Danielle P. 2013. When ideology clashes with reality: racial discrimination and black identity in contemporary Cuba. *Ethnic and Racial Studies* 36(10):1619–1636. DOI: 10.1080/01419870.2013.783928.

Clough, Patricia Ticineto, ed. 2007. *The affective turn. Theorizing the social*. Durham, NC: Duke University Press.

Clough, Patricia Ticineto. 2008. The affective turn: political economy, biomedia and bodies. *Theory, Culture & Society* 25(1):1–22. DOI: 10.1177/0263276407085156.

Cohen, Scott. 2010. Searching for escape, authenticity and identity: experiences of "lifestyle travellers". In *The tourism and leisure experience: consumer and managerial perspectives*. Michael Morgan, Peter Lugosi, and Brent Ritchie, eds. Bristol: Channel View Publications, pp. 27–42.

Cole, Jennifer, and Christian Groes, eds. 2016. *Affective circuits: African migrations to Europe and the pursuit of social regeneration*. Chicago, IL: University of Chicago Press.

Comaroff, Jean. 1985. *Body of power, spirit of resistance. The culture and history of a South African people*. Chicago, IL: University of Chicago Press.

Connell, John, and Chris Gibson. 2004. World music: deterritorializing place and identity. *Progress in Human Geography* 28(3):342–361. DOI: 10.1191/0309132504ph493oa.

Connell, Raewyn W. 1995. *Masculinities*. Cambridge: Polity Press.

Crane, Diana. 2015. Art worlds. In *The Blackwell encyclopedia of sociology*. George Ritzer, ed. Wiley Online Library. DOI: 10.1002/9781405165518.wbeosa065.pub2.

Cressey, Paul G. 1932. *The taxi-dance hall: a sociological study in commercialized recreation and city life*. Chicago, IL: University of Chicago Press.

Cresswell, Tim. 2006. "You cannot shake that shimmie here": producing mobility on the dance floor. *Cultural Geographies* 13(1):55–77. DOI: 10.1191/1474474006eu350oa.

Cresswell, Tim. 2010. Towards a politics of mobility. *Environment and Planning D: Society and Space* 28(1):17–31. DOI: 10.1068/d11407.

Crosby, Jill Flanders. 1997. The dancer's way of knowing. Merging practice and theory in the doing and writing of ethnography. *Etnofoor* X(1/2):65–81.

Csikszentmihalyi, Mihaly. 1990. *Flow. The psychology of optimal experience*. New York: Harper Perennial.

Dahinden, Janine. 2009. Are we all transnational now? Network transnationalism and transnational subjectivity: the differing impacts of globalization on the inhabitants of a small Swiss city. *Ethnic and Racial Studies* 32(8):1365–1386.

Dahinden, Janine. 2010. The dynamics of migrants' transnational formations: between mobility and locality. In *Diaspora and transnationalism*. Rainer Bauböck and Thomas Faist, eds. Amsterdam: Amsterdam University Press, pp. 51–71.

Dahinden, Janine. 2013. Cities, migrant incorporation, and ethnicity: a network perspective on boundary work. *International Migration and Integration* 14:39–60. DOI: 10.1007/s12134-011-0224-2.

Dahinden, Janine. 2016. A plea for the "de-migranticization" of research on migration and integration. *Ethnic and Racial Studies* 39(13):2207–2225. DOI: 10.1080/01419870.2015.1124129.

Dahinden, Janine. 2017. Transnationalism reloaded: the historical trajectory of a concept. *Ethnic and Racial Studies* 40(9):1474–1485. DOI: 10.1080/01419870.2017.1300298.

Daniel, Yvonne. 1995. *Rumba: dance and social change in contemporary Cuba*. Bloomington, IN: Indiana University Press.

Daniel, Yvonne. 2002. Cuban dance: an orchard of Caribbean creativity. In *Caribbean dance from Abakuá to Zouk: how movement shapes identitiy*. Susanna Sloat, ed. Gainesville, FL: University Press of Florida, pp. 23–55.

Davis, Kathy. 2015a. *Dancing Tango. Passionate encounters in a globalizing world*. New York: New York University Press.

Davis, Kathy. 2015b. Should a feminist dance tango? Some reflections on the experience and politics of passion. *Feminist Theory* 16(1):3–21. DOI: 10.1177/1464700114562525.

Davis, Kathy. 2018a. Auto/biography: bringing in the "I". In *Handbuch Biographieforschung*. Helma Lutz, Martina Schiebel, and Elisabeth Tuider, eds. Wiesbaden: Springer, pp. 633–646. DOI: 10.1007/978-3-658-18171-0_55.

Davis, Kathy. 2018b. From transnational biographies to transnational cultural space. In *Handbuch Biographieforschung*. Helma Lutz, Martina Schiebel, and Elisabeth Tuider, eds. Wiesbaden: Springer, pp. 659–668. DOI: 10.1007/978-3-658-18171-0_55.

Deleuze, Gilles, and Félix Guattari. 1998 (1980). *A thousand plateaus: capitalism and schizophrenia*. Minneapolis, MN: University of Minnesota Press.

Desmond, Jane C. 1993. Embodying difference: issues in dance and cultural studies. *Cultural Critique* 26:33–63. DOI: 10.2307/1354455.

Deutsch, Francine M. 2007. Undoing gender. *Gender & Society* 21(1):106–127. DOI: 10.1177/0891243206293577.

Ditmore, Melissa. 2007. Calcutta, sex workers organize. In *The affective turn. Theorizing the social*. Patricia T. Clough, ed. Durham, NC: Duke University Press, pp. 170–186.

Duany, Jorge. 2002. Mobile livelihoods: the sociocultural practices of circular migrants between Puerto Rico and the United States. *International Migration Review* 36(2):355–388. DOI: 10.1111/j.1747-7379.2002.tb00085.x.

Eide, Elisabeth. 2010. Strategic essentialism and ethnification: hand in glove? *Nordicom Review* 31(2):63–78.

Elliot, Alice. 2016. Gender. In *Keywords of mobility. Critical engagements*. Noel B. Salazar and Kiran Jayaram, eds. New York: Berghahn, pp. 73–92.

Erel, Umut. 2010. Migrating cultural capital: Bourdieu in migration studies. *Sociology* 44 (4):642–660. DOI: 10.1177/0038038510369363.

Escalona, Saul. 2014. Allons à la fête, on danse salsa. New routes for salsa in France. In *Salsa world. A global dance in local contexts*. Sydney Hutchinson, ed. Philadelphia, PA: Temple University Press, pp. 173–181.

Faist, Thomas. 2000. Transnationalization in international migration: implications for the study of citizenship and culture. *Ethnic and Racial Studies* 23(2):189–222. DOI: 10.1080/014198700329024.

Faist, Thomas. 2004. Social space. In *Encyclopedia of social theory*. George Ritzer, ed. Thousand Oaks, CA: Sage, pp. 331–332.

Faist, Thomas. 2013. The mobility turn: a new paradigm for the social sciences? *Ethnic and Racial Studies* 36(11):1637–1646. DOI: 10.1080/01419870.2013.812229.

Farnell, Brenda. 2012. Commentary: movement, mobility, and action. *Journal for the Anthropological Study of Human Movement* (2), http://jashm.press.uillinois.edu/17.2/farnell.html.

Febres, Mayra. 1997. Salsa as translocation. In *Everynight life: culture and dance in Latin/o America*. Celeste Fraser Delgado and José Esteban Muñoz, eds. London: Duke University Press.

Fernandez, Nadine T. 2013. Moral boundaries and national borders: Cuban marriage migration to Denmark. *Identities* 20(3):270–287. DOI: 10.1080/1070289X.2013.806266.

Fernandez-Selier, Yesenia. 2013. The making of the rumba body: René Rivero and the rumba craze. *Cuba global/Global Cuba* 1:85–100.

Flick, Uwe. 2014. *An Introduction to qualitative research*. 5th edition. London: Sage.

Fraser Delgado, Celeste. 2014. Review. *Dance Research Journal* 46(2):105–109.

Freakley, Vivien, and Jonothan Neelands. 2003. The UK artist's world of work. *Research in Dance Education* 4(1):51–61. DOI: 10.1080/14647890308305.

Fuentes, Leonardo Padura. 2003. *Faces of salsa: a spoken history of the music*. Washington, DC: Smithsonian Books.

Gagné, Nana Okura. 2014. Romance and sexuality in Japanese Latin dance clubs. *Ethnography* 15(4):446–468. DOI: 10.1177/1466138113490605.

Gans, Herbert J. 1979. Symbolic ethnicity: the future of ethnic groups and cultures in America. *Ethnic and Racial Studies* 2(1):1–20. DOI: 10.1080/01419870.1979.9993248.

García, Cindy. 2013. *Salsa crossings: dancing Latinidad in Los Angeles*. Durham, NC: Duke University Press.

García, David F. 2009. Embodying music/disciplining dance. The mambo body in Havana and New York City. In *Ballroom, boogie, shimmy sham, shake: a social and popular dance reader*. Julie Malnig, ed. Urbana, IL: University of Illinois Press, pp. 165–181.

Garfinkel, Harold. 1967. *Studies in ethnomethodology*. Englewood Cliffs, NJ: Prentice-Hall.

Gaudette, Pascal. 2013. Jembe Hero: West African drummers, global mobility and cosmopolitanism as status. *Journal of Ethnic and Migration Studies* 39(2):295–310. DOI: 10.1080/1369183x.2013.723259.

Gay, Du, Stuart Hall Paul, Linda Jones, Hugh Mackay, and Keith Negus. 1997. *Doing cultural studies. The story of the Sony Walkman*. London: Sage.

Gibert, Marie-Pierre. 2011. Transnational ties and local Involvement: North African musicians in and beyond London. *Music and Arts in Action* 3(3):92–115.

Giddens, Anthony. 1991. *Modernity and self-identity. Self and society in late-modernity*. Cambridge: Polity Press.

Gill, Rosalind. 2003. From sexual objectification to sexual subjectification: the resexualisation of women's bodies in the media. *Feminist Media Studies* 3(1):100–106.

Gilroy, Paul. 1991. *"There ain't no black in the union jack": the cultural politics of race and nation*. University of Chicago Press.

Gimlin, Debra. 2007. What is "body work"? A review of the literature. *Sociology Compass* 1(1):353–370. DOI: 10.1111/j.1751-9020.2007.00015.x.

Glaser, Barney, and Anselm Strauss. 1967. *The discovery of grounded theory. Strategies for qualitative research*. Chicago, IL: Aldine.

Glick Schiller, Nina. 2015. Explanatory frameworks in transnational migration studies: the missing multi-scalar global perspective. *Ethnic and Racial Studies* 38(13):2275–2282. DOI: 10.1080/01419870.2015.1058503.

Glick Schiller, Nina, Linda Basch, and Christina Blanc-Szanton. 1995. From immigrant to transmigrant: theorizing transnational migration. *Anthropological Quarterly* 68(1):48–63.

Glick Schiller, Nina, and Ulrike H. Meinhof. 2011. Singing a new song? Transnational migration, methodological nationalism and cosmopolitan perspectives. *Music and Arts in Action* 3(3):21–39.

Glick Schiller, Nina, and Noel B. Salazar. 2013. Regimes of mobility across the globe. *Journal of Ethnic and Migration Studies* 39(2):183–200. DOI: 10.1080/1369183x.2013.723253.

Goffman, Erving. 1963. *Behaviour in public places*. New York: Free Press.

Goffman, Erving. 1977. The arrangement between the sexes. *Theory and Society* 4 (3):301–331.

Gotfrit, Leslie. 1988. Women dancing back: disruption and the politics of pleasure. *The Journal of Education* 170(3):122–141.

Granovetter, Mark S. 1983. The strength of weak ties: a network theory revisited. *Sociological Theory* 1:201–233.

Gregg, Melissa. 2009. Learning to (love) labour: production cultures and the affective turn. *Communication and Critical/Cultural Studies* 6(2):209–214. DOI: 10.1080/147914209 02868045.

Gupta, Akhil, and James Ferguson. 1992. Beyond "culture": space, identity, and the politics of difference. *Cultural Anthropology* 7(1):6–23.

Hage, Ghassan. 2005. A not so multi-sited ethnography of a not so imagined community. *Anthropological Theory* 5(4):463–475. DOI: 10.1177/1463499605059232.

Hakim, Catherine. 2010. Erotic capital. *European Sociological Review* 26(5):499–518.

Hall, Derek R. 1992. Tourism development in Cuba. In *Tourism and the less developed countries*. David Harrison, ed. London: Belhaven Press, pp. 101–120.

Hamilton, Kathy, and Paul Hewer. 2009. Salsa magic: an exploratory netnographic analysis of the salsa experience. *Advances in Consumer Research* 36:502–508.

Hannam, Kevin, Mimi Sheller, and John Urry. 2006. Editorial: mobilities, immobilities and moorings. *Mobilities* 1(1):1–22. DOI: 10.1080/17450100500489189.

Hannerz, Ulf. 1996. *Transnational connections: culture, people, places*. London: Routledge.

Hannerz, Ulf. 2003. Being there. And there. And there! Reflections on multi-site ethnography. *Ethnography* 4(2):201–216.

Haraway, Donna. 1988. Situated knowledges: the science question in feminism and the privilege of partial perspective. *Feminist Studies* 14(3):575–599. DOI: 10.2307/3178066.

Hardt, Michael. 1999. Affective labor. *Boundary 2* 26(2):89–100.

Headland, Thomas N., Kenneth L. Pike, and Marvin Harris, eds. 1990. *Emics and etics: the insider/outsider debate, frontiers of anthropology*. Newbury Park, CA: Sage.

Hertz, Ellen. 2009. L'événement: l'espace-temps de la reconnaissance. In *Réinventer l'anthropologie? Les sciences de la culture à l'épreuve des globalisations*. Francine Saillant, ed. Montréal: Liber, pp. 205–220.

Heyman, Josiah McC., and Howard Campbell. 2009. The anthropology of global flows: a critical reading of Appadurai's "disjuncture and difference in the global cultural economy". *Anthropological Theory* 9(2):131–148. DOI: 10.1177/1463499609105474.

Hirschauer, Stefan. 1994. Die soziale Fortpflanzung der Zwei-Geschlechtlichkeit. *Kölner Zeitschrift für Soziologie und Sozialpsychologie* 46(4):668–692.

Hirschauer, Stefan. 2001. Das Vergessen des Geschlechts: zur Praxeologie einer Kategorie sozialer Ordnung. *Kölner Zeitschrift für Soziologie und Sozialpsychologie Sonderheft* 41:208–235.

Hochschild, Arlie Russell. 1983. *The managed heart: commercialization of human feeling*. Berkeley, CA: University of California Press.

Holmes, Su, and Sean Redmond. 2006. *Framing celebrity: new directions in celebrity culture.* London: Routledge.

Hughes, Everett C. 1958. *Men and their work.* Glencoe, IL: Free Press.

Hutchinson, Sydney. 2004. Mambo on 2: the birth of a new form of dance in New York City. *Centro Journal* 16(2):109–137.

Hutchinson, Sydney. 2009. Introduction. *The Journal of American Folklore* 122(486):378–390.

Hutchinson, Sydney, ed. 2014a. *Salsa world. A global dance in local contexts.* Philadelphia, PA: Temple University Press.

Hutchinson, Sydney. 2014b. What's in a number? From local nostalgia to global marketability in New York's on-2 salsa. In *Salsa world. A global dance in local contexts.* Sydney Hutchinson, ed. Philadelphia, PA: Temple University Press, pp. 26–45.

Iwanaga, Kengo. 2014. Diffusion and change in salsa dance styles in Japan. In *Salsa world. A global dance in local contexts.* Sydney Hutchinson, ed. Philadelphia, PA: Temple University Press, pp. 200–211.

Jackson, Peter, Philip Crang, and Claire Dwyer. 2004. *Transnational spaces.* New York: Routledge.

Jayaram, Kiran. 2016. Capital. In *Keywords of mobility. Critical engagements.* Noel B. Salazar and Kiran Jayaram, eds. New York: Berghahn, pp. 13–32.

Jenkins, Richard. 1994. Rethinking ethnicity: identity, categorization and power. *Ethnic and Racial Studies* 17(2):197–223. DOI: 10.1080/01419870.1994.9993821.

Jöns, Heike. 2011. Transnational academic mobility and gender. *Globalisation, Societies and Education* 9(2):183–209. DOI: 10.1080/14767724.2011.577199.

Kabir, Ananya. 2013. The European salsa congress. Music and dance in transnational circuits. In *A companion to diaspora and transnationalism.* Ato Quayson and Girish Daswani, eds. Blackwell Publishing, pp. 263–276.

Kalegoropoulou, Sofia. 2013. Greek dance and everyday ntionalism in contemporary Greece. *Dance Research Aotearoa* 1(1):55–74.

Kalir, Barak. 2013. Moving subjects, stagnant paradigms: can the "mobilities paradigm" transcend methodological nationalism? *Journal of Ethnic and Migration Studies* 39(2):311–327. DOI: 10.1080/1369183x.2013.723260.

Kaufmann, Vincent, Manfred Max Bergman, and Dominique Joye. 2004. Motility: mobility as capital. *International Journal of Urban and Regional Research* 28(4):745–756.

Kealiinohomoku, Joann. 1983. An anthropologist looks at ballet as a form of ethnic dance. In *What is dance? Readings in theory and criticism.* Roger Copeland and Marshall Cohen, eds. Oxford: Oxford University Press, pp. 533–549.

King, Anthony. 2000. Thinking with Bourdieu against Bourdieu: a "practical" critique of the habitus. *Sociological Theory* 18(3):417–433. DOI: 10.1111/0735-2751.00109.

Kirschbaum, Charles. 2007. Careers in the right beat: US jazz musicians' typical and non-typical trajectories. *Career Development International* 12(2):187–201. DOI: 10.1108/13620430710733659.

Kiwan, Nadia, and Ulrike H. Meinhof. 2011. *Cultural globalization and music. African artists in transnational networks.* New York: Palgrave Macmillan.

Klette Bøhler, Kjetil. 2013. Grooves, pleasures and politics in salsa Cubana. The musicality of Cuban politics – and the politics of salsa Cubana. PhD dissertation, Department of Musicology, University of Oslo, Oslo.

Knoblauch, Hubert. 2005. Focused ethnography. *Forum Qualitative Sozialforschung/Forum: Qualitative Social Research* (3), www.qualitative-research.net/index.php/fqs/article/view/20. DOI: 10.17169/fqs-6.3.20.

Kofman, Eleonore, and Parvati Raghuram. 2015. *Gendered migrations and global social reproduction*. Basingstoke: Palgrave Macmillan.

Lahire, Bernard. 2001. Champ, hors-champ, contrechamp. In *Le travail sociologique de Pierre Bourdieu. Dettes et critiques*. Bernard Lahire, ed. Paris: La Découverte, pp. 23–57.

Laillier, Joël. 2011. La dynamique de la vocation: les évolutions de la rationalisation de l'engagement au travail des danseurs de ballet. *Sociologie du Travail* 53(4):493–514. DOI: 10.1016/j.soctra.2011.08.010.

Lamont, Michèle, and Virág Molnár. 2002. The study of boundaries across the social sciences. *Annual Review of Sociology* 28:167–195.

Lazzarato, Maurizio. 1996. Immaterial labor. In *Radical thought in Italy: a potential politics*. Paolo Virno and Michael Hardt, eds. Minneapolis, MN: University of Minnesota Press, pp. 133–150.

Leemann, Regula Julia. 2010. Gender inequalities in transnational academic mobility and the ideal type of academic entrepreneur. *Discourse: Studies in the Cultural Politics of Education* 31(5):605–625. DOI: 10.1080/01596306.2010.516942.

Lin, Nan. 1999. Building a network theory of social capital. *Connections* 22(1):28–51.

Lindholm, Charles. 2008. *Culture and authenticity*. Oxford: Blackwell Publishing.

Lipphardt, Anna. 2012. Artists on the move. Theoretical perspectives, empirical implications. In *a.RTISTS IN TRANSIT. How to become an artist in residence*. Annette Hollywood and Andreas Schmid, eds. Berlin: Internationale Gesellschaft der bildenden Künste, pp. 109–122.

Llano, Isabelle. 2014. Salsa in Barcelona and Spain. In *Salsa world. A global dance in local contexts*. Sydney Hutchinson, ed. Philadelphia, PA: Temple University Press, pp. 182–199.

MacLeod, Nicola E. 2006. The placeless festival: identity and place in the post-modern festival. In *Festivals, tourism and social change*. David Picard and Mike Robinson, eds. Clevedon: Channel View Publication, pp. 222–237.

Manuel, Peter. 1994. Puerto Rican music and cultural identity: creative appropriation of Cuban sources from danza to salsa. *Ethnomusicology* 38(2):249–280.

Manuel, Peter. 1995. *Caribbean currents: Caribbean music from Rumba to Reggae*. Philadelphia, PA: Temple University Press.

Marcus, George E. 1995. Ethnography in/of the world system: the emergence of multi-sited ethnography. *Annual Review of Anthropology* 24:95–117. DOI: 10.2307/2155931.

Marion, Jonathan S. 2012. Circulation as destination: considerations from the translocal culture of competitive ballroom dance. *Journal for the Anthropological Study of Human Movement* (2), http://jashm.press.uillinois.edu/17.2/marion2.html.

Marion, Jonathan S. 2014. *Ballroom dance and glamour*. London: Bloomsbury.

Martiniello, Marco, Nicolas Puig, and Gilles Suzanne. 2009. Editiorial: créations en migrations. *Revue européenne des migrations internationales* 25(2):7–11.

Martiniello, Marco, and Andrea Rea. 2014. The concept of migratory careers: elements for a new theoretical perspective of contemporary human mobility. *Current Sociology* 62 (7):1079–1096. DOI: 10.1177/0011392114553386.

Massey, Doreen. 1994. *Space, place, and gender*. Minneapolis, MN: University of Minnesota Press.

Massey, Douglas S., Rafael Alarcón, Jorge Durand, and González. Humberto. 1987. *Return to Aztlan. The social process of international migration from Western Mexico*. Berkeley: University of California Press.

Mathieu, Chris, ed. 2011. *Careers in creative industries*. New York: Routledge.

Mau, Steffen, Fabian Gülzau, Lena Laube, and Natascha Zaun. 2015. The global mobility divide: how visa policies have evolved over time. *Journal of Ethnic and Migration Studies* 41 (8):1192–1213. DOI: 10.1080/1369183X.2015.1005007.

Mazzucato, Valentina. 2009. Bridging boundaries with a transnational research approach: a simultaneous matched sample methodology. In *Multi-sited ethnography. Theory, praxis and locality in contemporary research*. Mark-Anthony Falzon, ed. Surrey: Ashgate, pp. 215–231.

McClure, Brigid. 2015. Dancing the self with others. Gender, power and affect in social salsa dancing. PhD dissertation, Department of culture, media and creative industries, King's College, London.

McMains, Juliet. 2001. Brownface: representations of Latin-Ness in Dancesport. *Dance Research Journal* 33(2):54–71. DOI: 10.2307/1477804.

McMains, Juliet. 2006. *Glamour addiction: inside the American Ballroom dance industry*. Middletown, CT: Wesleyan University Press.

McMains, Juliet. 2009. Dancing Latin/Latin dancing. Salsa and dance sport. In *Ballroom, boogie, shimmy sham, shake. A social and popular dance reader*. Julie Malnig, ed. University of Illinois Press, pp. 302–322.

McMains, Juliet. 2015. *Spinning Mambo into salsa: Caribbean dance in global commerce*. Oxford: Oxford University Press.

McMains, Juliet. 2016. "Hot" Latin dance. Ethnic identity and stereotype. In *The Oxford handbook of dance and ethnicity*. Anthony Shay and Barbara Sellers-Young, eds. Oxford: Oxford University Press, pp. 480–500.

Meinhof, Ulrike H., and Anna Triandafyllidou. 2006. Beyond the diaspora: transnational practices as transcultural capital. In *Transcultural Europe. Cultural policy in a changing Europe*. Ulrike H. Meinhof and Anna Triandafyllidou, eds. Basingstoke: Palgrave Macmillan, pp. 200–222.

Menger, Pierre-Michel. 1999. Artistic labor markets and careers. *Annual Review of Sociology* 25:541–574.

Messerschmidt, James W. 2009. Doing gender. *Gender & Society* 23(1):85–88. DOI: 10.1177/0891243208326253.

Morales, Ed. 2003. *The Latin beat: the rhythms and roots of Latin music from bosa nova to salsa and beyond*. Cambridge: Da Capo.

Moret, Joëlle. 2016. Cross-border mobility, transnationality and ethnicity as resources: European Somalis' post-migration mobility practices. *Journal of Ethnic and Migration Studies* 42 (9):1455–1472. DOI: 10.1080/1369183X.2015.1123089.

Moret, Joëlle. 2018. *European Somalis' post-migration movements. Mobility capital and the transnationalisation of resources*. IMISCOE Research Series. Dordrecht: Springer. DOI: 10.1007/978-3-319-95660-2.

Moret, Joëlle, Apostolos Andrikopoulos, and Janine Dahinden. 2019. Contesting categories: cross-border marriages from the perspectives of the state, spouses and researchers. *Journal of Ethnic and Migration Studies* 1–18. DOI: 10.1080/1369183X.2019.1625124.

Morokvasic-Muller, Mirjana. 1999. La mobilité transnationale comme ressource: le cas des migrants de l'Europe de l'Est. *Cultures et conflits* 33–34:105–122.

Mueller, Alain. 2016. Beyond ethnographic scriptocentrism: modelling multi-scalar processes, networks, and relationships. *Anthropological Theory* 16(1):98–130. DOI: 10.1177/1463499615626621.

Nentwich, Julia C., and Elisabeth K. Kelan. 2014. Towards a topology of "doing gender": an analysis of empirical research and its challenges. *Gender Work and Organization* 21(2):121–134. DOI: 10.1111/gwao.12025.

Ness, Sally Ann. 1992. *Body, movement, and culture: kinesthetic and visual symbolism in a Philippine community*. Philadelphia, PA: University of Pennsylvania Press.

Neumayer, Eric. 2010. Visa restrictions and bilateral travel. *The Professional Geographer* 62(2):171–181. DOI: 10.1080/00330121003600835.

Neveu Kringelbach, Hélène, and Jonathan Skinner. 2012. Introduction. The movement of dancing cultures. In *Dancing cultures. Globalization, tourism and identity in the anthropology of dance*. Hélène Neveu Kringelbach and Jonathan Skinner, eds. Oxford: Berghahn, pp. 1–25.

Novack, Cynthia J. 1990. *Sharing the dance. Contact improvisation and American culture*. Madison, WI: University of Wisconsin Press.

Nowicka, Magdalena. 2013. Positioning strategies of polish entrepreneurs in Germany: transnationalizing Bourdieu's notion of capital. *International Sociology* 28(1):29–47. DOI: 10.1177/0268580912468919.

Nowicka, Magdalena, and Maria Rovisco. 2009. Introduction. Making sense of cosmopolitanism. In *Cosmopolitanism in practice*. Magdalena Nowicka and Maria Rovisco, eds. London: Routledge, pp. 1–18.

Pachucki, Mark A., Sabrina Pendergrass, and Michèle Lamont. 2007. Boundary processes: recent theoretical developments and new contributions. *Poetics* 35(6):331–351. DOI: 10.1016/j.poetic.2007.10.001.

Papadopoulos, Maria. 2003. Salsa no tiene frontera. Eine Szene ohne Grenzen? In *Global Heimat. Ethnographische Recherchen im transnationalen Frankfurt*. Sven Bergmann and Regina Römhild, eds. Frankfurt/Main: Universität Frankfurt Institut für Kulturanthropologie, pp. 75–104.

Pathirage, Jagath, and Michael Collyer. 2011. Capitalizing social networks: Sri Lankan migration to Italy. *Ethnography* 12(3):315–333. DOI: 10.1177/1466138110362013.

Pedwell, Carolyn, and Anne Whitehead. 2012. Affecting feminism: questions of feeling in feminist theory. *Feminist Theory* 13(2):115–129. DOI: 10.1177/1464700112442635.

Peraldi, Michel. 2007. The station of alicante is the centre of the world. Wars at the borders and peace in the market along the North African routes to Europe. *History and Anthropology* 18(3):389–404. DOI: 10.1080/02757200701727809.

Peterson, Richard A. 2005. In search of authenticity. *Journal of Management Studies* 42 (5):1083–1098.

Picard, David, and Mike Robinson. 2006. Remaking worlds: festivals, tourism and change. In *Festivals, tourism and social change. Remaking worlds*. David Picard and Mike Robinson, eds. Clevedon: Channel View Publications, pp. 1–31.

Piedra, José. 1997. Hip poetics. In *Everynight life: culture and dance in Latin/o America*. Celeste Fraser Delgado and José Esteban Muñoz, eds. Durham, NC: Duke University Press, pp. 93–104.

Pietrobruno, Sheenagh. 2006. *Salsa and its transnational moves*. Lanham: Lexington Books.

Pink, Sarah, and Jennifer Morgan. 2013. Short-term ethnography: intense routes to knowing. *Symbolic Interaction* 36(3):351–361.

Portes, Alejandro, Luis Eduardo Guarnizo, and William J. Haller. 2002. Transnational entrepreneurs: an alternative form of immigrant economic adaptation. *American Sociological Review* 67(2):278–298. DOI: 10.2307/3088896.

Pries, Ludger. 2001. The disruption of social and geographic space: Mexican-US migration and the emergence of transnational social spaces. *International Sociology* 16(1):55–74. DOI: 10.1177/0268580901016001005.

Pries, Ludger. 2008. Transnational societal spaces: which units of analysis, reference and measurement. In *Rethinking transnationalism: the Meso-link of organizations*. Ludger Pries, ed. Abingdon: Routledge, pp. 1–20.

Puccio, Deborah. 2000. Sous le signe de la salsa. Les danses latino-américaines à Toulouse. *Terrain. Revue d'ethnologie de l'europe* 35:23–40.

Pušnik, Marusa, and Kristina Sicherl. 2010. Relocating and personalising salsa in Slovenia: to dance is to communicate. *Anthropological Notebooks* 16(3):107–123.

Qacha, Fatima. 2013. Transmigration solitaire et recherche de revenus d'une femme maro-caine. In *Transmigrants et nouveaux étrangers*. Alain Tarrius, Lamia Missaoui, and Fatima Qacha, eds. Toulouse: Presses Universitaires du Midi, pp. 147–178.

Quayson, Ato. 2014. Este loco, loco: transnationalism and the shaping of Accra's salsa scene. In *Oxford street, Accra. City life and the itineraries of transnationalism*. Ato Quayson, ed. Durham, NC: Duke University Press, pp. 159–182.

Quintero Rivera, Angel. 1998. *Salsa, sabor y control!: sociología de la música "tropical"*. Mexico: Siglo Veintiuno Editores.

Randeria, Shalini. 1999. Geteilte Geschichte und verwobene Moderne. In *Zukunftsent-würfe. Ideen für eine Kultur der Veränderung*. J. Rüsen, ed. Frankfurt/Main: Campus, pp. 87–96.

Reed, Susan A. 1998. The politics and poetics of dance. *Annual Review of Anthropology* 27 (1):503–532. DOI: 10.1146/annurev.anthro.27.1.503.

Reisinger, Yvette, and Carol J. Steiner. 2006. Reconceptualizing object authenticity. *Annals of Tourism Research* 33(1):65–86. DOI: 10.1016/j.annals.2005.04.003.

Renta, Priscilla. 2014. The global commercialization of salsa dancing and sabor. In *Salsa world. A global dance in local contexts*. Sydney Hutchinson, ed. Philadelphia, PA: Temple University Press, pp. 117–215.

Riaño, Yvonne, and Nadia Baghdadi. 2007. Je pensais que je pourrais avoir une relation plus égalitaire avec un Européen ». Le rôle du genre et des imaginaires géographiques dans la migration des femmes. *Nouvelles Questions Féministes* 26(1):38–53. DOI: 10.3917/nqf.261.0038.

Riccio, Bruno. 2001. From "ethnic group" to "transnational community"? Senegalese migrants' ambivalent experiences and multiple trajectories. *Journal of Ethnic and Migration Studies* 27(4):583–599. DOI: 10.1080/13691830120090395.

Rich, Adrienne. 1986. Notes towards a politics of location. In *Blood, bread, and poetry: selected prose, 1979–1985*. Adrienne Rich, ed. New York: Norton, pp. 210–231.

Richter, Marina. 2012. Researching transnational social spaces: a qualitative study of the Spanish second generation in Switzerland. *Forum Qualitative Sozialforschung/Forum: Quali-tative Social Research* 13:3. DOI: 10.17169/fqs-13.3.1678.

Riemann, Gerhard, and Fritz Schütze. 1991. "Trajectory" as a basic theoretical concept for analyzing suffering and disorderly social processes. In *Social organization and social process: essays in honor of Anselm Strauss*. David Maines, ed. New York: Aldine de Gruyter, pp. 333–357.

Risman, Barbara J. 2009. From doing to undoing: gender as we know it. *Gender & Society* 23 (1):81–84. DOI: 10.1177/0891243208326874.

Robertson, Roland. 1992. *Globalization: social theory and global culture*. London: Sage.

Robitaille, Laurence. 2013. Capoeira as a resource: multiple uses of culture under conditions of transnational neoliberalism. PhD dissertation, Communication and Culture, York University, Toronto.

Román-Velazquez, Patria. 2002. Locating salsa. In *Popular music studies*. David Hesmondhalgh and Keith Negus, eds. London: Bloomsbury, pp. 210–220.

Romàn-Velazquez, Patria. 2002b. The making of a salsa music scene in London. In *Situating salsa. Global markets and local meaning in Latin popular music*. Lise Waxer, ed. New York: Routledge, pp. 259–287.

Rosenthal, Gabriele. 1993. Reconstruction of life stories: principles of selection in gen-erating stories for narrative biographical interviews. *The Narrative Study of Lives* 1 (1):59–91.

Ryan, Louise. 2015. Friendship-making: exploring network formations through the narratives of Irish highly qualified migrants in Britain. *Journal of Ethnic and Migration Studies* 41 (10):1664–1683. DOI: 10.1080/1369183X.2015.1015409.

Ryan, Louise, and Jon Mulholland. 2014. French connections: the networking strategies of French highly skilled migrants in London. *Global Networks* 14(2):148–166. DOI: 10.1111/glob.12038.

Ryen, Anne. 2004. Ethical issues. In *Qualitative research practice*. Clive Seale, Giampietro Gobo, Jaber F. Gubrium, and David Silverman, eds. London: Sage, pp. 218–235. DOI: 10.4135/9781848608191.

Salazar, Noel B. 2011. The power of imagination in transnational mobilities. *Identities* 18 (6):576–598. DOI: 10.1080/1070289x.2011.672859.

Salazar, Noel B., Alice Elliot, and Roger Norum. 2017. Studying mobilities: theoretical notes and methodological queries. In *Methodologies of mobility: ethnography and experiment*. Alice Elliot, Roger Norum and Noel B. Salazar, eds. New York: Berghahn, pp. 1–24.

Salazar, Noel B., and Alan Smart. 2011. Anthropological takes on (im)mobility. *Identities* 18 (6):i–ix. DOI: 10.1080/1070289x.2012.683674.

Salzbrunn, Monika. 2017. Musique, religion, appartenances multiples: une approche de l'événement. *Sociétés Plurielles* (1):1–23.

Savigliano, Marta E. 1995. *Tango and the political economy of passion*. Boulder, CO: Westview Press.

Savigliano, Marta E. 2010. Notes on Tango (as) Queer (commodity). *Anthropological Notebooks* 16(3):135–143.

Schaer, Martine, Janine Dahinden, and Alina Toader. 2017. Transnational mobility among early-career academics: gendered aspects of negotiations and arrangements within heterosexual couples. *Journal of Ethnic and Migration Studies* 43(8):1292–1307. DOI: 10.1080/1369183X.2017.1300254.

Schapendonk, Joris. 2015. What if networks move? Dynamic social networking in the context of African migration to Europe. *Population, Space and Place* 21(8):809–819. DOI: 10.1002/psp.1860.

Schapendonk, Joris, Ilse van Liempt, and Bas Spierings. 2015. Travellers and their journeys: a dynamic conceptualization of transient migrants' and backpackers' behaviour and experiences on the road. *Migration Studies* 3(1):49–67. DOI: 10.1093/migration/mnu033.

Scheibelhofer, Elisabeth. 2008. Gender still matters: mobility aspirations among European scientists working abroad. In *Gendered mobilities*. Tim Cresswell and Tanu Priya Uteng, eds. Aldershot, England and Burlington, VT: Ashgate, pp. 115–128.

Schensul, Jean S., and Margaret D. LeCompte, eds. 1999. *Essential ethnographic methods: observations, interviews, and questionnaires (book 2 in ehtnographer's toolkit)*. Walnut Creek, CA: Alta Mira Press.

Schmoll, Camille. 2005. Pratiques spatiales transnationales et stratégies de mobilité de commerçantes tunisiennes. *Revue européenne des migrations internationales* 25(1):131–154.

Schmutz, Vaughn, and Alison Faupel. 2010. Gender and cultural consecration in popular music. *Social Forces* 89(2):685–707. DOI: 10.1353/sof.2010.0098.

Schneider, Britta. 2010. Multilingual cosmopolitanism and monolingual commodification: language ideologies in transnational salsa communities. *Language in Society* 39:647–668. DOI: 10.1017/S0047404510000643.

Schneider, Britta. 2013. Heteronormativity and queerness in transnational heterosexual salsa communities. *Discourse & Society* 24(5):553–571. DOI: 0.1177/0957926513486071.

Schulze, Marion. 2015. *Hardcore and gender. Soziologische Einblicke in eine globale Subkultur.* Bielefeld: Transcript.

Schwandt, Thomas. 1998. Constructivist, interpretivist approaches to human inquiry. In *The landscape of qualitative research. Theories and issues.* Norman K. Denzin and Yvonna S. Lincoln, eds. Thousand Oaks, CA: Sage, pp. 221–259.

Schweizer, Thomas. 1988. Netzwerkanalyse als moderne Strukturanalyse. In *Netzwerkanalyse. Ethnologische perspektiven.* Thomas Schweizer, ed. Berlin: Reimer, pp. 1–34.

Shamir, Ronen. 2005. Without borders? Notes on globalization as a mobility regime. *Sociological Theory* 23(2):197–217. DOI: 10.1111/j.0735-2751.2005.00250.x.

Sheller, Mimi. 2011. Mobility. *Sociopedia.isa.* DOI: 10.1177/205684601163.

Sheller, Mimi, and John Urry. 2006. The new mobilites paradigm. *Environment and Planning A* 38:207–226.

Shinozaki, Kyoko. 2014. Career strategies and spatial mobility among skilled migrants in Germany: the role of gender in the work-family interaction. *Tijdschrift voor economische en sociale geografie* 105(5):526–541. DOI: 10.1111/tesg.12111.

Simoni, Valerio. 2016. *Tourism and informal encounters in Cuba.* New York: Berghahn.

Singer, Roberta. 1983. Tradition and innovation in contemporary Latin popular music in New York City. *Latin American Music Review* 4(2):183–202.

Skinner, Jonathan. 2007. The salsa class: a complexity of globalization, cosmopolitans and emotions. *Global Studies in Culture and Power* 14(4):185–506. DOI: 10.1080/10702890701578480.

Skinner, Jonathan. 2008. Women dancing back – and forth: resistance and self-regulation in belfast salsa. *Dance Research Journal* 40(1):65–77.

Skinner, Jonathan. 2010. Leading questions and body memories: a case of phenomenology and physical ethnography in the dance interview. In *Keeping an open "I": memory and experience as resources in ethnography.* Anselma Gallinat and Peter Collins, eds. Oxford: Berghahn, pp. 111–128.

Skinner, Jonathan. 2011. Displeasure on "pleasure Island": tourist expectation and desire on and off the Cuban dance floor. In *Great expectations: Imagination, Anticipation, and Enchantment in Tourism.* Jonathan Skinner and Dimitrios Theodossopoulos, eds. Oxford: Berghahn, pp. 116–136.

Sklar, Deidre. 2000. Reprise: on dance ethnography. *Dance Research Journal* 32(1):70–77. DOI: 10.2307/1478278.

Sklar, Deidre. 2001. *Dancing with the virgin: body and faith in the fiesta of Tortuga, New Mexico.* Berkeley, CA: University of California Press.

Sorignet, Pierre-Emmanuel. 2014. Le métier de danseur. Retour sur une enquête. *Staps* 1 (103):119–131.

Spencer, Paul. 1986. *Society and the dance: the social anthropology of process and performance.* Cambridge: Cambridge University Press.

Spivak, Gayatri Chakravorty. 2012 (1988). *Other worlds essays in cultural politics.* Abingdon: Routledge.

Strauss, Anselm, and Barney Glaser. 1970. *Anguish: the case study of a dying trajectory.* Mill Valley, CA: Sociology Press.

Svensson, Lennart G. 2015. Occupations and professionalism in art and culture. *Professions and Professionalism* 5(2):1–14.

Szasz, Margaret Connell. 1994. Introduction. In *Between Indian and white worlds: the cultural broker.* Margaret Connell Szasz, ed. Norman, OK: University of Oklahoma Press, pp. 3–20.

Tarrius, Alain. 1993. Territoires circulatoires et espaces urbains: Différentiation des groupes migrants. *Annales de la Recherche Urbaine* 59–60:51–60.

Tarrius, Alain. 2001. Au-delà des États-nations: des sociétés de migrants. *Revue Européenne des Migrations Internationales* 17(2):37–61.

Tarrius, Alain. 2002. *La mondialisation par le bas. les nouveaux nomades des économies souterraines.* Paris: Editions Balland.

Taylor, Charles. 1992. *Multiculturalism and "the politics of recognition".* Princeton, NJ: Princeton University Press.

Törnqvist, Maria. 2012. Troubling romance tourism: sex, gender and class inside the Argentinean tango clubs. *Feminist Review* 102:21–40.

Törnqvist, Maria. 2013. *Tourism and the globalization of emotions. The intimate economy of Tango.* New York: Routledge.

Tsing, Anna. 2000. The global situation. *Cultural Anthropology* 15(3):327–360.

Turner, Victor. 1969. *The ritual process: structure and anti-structure.* Chicago, IL: Aldine de Gruyter.

Urquía, Norman. 2005. The re-branding of salsa in London's dance clubs: how an ethnicised form of cultural capital was institutionalised. *Leisure Studies* 24(4):385–397. DOI: 10.1080/02614360500200698.

Urry, John. 1995. *Consuming places.* London: Routledge.

Urry, John. 2003. Social networks, travel and talk. *The British Journal of Sociology* 54 (2):155–175. DOI: 10.1080/0007131032000080186.

Urry, John. 2007. *Mobilities.* Cambridge: Polity Press.

Vertovec, Steven. 1999. Conceiving and researching transnationalism. *Ethnic and Racial Studies* 22(2):447–462. DOI: 10.1080/014198799329558.

Viladrich, Anahí. 2013. *More than two to Tango. Argentine Tango immigrants in New York City.* Tucson: University of Arizona Press.

Villa, Paula-Irene. 2003. Mit dem Ernst des Körpers spielen: Körper, Diskurse und Emotionen im Argentinischen Tango. In *Aufs Spiel gesetzte Körper. Aufführungen des Sozialen in Sport und populärer Kultur.* Thomas Alkemeyer, Bernhard Boschert, Robert Schmidt, and Gunter Gebauer, eds. Konstanz: UVK, pp. 131–154.

Villa, Paula-Irene. 2010. Verkörperung ist immer mehr. In *Fokus Intersektionalität.* Helma Lutz, Maria Vivar, and Linda Supik eds. VS Verlag für Sozialwissenschaften, pp. 203–221. DOI: 10.1007/978-3-531-92555-4_11.

Wacquant, Loïc. 2004. *Body and soul: notebooks of an apprentice boxer.* Oxford: Oxford University Press.

Wacquant, Loïc. 2015. For a sociology of flesh and blood. *Qualitative Sociology* 38(1):1–11. DOI: 10.1007/s11133-014-9291-y.

Wade, Lisa. 2011. The emancipatory promise of the habitus: lindy hop, the body, and social change. *Ethnography* 12(2):224–246. DOI: 10.1177/1466138111398231.

Wagner, Izabela. 2006. Career coupling: career making in the elite world of musicians and scientists. *Qualitative Sociology Review* 2:3.

Wagner, Izabela. 2015. *Producing excellence: the making of virtuosos.* New Brunswick: Rutgers University Press.

Wagner, Izabela. 2016. Discovering the secret of excellence: Everett Hughes as a source of inspiration in researching creative careers. In *The anthem companion to Everett Hughes.* Rick Helmes-Hayes and Marco Santoro, eds. London: Anthem, pp. 193–210.

Wall, Tim. 2013. *Studying popular music culture.* London: Sage.

Warner, Michael. 1991. Introduction: fear of a queer planet. *Social Text* 29:3–17.

Washburne, Christopher. 2008. *Sounding salsa: performing Latin music in New York city*. Philadelphia, PA: Temple University Press.

Waxer, Lise, ed. 2002a. *Situating salsa. Global markets and local meanings in Latin American popular music*. New York: Routledge.

Waxer, Lise. 2002b. Llegó la salsa: the rise of salsa in Venezuela and Colombia. In *Situating salsa. Global markets and local meanings in latin popular music*. Lise Waxer, ed. New York: Routledge, pp. 219–246.

West, Candace, and Don H. Zimmerman. 1987. Doing gender. *Gender and Society* 1 (2):125–151.

West, Candace, and Don H. Zimmerman. 2009. Accounting for doing gender. *Gender & Society* 23(1):112–122. DOI: 10.1177/0891243208326529.

Whiteley, Sheila. 2000. *Women and popular music: sexuality, identity, and subjectivity*. London: Routledge.

Wicker, Hans-Rudolf. 1997. From complex culture to cultural complexity. In *Debating cultural hybridity. Multi-cultural identities and the politics of anti-racism*. Pnina Werbner and Tariq Modood, eds. London: Zed Books, pp. 29–45.

Wieschiolek, Heike. 2003. Ladies, just follow his lead! Salsa, gender and identity. In *Sport, dance and embodied identities*. Eduardo P. Archetti and Noel Dyck, eds. Berg: Oxford, pp. 115–137.

Wilcox, Emily. 2012. Dancers doing fieldwork: socialist aesthetics and bodily experience in the people's republic of China. *Journal for the Anthropological Study of Human Movement*, http://jashm.press.uillinois.edu/17.2/wilcox.html.

Wimmer, Andreas. 2009. Herder's heritage and the boundary-making approach: studying ethnicity in immigrant societies. *Sociological Theory* 27:244–270.

Wimmer, Andreas, and Nina Glick Schiller. 2002. Methodological nationalism and beyond: nation-state building, migration and the social sciences. *Global Networks* 2(4):301–334.

Witzel, Andreas. 2000. Das problemzentrierte interview. *Forum Qualitative Sozialforschung* (1), www.qualitative-research.net/index.php/fqs/article/viewArticle/1132/2519. DOI: 10.1007/978-3-8349-9441-7_29.

Wulff, Helena. 1998. *Ballet across borders. Career and culture in the world of dancers*. New York: Berg.

Wulff, Helena. 2003. The Irish body in motion: moral politics, national identity and dance. In *Sport, dance and embodied identities*. Noel Dyck and Eduardo P. Archetti, eds. Oxford: Berg, pp. 179–196.

Index

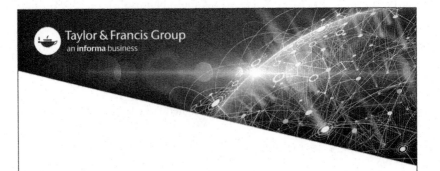